OXFORD WORLD'S CLASSICS

MYTHS FROM MESOPOTAMIA

STEPHANIE DALLEY has worked on various excavations in the Middle East and has published cuneiform tablets found there by the British Archaeological Expedition to Iraq as well as a book for the general reader about those discoveries, *Mari and Karana* (1984). She has taught Akkadian at the Universities of Edinburgh and Oxford and is now Shillito Fellow in Assyriology at the Oriental Institute, Oxford, and a Senior Research Fellow of Somerville College. She is editor and main author of *The Legacy of Mesopotamia* (Oxford University Press).

Ninurta attacks Anzu to regain the stolen Tablet of Destinies. From a stone sculpture found in the temple of Ninurta at Nimrud, Iraq. (Layard, *Monuments of Nineveh, ii, plate 5*)

OXFORD WORLD'S CLASSICS

Myths from Mesopotamia
Creation, the Flood, Gilgamesh, and Others

*Edited and translated
with an Introduction and Notes by*
STEPHANIE DALLEY

Revised edition

OXFORD
UNIVERSITY PRESS

OXFORD

UNIVERSITY PRESS

Great Clarendon Street, Oxford OX2 6DP

Oxford University Press is a department of the University of Oxford.
It furthers the University's objective of excellence in research, scholarship,
and education by publishing worldwide in

Oxford New York

Auckland Bangkok Buenos Aires Cape Town Chennai
Dar es Salaam Delhi Hong Kong Istanbul Karachi Kolkata
Kuala Lumpur Madrid Melbourne Mexico City Mumbai Nairobi
São Paulo Shanghai Taipei Tokyo Toronto

Oxford is a registered trade mark of Oxford University Press
in the UK and in certain other countries

Published in the United States
by Oxford University Press Inc., New York

First published 1989 by Oxford University Press
First issued as a World's Classics paperback 1991
Reissued as an Oxford World's Classics paperback 1998
Revised edition 2000

British Library Cataloguing in Publication Data

Data available

Library of Congress Cataloging in Publication Data

Data available

ISBN–13: 978–0–19–283589–5
ISBN–10: 0–19–283589–0

13

Printed in Great Britain by
Clays Ltd, St Ives plc

Inscriptions here of various names I view'd,
The greater part by hostile time subdu'd;
Yet wide was spread their fame in ages past,
And Poets once had promis'd they should last.

The Temple of Fame
Alexander Pope (AD 1715)

PREFACE

Such huge strides have been made in our understanding of the cuneiform script and the Akkadian language during the past three decades, and so many new clay tablets have come to light, that new translations need no justification. In the same measure, scholarship will continue in future to improve on present efforts, so these translations offer by no means a final or definitive work, although the recent completion of von Soden's superb dictionary means that an era of struggling misinterpretation is drawing to a close. This book is intended to give an accurate, up-to-date rendering of the best-preserved texts in current, readable English, avoiding the poetic mannerisms and archaisms that have often characterized translations in the past; but it is not intended as a substitute for proper editions in which difficulties can be aired at length. Such editions for several of the myths are now long overdue.

When the first stumbling but brilliant attempts were made, about a century ago, to translate these most ancient of stories, an excited public demanded confirmation of biblical truth to uphold religious beliefs based on the Old Testament in the face of evolutionary theory. Today ancient Mesopotamian stories are used less to bolster fundamentalism, more to provide comparative material for biblical and early Greek traditions, as well as for wider studies in the cultural development of mankind. Few would now deny that ancient Mesopotamia lies at the roots of our own civilization, but only as part of widespread contributory factors.

The language in which the stories were written is flexible in different ways from English. In particular the range of meaning found in a single word, and the varying use of tenses in verbs, as well as punning and alliteration, cannot be conveyed by strict equivalence in English, so they are indicated mainly in the notes, although a few crucial puns are given by alternative translations in the main text. The introductory material and the notes have been restricted largely to basic information gleaned and sifted from specialist research. Numerous fine points of textual detail come from von Soden's *Akkadisches Handwörterbuch* and from the *Chicago Assyrian Dictionary*. However, the notes to translations are meant only as a guide for the general reader, and are not intended to be comprehensive. Most of the stories have considerable gaps, for which estimated lengths are given where possible, to remind the reader of the fragmented nature of the source material. As new clay tablets come to light, it may gradually be possible to fill the gaps in each version of the stories, but we are still far from such a theoretical and anticipatory state of bliss. Different versions of a story are occasionally combined in order to present a coherent text, but on the few occasions when this is so, the patchwork nature of the translation is indicated. The versions are labelled according to the period of the actual tablets on which they were written (see Sigla and Abbreviations), although it must be remembered that a tablet may be of a later date than the version of the story written upon it. Names are variously spelt according to the form used on tablets of various periods, so, for example, Anum is the older form of Anu, Huwawa is the older form of Humbaba.

Detailed bibliography is now enormous. Here listed are only the main writings from which an enquiring reader, polyglot and persevering, may pursue the subject further, together with a few recent articles to which the notes refer on points of detail. The work does not aim to be original, and depends very heavily upon more than a century's scholarly effort by many brilliant and perceptive minds, but no one translator could agree with every reading or interpretation, and discarded interpretations are not aired in the notes. A few original contributions by this translator are included: recognition that the *Tale of Buluqiya* in the *Arabian Nights* is related to the *Epic of Gilgamesh*; connection of an episode in *Nergal and Ereshkigal* to a ritual practice; and a few small points which are indicated in the notes by the author's initials.

I am deeply indebted both to Dr Jeremy Hughes, with whom I read most of the texts in detail over several years, and to Henrietta McCall, whose patient checking and positive criticism have improved the work immeasurably. Without their support and encouragement the book could not have been contemplated, let alone completed with enjoyment. Also vital to the work were the unparalleled facilities of the Griffith Institute library in Oxford. I am grateful to Dr Simo Parpola for making available to me his own 'musical score' typescript of the Gilgamesh texts,

and to Theresa Fitzherbert and Kay Lattimore for typing with
good humour from pencilled notebooks. Finally, Hilary Feld-
man of Oxford University Press commissioned the translations
for which I owe her many thanks.

S.M.D.

Oxford
October 1988

PREFACE TO REVISED EDITION

Several important pieces of new text have come to light since
the first edition was completed. They have surfaced from
recent excavations of the Iraqi Department of Antiquities at
Sippar, and from work done in the British Museum. One piece
reveals at last how *The Epic of Gilgamesh* began, in its Standard
Version. The new passages which have been published in full
editions have been added, partly at the end of the volume, if
they were too long to be inserted into the existing pages; the
point of insertion is clearly noted on the appropriate page.
These include a major episode in *Atrahasis*, and one in *The Epic
of Creation*. Smaller improvements have been incorporated in
the appropriate place, often filling a gap due to damaged text,
from a new duplicate. The name of the scribe who wrote a
main version of *Atrahasis* has been reread for the fourth time.
Two interesting new fragments from *The Epic of Gilgamesh* have
not yet been published, but are given in translation by George
(1999). They concern the formal adoption of Enkidu by
Ninsun, and the grave-goods made for Enkidu. Their content
is paraphrased at appropriate points for this revision. As a
result of improved understanding, I have added a paragraph
to the end of the introduction to *Atrahasis*, replaced note 44 on
p. 38, and changed my translation of *lullû* from 'mortal man' to
'primeval man', a coherent set of changes which are
particularly significant for understanding the myth. A short
paragraph has also been added at the end of the introduction
to *The Epic of Gilgamesh*. In note 21 on p. 275 an important
collation of one damaged sign has required a change showing

that Ashur's chariot contained not the king Sennacherib but the god's victorious weapons in the cosmic battle celebrated in Assyria at the New Year Festival. The important new evidence for the storm-god of Aleppo as hero of a cosmic battle against the Sea in the time of Hammurabi is detailed in note 52 on p. 277. In addition, a few minor corrections, alterations, and updatings have been made.

The publications from which the changes chiefly derive are:

Clifford, R. J. 1994, *Creation Accounts in the Ancient Near East and in the Bible*, Catholic Biblical Quarterly Monograph Series 26 (Washington, DC).

Dalley, S. 1999, 'Authorship, Variation and Canonicity in Gilgamesh and other ancient texts', *Interaction, Journal of the Tureck Bach Research Foundation*, 2, pp. 31–47.

Durand, J.-M. 1993, 'Le mythologème du combat entre le dieu de l'orage et la Mer en Mésopotamie', *Mari Annales de Recherches Interdisciplinaires*, 7, pp. 41–61.

Foster, B. R. 1993, *Before the Muses* (Bethesda, Md.).

George, A. R. 1999, *The Epic of Gilgamesh. A New Translation* (London).

George, A. R., and Al-Rawi, F. N. H. 1990, 'Tablets from the Sippar Library II. Tablet II of the Babylonian Creation Epic', *Iraq*, 52, pp. 149–58.

George, A. R., and Al-Rawi, F. N. H. 1996, 'Tablets from the Sippar Library VI. Atrahasis', *Iraq*, 58, pp. 147–90.

Horowitz, W. 1998, *Mesopotamian Cosmic Geography* (Eisenbrauns).

Kwasman, T., and George, A. R. 1999, 'A new join to the Epic of Gilgamesh tablet 1', *Nouvelles Assyriologiques Brèves et Utilitaires.*

Wilcke, C. 1999, 'Weltuntergang als Anfang', in *Weltende*, ed. Adam Jones (Wiesbaden), 63–112.

I would like to thank Martin L. West for making his criticisms of the first edition available to me, and to Helge Kvanvig for useful discussion of Wilcke's 'Weltuntergang als Anfang'.

A translation of the first edition into Arabic by Dr Najwa Nasr of the Faculty of Letters, Lebanese University, Beirut, was published by Beisan Press in 1998.

CONTENTS

LIST OF FIGURES

SIGLA AND ABBREVIATIONS

[ ]   Square brackets indicate short gaps in text due to damage of tablet clay. Text inside brackets is restored, often from parallel versions.

( )   Round brackets indicate words inserted to give a better rendering in English, or explanatory insertions.

[( )] Square brackets enclosing round brackets indicate uncertainty as to whether or not there is a gap in the text.

. . . Omission dots indicate an unknown word or phrase.

OBV   Old Babylonian Version, i.e. text from the early second millennium BC.

MAV   Middle Assyrian Version, i.e. text from the late second millennium found in Assyria.

SBV   Standard Babylonian Version, i.e. the form of a work that was current in fairly standardized version in libraries of both Assyria and Babylonia in the early to mid-first millennium BC.

LV   Late Version, i.e. text dating between 612 BC and the end of the Seleucid era, from Babylonia.

Upper case roman numerals are used for tablet numbers within an epic; lower case for columns within a tablet.

AHw   W. von Soden, *Akkadisches Handwörterbuch.*

CAD   *Chicago Assyrian Dictionary.*

RlA   *Reallexikon der Assyriologie.*

INTRODUCTION

These stories all concern the deities and people of Mesopotamia, a rich, alluvial country which lies between the great rivers Tigris and Euphrates in modern Iraq. Their background is that of a very ancient, largely urban society, supported by agriculture and pastoralism, in which prosperity was assured by firm government capable of controlling irrigation for agriculture, and by extensive trading. Unpredictable weather scarcely affected life, and the forces of nature could be held in check, so the gods were usually compliant and democratic, taking their decisions by discussion in an assembly. Less predictable elements tended to be associated with sea and with mountains, both of which lie beyond the boundaries of Mesopotamia proper, and with incursions of nomads from deserts and mountainous tracts. Leisure at the courts of kings or on long trading caravans gave time and opportunity for telling stories, which even in their earliest written forms show the influence of 'contest' literature, one of the earliest Sumerian literary forms known, in a spirit of inventive competition for the sake of entertainment.

The stories were all written in Akkadian, a broad term which comprises the Semitic Babylonian and Assyrian dialects that were spoken and written for over two thousand years down to the time of Alexander's successors, the Seleucids. Clay tablets, which are excavated in great quantities on archaeological sites in the Middle East, yet so often are extricated in a damaged and fragmentary condition, were the chief medium for the wedge-shaped (cuneiform) writing of Akkadian. So it may never be possible to understand all the stories completely; most of them are over four thousand years old, and have come to us in fragments of friable clay from complex literary traditions written in an ambiguous and exceptionally complicated writing system.

Royal epics relating the exploits of known, historical kings are not included here because they are not yet extant in a sufficiently coherent form for translation, but fragments exist from

epics of Sargon of Agade (*c.*2390 BC),[1] Zimri-Lim of Mari
(*c.*1850 BC), Adad-nirari of Assyria (*c.*1300 BC), Tukulti-Ninurta
I of Assyria (*c.*1220 BC), Nebuchadnezzar I of Babylon (*c.*1120
BC), and Nabopolassar of Babylon (*c.*620 BC) among others, and
their existence shows that the epic tradition continued to be
creative throughout the history of that civilization.

Akkadian literature in its written form is different in concept
from later written literature. Through the study of several
versions of one story, it has become clear that one version may
omit an episode crucial to the sequence, or it may be so elliptical
or telescoped as to be unintelligible without the help of another,
more explicit version. This is a recognized feature of Sumerian
literature, which preceded Akkadian, and is also true to a lesser
extent of stories written in Akkadian. A later version is not
necessarily fuller than an earlier one: for example, the latest
version of *Ishtar's Descent* from Nineveh is slightly briefer than
the earlier version from Assur, and less than half the length of
the Sumerian story, which is even earlier. We should probably
understand some of the abrupt changes of theme as bare
skeletons which were fleshed out in practice by skilled narrators,
rather as early musical notation gave only the guidelines needed
to remind the musician of appropriate melody and rhythms,
leaving embellishments and flourishes to his own skills and
to popular taste. This may help to explain why much
Akkadian literature is relatively poor in vocabulary and des-
criptive imagery compared with Ugaritic myths and Homeric
epics.

So oral tradition continued to develop alongside written
literature, and the primary purpose of recording stories in
writing was not necessarily to supply individual readers with a
coherent and connected account. Ancient stories were used for a
multitude of purposes, often in extracts: attached to a ritual, to
give authenticity or to provide an aetiology; to give the weight
of some ancient tradition to a custom or to an incantation. Some
of the most famous author-scribes were also incantation-priests.
Authorship of the oldest, traditional works was attributed to

---

[1] Dates earlier than the mid-second millennium BC are given according to the 'long'
chronology, which takes the first year of Hammurabi's reign in Babylon as 1848 BC, 56
years longer than the 'middle' chronology, following Huber 1982, Hassan and Robinson
1987, Clayden 1989.

sages who were sent before the Flood by the god Ea to bring civilization to mankind, and authors after the Flood were honoured with sage-like status. Many of the most famous, named scribes from whom later scribes claimed descent, lived during the Kassite period (*c.*1650–1150 BC) in the Late Bronze Age, a time which is now recognized as one of particular scribal activity, both in collecting and composing literature.

The modern reader is often at a disadvantage in expecting oral and written literature to be pretty much identical, and he is largely ignorant of the cultural and linguistic background in which the tales were transmitted. Nevertheless, many stylistic techniques can be outlined, not all of them apparent in translation. Metre, in the strict sense in which Greek and Latin literature is composed, may be absent, but more basic groups of main beats in a line are certainly the rule. Punning and word-play are revelled in, and sometimes they are crucial to the plot; at other times they are highly esoteric and would only have been appreciated by expert scribes. Alliteration, rhetorical questions, chiasma, inclusio, similes; verb pairs with contrasting tenses; a build-up of tension through repetition with slight variation; fixed epithets and formulaic lines such as still delight children throughout the world: all these devices enliven the Akkadian text. Length of line on a tablet is not directly connected to the concept of a metrical line, as various arrangements in different versions show. At all periods the concept of metre and poetic structure was a highly flexible one which allowed for alteration and development by subsequent narrators, making composition a fluid and adaptable art.

Plagiarism and adaptability are characteristics of written literature in ancient Mesopotamia, and modern attempts to define closely and exclusively different categories of composition have only limited validity. Thus it is rash to attempt grand generalizations about the definition of myth, epic, or legend, or about the priority of myth over ritual. Individual examples must speak for themselves; many kinds of combinations can be found, but all are entertaining stories.

There is, to some extent, a concept of canonization in that a particular version of an epic might be well-written, deposited in a library, and copied by later scribes for other libraries. Tukulti-Ninurta I of Assyria sacked Babylon in the thirteenth century BC and looted its libraries for his own collections. All the great temples would have had their own libraries, and the last great kings of Assyria who ruled from Nineveh in the early seventh century BC stocked the libraries of their palaces and temples with copies taken from texts in the temple libraries of Babylonia. Because of the looting and copying, tablets found in the cities of Assyria and of Babylonia contain more or less identical versions of myths, and this has led some scholars to deduce widespread conservatism of scribal practice in which texts were faithfully transmitted and variation is all accidental and unintentional. Such homogeneity within Mesopotamia gives a false impression, however, for if one looks further afield, to Tell el-Amarna or to Bogazköy, one sees that great variation did indeed exist, to which in particular the two versions of *Nergal and Ereshkigal* bear witness, and the divergence cannot possibly be explained by scribal error. Many such myths must have existed which were not composed in Babylonia, nor diffused from there with fidelity to a hypothetical original. The newly found third tablet of *Anzu* with its colophon giving Hanigalbat (far to the north-west of Assyria) as the original source of the text contributes a healthy reminder that independent cuneiform libraries existed outside Assyria and Babylonia. Each epic was referred to in antiquity by its opening line or first words, so the early version of *Gilgamesh* has a different title from the standard version because the latter added a new prologue. The titles that are used in this book are modern.

Akkadian myths and epics were universally known during antiquity, and they were not restricted to the Akkadian language. Some were definitely told in Sumerian, Hittite, Hurrian, and Hebrew; the story itself flourishes beyond the boundaries of any particular language or ethnic group. This happened partly because Akkadian was the language of diplomacy throughout the ancient Near East from the mid-second to mid-first millennium BC, even in Egypt, Anatolia, and Iran, and trainee scribes in those far-flung countries practised their skills on Akkadian literary texts; also because strong nomadic and mercantile elements in the population travelled enormous distances, because national boundaries frequently changed, and because trading colonies abroad were ubiquitous. Therefore Akkadian stories share common ground with tales in the Old Testament, the *Iliad*, the *Odyssey*, the works of Hesiod, and the *Arabian Nights*; they were popular with an international audience at the dawn of history.

CHRONOLOGICAL CHART

BC	Periods in Assyria and Babylonia	Periods outside Mesopotamia	Events that may be relevant for literary transmission
3000	Early Dynastic		
		Egyptian Pyramids	Akkadian influx (?)
2500	Dynasty of Agade Gutian Raids 3rd Dynasty of Ur		
		Old Assyrian trading colonies in Anatolia	
	Isin-Larsa		Amorite influx
2000	Old Babylonian	Hittite Old Kingdom	
	Kassite	Hittite Empire Mittani Empire (Hanigalbat) Amarna Age	Hittites raid Babylon c.1651
1500			Hanigalbat rules Assyria Akkadian is language of diplomacy
	Middle Assyrian		Assyrians conquer Hanigalbat c.1250 Assyrians conquer Babylon c.1225
1000			Aramaean influx Phoenician expansion
	Neo-Assyrian		Assyrians conquer Babylon 728 Fall of Nineveh to Medes 612 Fall of Babylon to Cyrus 539
	Neo-Babylonian		
500	Achaemenid Persian	Greek	Return of Jews to Judah Fall of Babylon to Alexander 331 Berossus writes *Babyloniaca* c.281
	Seleucid Greek Parthian	Roman	
AD			
	Sassanian		Arab influx
500		Byzantine	
	Islamic		Damascius at court of Chosroes I c.550

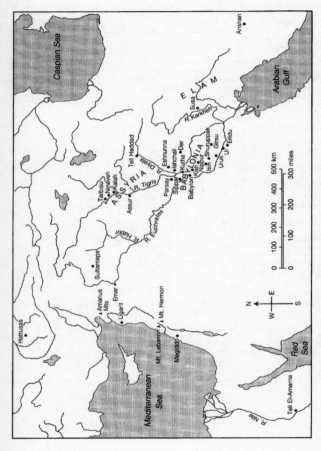

Fig. 1. Map of the Near East showing where Akkadian myths have been found, and places named in the myths

Atrahasis

Atrahasis the wise man, who built an ark and saved mankind from destruction, is a figure of immense prestige and antiquity to whom various literary and religious traditions were attached. He was known by a variety of names and epithets which were translated into different languages, sometimes with reinterpreted meanings, sometimes abbreviated, and in this way his fame spread over huge distances through a span of some five thousand years. In Mesopotamian literature he was the survivor of the Flood, together with his wife, and was granted a form of immortality by the great gods. The story of the Flood was one of the most popular tales of ancient times, and is found in several ancient languages, reworked to suit different areas and cultures so that different settings and details are found in each version. The specific information which follows helps to illustrate how widely diffused the man and the story became in the ancient world.

ATRAHASIS IN HISTORY

According to one version of the Sumerian king list, in the years just before the Flood swept over the earth, Ubara-Tutu (who is named as the father of Atrahasis in *Gilgamesh*) was king of Shuruppak, modern Tell Fara in central southern Mesopotamia, where some of the earliest writings known in the whole world have been unearthed. According to a different version of the Sumerian king list, Atrahasis, called there by his Sumerian name Ziusudra, himself ruled the city Shuruppak, preceded by his father who was named like the city, Shuruppak and who was presumably regarded as the eponymous ancestor of the citizens there.[1] A wisdom composition known as *The Instructions of Shuruppak* is now attested on clay tablets from the Early Dynastic period in the early third millennium BC, and contains

[1] He is preceded in that list by Ubara-Tutu, and so was not the first king of Shuruppak.

sage advice given by Shuruppak to his son Ziusudra. Thus
Atrahasis was a notable figure at the dawn of history, and
literary tradition was attached to him at an extremely early
period.

THE NAMES OF ATRAHASIS

'Extra-wise' is the meaning of his name in *Atrahasis*; he is Ut-
napishtim and Uta-na'ishtim in *Gilgamesh*, a name which can
mean 'He found life'. Sumerian Ziusudra is an approximate
translation of Akkadian Ut-napishtim together with his epithet,
in which the element *sudra* corresponds to Atrahasis' epithet
rūqu, 'the far-distant'. The name used by Berossus[2] for the
survivor of the Flood is Xisuthros, probably a phonetic rendering
of Ziusudra. Prometheus, Deucalion's father, may possibly be an
approximate Greek translation of Atrahasis, and it is just possible that an abbreviation of (Uta)-na'ish(tim) was pronounced
'Noah' in Palestine from very early times. Atrahasis is also
found as the name or epithet of a man who features in a Hittite
story about Kumarbi. It has been suggested that the name
Ulysses, used by the Romans for Odysseus, comes from the
Hittite *ullu(ya)š*, as a translation of Atrahasis' epithet 'the far-
distant', and that the names Odysseus and Outis may be based
on a pronunciation of the logogram for Ut-napishtim, which is
UD.ZI.[3] The name or epithet Atrahasis is used for the skilful god
of craftsmanship Kothar-wa-hasis in Ugaritic mythology, and is
abbreviated to Chousor in the Greek account of Syrian origins
related by Philo of Byblos. A similar abbreviation is used in the
name of the Islamic sage Al-khiḍr (also called al-Khaḍir), who
guarded the Fountain of Life, and gave water from it to King
Sakhr (meaning 'rock') who thus became immortal. This episode
is related, in one of the *Arabian Nights*, to the Gilgamesh of
Islamic narrative, Buluqiya, who, having travelled through
many lands, lost his faithful adviser Affan in a fruitless attempt
to obtain the ring of Suleiman, with which he might travel to the

---

[2] Berossus was a Babylonian priest who wrote a book called *Babyloniaca* in the third
century BC to make the culture and history of his country known to the Greeks.

[3] Schretter 1974, 13. There is no evidence, however, that UD.ZI was ever pronounced
phonetically.

Fountain of Life and drink the water of immortality. The name Al-Khiḍr here bears a new etymology, 'the green one'. Al-khiḍr as a holy man of Islam is buried at Baniyas on the Golan Heights, where a tributary of the Jordan river gushes out of a rock. In all these appellations it is impossible to distinguish a 'real' name from an epithet.

THE TEXT

Clay tablets inscribed with the Old Babylonian version of the epic can be dated around 1700 BC. Each tablet is divided into eight columns, four on the obverse and four on the reverse. Some passages in Late Assyrian versions, discovered in the palace library of the great king Assurbanipal, appear to follow the Old Babylonian version fairly closely, but with additions and considerable alteration in phrasing and vocabulary, as far as can be ascertained from the small quantity of text that survives.

THE AUTHOR, IPIQ-AYA[4]

Rarely is an author named for such an early text. Ipiq-Aya was writing during the reign of Ammi-ṣaduqa, king of Babylon (1702–1682 BC), on eight-column tablets, each column comprising about fifty-five lines, and he probably lived in Sippar, where the tablets almost certainly originated. Ipiq-Aya was presumably the compiler and arranger of traditional material, and the extent of his personal contribution to it cannot be assessed. To understand his role, we may look to Enheduana, daughter of Sargon of Agade (2390–2335 BC), holder of the most prestigious temple office at Ur, and traditionally the authoress of the Sumerian Collection of Temple Hymns. We now know much of that work existed long before her lifetime, and was revised and augmented after her death; this did not undermine her credibility as an author in antiquity, but rather enhanced it.

At Sippar the temple of the sun-god Shamash was particularly famous, in Old Babylonian times when Ipiq-Aya lived there, for

---

[4] Previously misread Ku-Aya, Nur-Aya, and Kasap-Aya.

its cloister of blue-blooded priestesses who were not allowed to
bear children. This version of *Atrahasis* may have been composed in order to justify their enforced infertility since it
presents the myth as justifying a social phenomenon which was
prevalent at that period.

CREATION OF MAN

According to *Atrahasis*, the mother goddess Mami, with the
help of the wise god Ea, created men out of clay mixed with the
blood of a slain god called Ilawela:[1] man's purpose in life was to
relieve the gods of hard labour. This account of man's creation
may be compared with that in the *Epic of Creation*, in which
Marduk used the blood of Qingu, the evil leader of the enemy
gods whom he had slain, to create mankind with the help of Ea;
clay is not mentioned, and no birth-goddess takes part, but the
purpose of man's creation is again to toil on the gods' behalf.
Neither account mentions the creation of animals, which is an
important preliminary to man's creation in Genesis (Priestly
source).

The account in Genesis describes God using earth (adamah)
to create the first man (Adam), animating him with the breath of
life. In Hesiod's *Works and Days*, written in Boeotia in Greek
around the late eighth century BC, the gods incite the smith-god
Hephaistos to make Pandora out of clay and water; both in
Greece and Mesopotamia deities associated with birth and
fertility are also patrons of mining, smelting, and coppersmith's
craft, because they create new forms from basic materials.

THE FLOOD

Atrahasis, the hero of the Flood story, was a citizen of Shuruppak in lower Mesopotamia. An extensive flood as a natural event
sometimes took place in that region, where the Euphrates in
spate can overflow and spill across the intervening land into the
lower-lying Tigris, which itself often breaks its own banks in
sudden spate, but a flood would be impossible on a similar scale
in Palestine, Syria, Anatolia, or Greece. Such floods occur quite

[1] Formerly read We-ila or Geshtu-e.

commonly in Iraq, and strata of silt deposits on Early Dynastic sites of the fourth millennium BC, found there by archaeologists, can be interpreted as recording various different floods in remote antiquity. That evidence does not, however, disclose whether one particular flood was more catastrophic than others; it only shows that no unusual break in cultural continuity was caused by such a deposit, and that the layer of flood silt found in excavations at Ur is certainly much earlier in date than the flood deposit found at Shuruppak. No flood deposits are found in third millennium strata, and Archbishop Usher's date for the Flood of 2349 BC, which was calculated by using numbers in Genesis at face value and which did not recognize how highly schematic Biblical chronology is for such early times, is now out of the question.

In *Atrahasis* the Flood was sent by the gods in order to reduce overpopulation, a situation which has been compared with an early Greek poem, the *Cypria* (loosely attributed to Homer in antiquity and known mainly from allusions and quotations), in which Zeus planned to reduce overpopulation by war. In *Atrahasis*, war is not used for this purpose. In the Priestly account of the Flood in Genesis, and in Ovid's *Metamorphoses*, man's wickedness is the cause of divine anger which results in the Flood. In *Gilgamesh* the Flood story is reused out of its original context, to mark the time in history after which it was no longer possible for a mortal to win immortality. The Flood is also important for Mesopotamian tradition because it marks the end of the period when true sages lived on earth and brought to mankind the arts of civilization from the gods. Later post-diluvian sages were sometimes authors or literary figures who worked for known kings of historical times, but they were not regarded as immortal, and were additional to the original seven. In *Erra and Ishum*, the god Marduk claims responsibility for sending the Flood and the Seven Sages, thus adapting two traditional themes which were closely connected.

There are indications that the story of the Flood as related in the Old Babylonian *Atrahasis*, and with considerable variation in the Ninevite recension of *Gilgamesh*, was not the only one in circulation in Babylonia. Berossus, writing from Babylonia for the Greeks in the third century BC, includes some details which are not known elsewhere except in the Priestly account in

Genesis. The latter may have been composed or finalized in the early Persian period (late sixth to early fifth centuries BC). Notable items are that the survivor of the Flood (Xisuthros, Noah) is the tenth antediluvian king in both Berossus and Genesis (Priestly source), that the month in which the Flood happened is named, and that the ten antediluvian kings whom Berossus cites ruled for 432,000 'years' (i.e. 86,400 × 5, five years being sixty months) and in Genesis (Priestly source) for 1,656 'years' (i.e. 86,400 weeks), so the two accounts may originally have shared a common chronological scheme.[5]

Berossus' account of the Flood story must be derived from a Sumerian version of the story, since he names the hero as Xisuthros (Ziusudra) rather than Atrahasis or Ut-napishtim, and this version connects the Flood with genealogical information. The Sumerian king list, compiled in the early second millennium, includes a brief note about the Flood, which in that text divides dynasties with enormous lengths of reign from more realistic numbers. A Sumerian story of Ziusudra and the Flood, still largely incomplete, appears to be a relatively late composition based on an Akkadian version of the story, and it lists the antediluvian cities in the same way as the Sumerian king list does. An Akkadian account of the Flood has also been found at Ugarit, a Late Bronze Age city on the Syrian coast.

It is probable that these ancient Near Eastern flood stories are versions of a tale which originated in lower Mesopotamia, though not necessarily in a single devastation. The variety of detail found in them illustrates the kaleidoscopic character of the folk tale, in which certain basic elements are widely used in new combinations and are adapted to national interests and different literary settings. For instance, in Genesis the dove brings back to Noah an olive leaf, which belongs to the flora of Palestine; olive trees do not grow in Mesopotamia.

Although *Atrahasis* emphasizes the catastrophic nature of the Flood, the ancient Babylonians were well aware that not everything was destroyed; *Erra and Ishum* makes it clear that the city of Sippar survived, a belief echoed by Berossus, who says that ancient writings were buried there before the Flood and later retrieved.

[5] Oppert 1903.

Various stories relating a catastrophic flood are told by Classical authors, focusing upon cities which lie far beyond Mesopotamia, and featuring Ogyges or Deucalion as the hero who survived. Lucian of Samosata (Assyrian Samsat) who wrote *The Syrian Goddess* in the second century AD describes a tradition popular in Hierapolis (modern Membidj) in central Syria, in which Deucalion was the hero, and it was claimed locally that the flood waters vanished down a natural cleft in the bedrock directly beneath the temple of the great goddess. This claim gave the city a focal role in formative cosmic events, and enhanced its prestige and authority. Apollodorus in the first century BC relates the tale of Deucalion, son of Prometheus, who survived a flood that began in Thessaly, in a floating chest or ark, and after nine days and nights drifted on to Mount Parnassus; the account links the flood, as does Genesis and the Sumerian king list, to early genealogies. Ovid in *Metamorphoses*, VIII alluded to an account of the Flood from Phrygia, which can be traced through scattered allusions and a motif on coins to two cities: Apamea Kibotos and Iconium (Konya), two major caravan centres of extreme antiquity. At Apamea the local hill claimed to be Mount Ararat, where the ark came to rest.

All these flood stories may be explained as deriving from the one Mesopotamian original, used in travellers' tales for over two thousand years, along the great caravan routes of Western Asia: translated, embroidered, and adapted according to local tastes to give a myriad of divergent versions, a few of which have come down to us. However, the possibility of several independent origins cannot be dismissed, for the idea of a universal flood may well have arisen to explain observations in different places of marine fossils in rocks high above sea level. At a time when there was no conception of how geological change took place, nor of how vast was the time-scale of evolution, moreover when the creation of man was generally supposed to have accompanied the creation of the earth in its present form, an enormous flood which man by chance survived would be the only way to account for the presence of such marine fossils, and may have been thought up by more than one inquiring mind.

Although the Flood story was known at Ugarit in Syria and Bogazköy in central Anatolia in the Late Bronze Age, it may not have survived the Dark Ages in that area, and so may be a latecomer into Greek mythology, for it is not mentioned by Homer or Hesiod. In Phrygia, where the hero is named on coins as Noah, the tale may have become popular when Jews settled there, and may have been attached at a later date to heroes of much greater antiquity. Where Flood stories are found in other parts of the world, missionaries and early Christian travellers may have disseminated them; there is no reason to suppose that they are indigenous.

OVERPOPULATION AND MORTALITY

When the gods created the first, primeval male and female human beings, they did not allot a life-span for them. This meant that everyone remained alive for centuries, continuing to reproduce until the earth was overcrowded. People died only when the gods were forced to relieve the pressure by sending, intermittently, plague, famine, or flood. Scholars now agree that damaged text near the end of the Epic refers to the gods' decision to institute death as a normal end to human life; the restoration is supported by a newly discovered piece of Sumerian text. This late decision rectified the mistake the gods made in the initial creation of man. In OBV *Gilgamesh* Siduri refers to this decision. The gods also decided to prevent some people breeding, and to institute infant and child mortality.

ATRAHASIS

OBV i   When the gods instead of man[1]
Did the work, bore the loads,
The gods' load was too great,
The work too hard, the trouble too much,[2]
The great Anunnaki made the Igigi
Carry the workload sevenfold.[3]
Anu their father was king,
Their counsellor warrior Ellil,
Their chamberlain was Ninurta,
Their canal-controller Ennugi.
They took the box (of lots) . . . ,
Cast the lots; the gods made the division.[4]
Anu went up to the sky,
[And Ellil (?)] took the earth for his people (?).
The bolt which bars the sea
Was assigned to far-sighted Enki.[5]
When Anu had gone up to the sky,
[And the gods of] the Apsu had gone below,
The Anunnaki of the sky
Made the Igigi bear the workload.
The gods had to dig out canals,
Had to clear channels, the lifelines of the land,
The Igigi had to dig out canals,
Had to clear channels, the lifelines of the land.
The gods dug out the Tigris river (bed)
And then dug out the Euphrates.
[   ] in the deep
[   ] they set up
[   ] the Apsu
[   ] of the land
[   ] inside it
[   ] raised its top
[   ] of all the mountains
They were counting the years of loads;

[   ] the great marsh,
They were counting the years of loads.
For 3,600 years they bore the excess,
Hard work, night and day.
They groaned and blamed each other,
Grumbled over the masses of excavated soil:[6]
   'Let us confront our [   ] the chamberlain,
   And get him to relieve us of our hard work!
   Come, let us carry [the Lord (?)],
   The counsellor of gods, the warrior, from his
      dwelling.
   Come, let us carry [Ellil],
   The counsellor of gods, the warrior, from his
      dwelling.'
Then Alla made his voice heard[7]
And spoke to the gods his brothers, (*gap of about 8 lines*)

ii   'Come! Let us carry
   The counsellor of gods, the warrior, from his
      dwelling.
   Come! Let us carry Ellil,
   The counsellor of gods, the warrior, from his
      dwelling.
   Now, cry battle!
   Let us mix fight with battle!'
The gods listened to his speech,
Set fire to their tools,
Put aside their spades for fire,
Their loads for the fire-god,
They flared up. When they reached
The gate of warrior Ellil's dwelling,
It was night, the middle watch,
The house was surrounded, the god had not
      realized.
It was night, the middle watch,
Ekur was surrounded, Ellil had not realized.
Yet Kalkal was attentive, and had it closed,
He held the lock and watched [the gate].
Kalkal roused [Nusku].
They listened to the noise of [the Igigi].
Then Nusku roused his master,

Made him get out of bed:
    'My lord, your house is surrounded,
    A rabble is running around your door!
    Ellil, your house is surrounded,
    A rabble is running around your door!'
Ellil had weapons brought to his dwelling.
Ellil made his voice heard
And spoke to the vizier Nusku,
    'Nusku, bar your door,
    Take up your weapons and stand in front of me.'
Nusku barred his door,
Took up his weapons and stood in front of Ellil.
Nusku made his voice heard
And spoke to the warrior Ellil,
    'O my lord, your face is (sallow as) tamarisk!⁸
    Why do you fear your own sons?
    O Ellil, your face is (sallow as) tamarisk!
    Why do you fear your own sons?
    Send for Anu to be brought down to you,
    Have Enki fetched into your presence.'
He sent for Anu to be brought down to him,
Enki was fetched into his presence,
Anu king of the sky was present,
Enki king of the Apsu attended.
The great Anunnaki were present.
Ellil got up and the case was put.
Ellil made his voice heard
And spoke to the great gods,
    'Is it against me that they have risen?
    Shall I do battle . . .?
    What did I see with my own eyes?
    A rabble was running around my door!'
Anu made his voice heard
And spoke to the warrior Ellil,
iii   'Let Nusku go out
    And [find out] word of the Igigi
    Who have surrounded your door.
    A command . . .
    To . . .'
Ellil made his voice heard

And spoke to the vizier Nusku,
   'Nusku, open your door,
   Take up your weapons [and stand before me!]
   In the assembly of all the gods,
   Bow, then stand [and tell them],
   "Your father Anu,
   Your counsellor warrior Ellil,
   Your chamberlain Ninurta
   And your canal-controller Ennugi[9]
   Have sent me to say,
   Who is in charge of the rabble?
   Who is in charge of the fighting?
   Who declared war?
   Who ran to the door of Ellil?"'
[Nusku opened] his door,
[Took up his weapons,] went [before (?)] Ellil
In the assembly of all the gods
[He bowed], then stood and told the message.
   'Your father Anu,
   Your counsellor warrior Ellil,
   Your chamberlain Ninurta
   And your canal-controller Ennugi
   Have sent me to say,
   "Who is in charge of the rabble?
   Who is in charge of the fighting?
   Who declared war?
   Who ran to the door of Ellil?"'
[   ]
Ellil [   ]
   'Every single one of us gods declared war!
   We have put [a stop] to the digging.
   The load is excessive, it is killing us!
   Our work is too hard, the trouble too much!
   So every single one of us gods
   Has agreed to complain to Ellil.'
Nusku took his weapons,
Went [and returned to Ellil]
   'My lord, you sent me to [   ].
   I went [   ]
   I explained [   ]

[   ]
Saying, "Every single one of us gods
Declared war.
We have put [a stop] to the digging.
The load is excessive, it is killing us,
Our work is too hard, the trouble too much,
So every single one of us gods
Has agreed to complain to Ellil!"'
Ellil listened to that speech.
His tears flowed.
Ellil spoke guardedly (?),
Addressed the warrior Anu,
   'Noble one, take a decree

iv   With you to the sky, show your strength—
    While the Anunnaki are sitting before you
    Call up one god and let them cast him for
       destruction!'
Anu made his voice heard
And spoke to the gods his brothers,
   'What are we complaining of?
    Their work was indeed too hard, their trouble was
      too much.
    Every day the earth (?) [resounded (?)].
    The warning signal was loud enough, we kept
      hearing the noise.
[   ] do
[   ] tasks (?)

*(gap partly filled, partly overlapped
by the following two SBV fragments)*

SBV   '(While) the Anunnaki are sitting before you,
    And (while) Belet-ili the womb-goddess is
      present,
    Call up one and cast him for destruction!'
Anu made his voice heard and spoke to [Nusku],
   'Nusku, open your door, take up your weapons,
    Bow in the assembly of the great gods, [then
      stand]
    And tell them [   ],
    "Your father Anu, your counsellor warrior Ellil,

Your chamberlain Ninurta and your canal-
controller Ennugi
Have sent me to say,
Who is in charge of the rabble? Who will be in
charge of battle?
Which god started the war?
A rabble was running around my door!'' '
When Nusku heard this,
He took up his weapons,
Bowed in the assembly of the great gods, [then
stood]
And told them [   ],
  'Your father Anu, your counsellor warrior Ellil,
  Your chamberlain Ninurta and your canal-
  controller Ennugi
  Have sent me to say,
  "Who is in charge of the rabble? Who is in
  charge of the fighting?
  Which god started the war?
  A rabble was running around Ellil's door." '

        (*gap of uncertain length*)

SBV   Ea made his voice heard
      And spoke to the gods his brothers,
        'Why are we blaming them?
        Their work was too hard, their trouble was too
        much.
        Every day the earth (?) [resounded (?)].
        The warning signal was loud enough, [we kept
        hearing the noise.]
        There is [   ]
        Belet-ili the womb-goddess is present—
        Let her create primeval man
        So that he may bear the yoke [( )],
        So that he may bear the yoke, [the work of Ellil],
        Let man bear the load of the gods!'

          (*gap*)

OBV   'Belet-ili the womb-goddess is present,
      Let the womb-goddess create offspring,

And let man bear the load of the gods!'
They called up the goddess, asked
The midwife of the gods, wise Mami,
   'You are the womb-goddess (to be the) creator of
      mankind!
   Create primeval man, that he may bear the yoke!
   Let him bear the yoke, the work of Ellil,
   Let man bear the load of the gods!'
Nintu made her voice heard
And spoke to the great gods,
   'It is not proper for me to make him.
   The work is Enki's;
   He makes everything pure!
   If he gives me clay, then I will do it.'
Enki made his voice heard
And spoke to the great gods,
   'On the first, seventh, and fifteenth of the month
   I shall make a purification by washing.
   Then one god should be slaughtered.
   And the gods can be purified by immersion.
   Nintu shall mix clay
   With his flesh and his blood.
   Then a god and a man
   Will be mixed together in clay.
   Let us hear the drumbeat forever after,[10]
   Let a ghost come into existence from the god's
      flesh,[11]
   Let her proclaim it as his living sign,[12]
   And let the ghost exist so as not to forget (the
      slain god).'
They answered 'Yes!' in the assembly,
The great Anunnaki who assign the fates.

On the first, seventh, and fifteenth of the month
He made a purification by washing.
Ilawela who had intelligence,[11]
They slaughtered in their assembly.
Nintu mixed clay
With his flesh and blood.
They heard the drumbeat forever after.

A ghost came into existence from the god's flesh,
And she (Nintu) proclaimed it as his living sign.

v   The ghost existed so as not to forget (the slain god).
After she had mixed that clay,
She called up the Anunnaki, the great gods.
The Igigi, the great gods,
Spat spittle upon the clay.
Mami made her voice heard
And spoke to the great gods,
  'I have carried out perfectly
  The work that you ordered of me.
  You have slaughtered a god together with his
      intelligence.
  I have relieved you of your hard work,
  I have imposed your load on man.
  You have bestowed noise on mankind.
  I have undone the fetter and granted freedom.'
They listened to this speech of hers,[13]
And were freed (from anxiety), and kissed her feet:
  'We used to call you Mami
  But now your name shall be Mistress of All
      Gods.'
Far-sighted Enki and wise Mami
Went into the room of fate.
The womb-goddesses were assembled.
He trod the clay in her presence;[14]

SBV   She kept reciting an incantation,
For Enki, staying in her presence, made her recite
    it.
When she had finished her incantation,
She pinched off fourteen pieces (of clay),
(And set) seven pieces on the right,
Seven on the left.
Between them she put down a mud brick.[15]
She made use of (?) a reed, opened it (?) to cut the
    umbilical cord,[16]
Called up the wise and knowledgeable
Womb-goddesses, seven and seven.
Seven created males,
Seven created females,

For the womb-goddess (is) creator of fate.
He . . .-ed them two by two,[17]
. . .-ed them two by two in her presence.
Mami made (these) rules for people:[18]
  'In the house of a woman who is giving birth
  The mud brick shall be put down for seven days.
  Belet-ili, wise Mami shall be honoured.
  The midwife shall rejoice in the house of the
      woman who gives birth
  And when the woman gives birth to the baby,
  The mother of the baby shall sever herself.
  A man to a girl [   ]

OBV   [   ] her bosom[19]
  A beard can be seen (?)
  On a young man's cheek.
  In gardens and waysides
  A wife and her husband choose each other.'
The womb-goddesses were assembled
And Nintu was present. They counted the months,
Called up the tenth month as the term of fates.

vi   When the tenth month came,
  She slipped in (?) a staff and opened the womb.[20]
  Her face was glad and joyful.
  She covered her head,
  Performed the midwifery,
  Put on her belt, said a blessing.
  She made a drawing in flour and put down a mud
      brick:
  'I myself created (it), my hands made (it).
  The midwife shall rejoice in the house of the
      qadištu-priestess.
  Wherever a woman gives birth
  And the baby's mother severs herself,
  The mud brick shall be put down for nine days.
  Nintu the womb-goddess shall be honoured.
  She shall call their . . . "Mami".[21]
  She shall [ ] the womb-goddess,
  Lay down the linen cloth (?).
  When the bed is laid out in their house,
  A wife and her husband shall choose each other.

Ishtar shall rejoice in the wife-husband
   relationship
In the father-in-law's house.
Celebration shall last for nine days,
And they shall call Ishtar "Ishhara".
[On the fifteenth day (?)], the fixed time of fate
She shall call [   ].

   (*gap of about 23 lines*)

A man [   ]
Clean the home [   ]
The son to his father [   ]
[   ]
They sat and [   ]
He was carrying [   ]
vii He saw [   ]
Ellil [   ]
They took hold of . . . ,
Made new picks and spades,
Made big canals
To feed people and sustain the gods.

   (*gap of about 13 lines*)

600 years, less than 600, passed,[22]
And the country became too wide, the people too
   numerous.
The country was as noisy as a bellowing bull.
The God grew restless at their racket,
Ellil had to listen to their noise.
He addressed the great gods,
   'The noise of mankind has become too much,
   I am losing sleep over their racket.
   Give the order that *šuruppu*-disease shall break
   out,

   (*gap of about 3 lines*)

Now there was one Atrahasis
Whose ear was open (to) his god Enki.
He would speak with his god
And his god would speak with him.

Atrahasis made his voice heard
And spoke to his lord,
   'How long (?) [will the gods make us suffer]?
   Will they make us suffer illness forever?'
Enki made his voice heard
And spoke to his servant:
   'Call the elders, the senior men![23]
   Start [an uprising] in your own house,
   Let heralds proclaim . . .
   Let them make a loud noise in the land:
   Do not revere your gods,[24]
   Do not pray to your goddesses,
   But search out the door of Namtara.
   Bring a baked loaf into his presence.
   May the flour offering reach him,
   May he be shamed by the presents
   And wipe away his "hand".'[25]
Atrahasis took the order,
Gathered the elders to his door.
Atrahasis made his voice heard
And spoke to the elders,
   'I have called the elders, the senior men!
viii   Start [an uprising] in your own house,
   Let heralds proclaim . . .
   Let them make a loud noise in the land:
   Do not revere your gods!
   Do not pray to your goddesses!
   Search out the door of Namtara.
   Bring a baked loaf into his presence.
   May the flour offering reach him;
   May he be shamed by the presents
   And wipe away his "hand".'
The elders listened to his speech;
They built a temple for Namtara in the city.
Heralds proclaimed . . .
They made a loud noise in the land.
They did not revere their god,
Did not pray to their goddess,
But searched out the door of Namtara,
Brought a baked loaf into his presence.

The flour offering reached him.
And he was shamed by the presents.
And wiped away his 'hand'.
The *šuruppu*-disease left them,
[The gods] went back to their [(regular) offerings]

(*2 lines missing to end of column*)

(*Catchline*)
600 years, less than 600 passed.

TABLET II

OBV i   600 years, less than 600, passed[26]
And the country became too wide, the people too
   numerous.
The country was as noisy as a bellowing bull.
The God grew restless at their clamour,
Ellil had to listen to their noise.
He addressed the great gods,
   'The noise of mankind has become too much.
   I am losing sleep over their racket.
   Cut off food supplies to the people!
   Let the vegetation be too scant for their hunger![27]
   Let Adad wipe away his rain.
   Below (?) let no flood-water flow from the
      springs.
   Let wind go, let it strip the ground bare,
   Let clouds gather (but) not drop rain,
   Let the field yield a diminished harvest,
   Let Nissaba stop up her bosom.
   No happiness shall come to them.
   Let their [   ] be dejected.'

   (*gap of about 34 lines to end of column*)

ii   (*gap of about 12 lines at beginning of
   column*)

'Call the [elders, the senior men],
Start an uprising in your house,
Let heralds proclaim . . .

Let them make a loud noise in the land:
Do not revere your god(s)!
Do not pray to your goddess!
Search out the door of Adad,
Bring a baked loaf into his presence.
May the flour offering reach him,
May he be shamed by the presents
And wipe away his ''hand''.'
(Then) he will make a mist form in the morning
And in the night he will steal out and make dew
    drop,
Deliver (?) the field (of its produce) ninefold, like
    a thief.'[28]

They built a temple for Adad in the city,
Ordered heralds to proclaim
And make a loud noise in the land.
They did not revere their god(s),
Did not pray to their goddess,
But searched out the door of Adad,
Brought a baked (loaf) into his presence.
The flour offering reached him;
He was shamed by the presents
And wiped away his 'hand'.
He made mist form in the morning
And in the night he stole out and made dew drop,
Delivered (?) the field (of its produce) ninefold, like
    a thief.
[The drought] left them,
[The gods] went back [to their (regular) offerings].

SBV iii Not three epochs had passed.
The country became too wide, the people too
    numerous.
The country was as noisy as a bellowing bull.
The gods grew restless at their noise.
Enlil organized his assembly again,
Addressed the gods his sons:
  'The noise of mankind has become too much,
  Sleep cannot overtake me because of their racket.
  Command that Anu and Adad keep the (air)
    above (earth) locked,
  Sin and Nergal keep the middle earth locked.

> As for the bolt that bars the sea,
>   Ea with his *lahmu*-creatures shall keep it locked'
> He ordered, and Anu and Adad kept the (air) above
>   (earth) locked,
> Sin and Nergal kept the middle earth locked.
> As for the bolt that bars the sea,
> Ea with his *lahmu*-creatures kept it locked.
> Then the very wise man Atra-hasis
> Wept daily.
> He would carry a *maššakku*-offering along the
>   riverside pasture,
> Although the irrigation-water was silent.
> Half-way through the night he offered a sacrifice.
> As sleep began to overtake him (?)
> He addressed the irrigation-water:
>   'May the irrigation-water take it, may the river
>   carry it,
>   May the gift be placed in front of Ea my lord.
>   May Ea see it and think of me!
>   So may I see a dream in the night.'
> When he had sent the message by water,
> He sat facing the river, he wept (?),
> The man wept (?) facing the river
> As his plea went down to the Apsu.
> Then Ea heard his voice.
> [He summoned his *lahmu*-creatures] and addressed
>   them.

(for the next 36 lines see Supplement 1 on pp. 338–9)

OBV iv   Above, [rain did not fill the canals (?)]
> Below, flood-water did not flow from the springs.
> Earth's womb did not give birth,
> No vegetation sprouted . . .
> People did not look [   ]
> The dark pastureland was bleached,
> The broad countryside filled up with alkali.[30]
> In the first year they ate old grain
> In the second year they depleted the storehouse.[31]
> When the third year came,
> Their looks were changed by starvation,

Their faces covered with scabs (?) like malt.
They stayed alive by ...   ... life.
Their faces looked sallow.
They went out in public hunched,
Their well-set shoulders slouched,
Their upstanding bearing bowed.
They took a message [from Atrahasis to the gods].
In front of [the assembly of the great gods],
They stood [and   ]
The orders [of Atrahasis they repeated]
In front of [   ]

(*gap of about 32 lines to end of column*)

SBV

iv [600 years, less than 600 years, passed.
The country became too wide, the people too
      numerous.]
He grew restless at their noise.
Sleep could not overtake him because of their
      racket.
Ellil organized his assembly,
Addressed the gods his sons,
  'The noise of mankind has become too much.
  I have become restless at their noise.
  Sleep cannot overtake me because of their racket.
  Give the order that *šuruppu*-disease shall break
      out,
  Let Namtar put an end to their noise straight
      away!
  Let sickness: headache, *šuruppu*, *ašakku*,
  Blow in to them like a storm.'
They gave the order, and *šuruppu*-disease did break
      out.
Namtar put an end to their noise straight away.
Sickness: headache, *šuruppu*, *ašakku*,
Blew into them like a storm.
The thoughtful man, Atrahasis[32]
Kept his ear open to his master Ea;
He would speak with his god,

[And his god (?)] Ea would speak with him.
Atrahasis made his voice heard and spoke,
Said to Ea his master,
  'Oh Lord, people are grumbling!
  Your [sickness] is consuming the country!
  Oh Lord Ea, people are grumbling!
  [Sickness] from the gods is consuming the
      country!
  Since you created us
  [You ought to] cut off sickness: headache,
      šuruppu and *ašakku*.'³³
Ea made his voice heard and spoke,
Said to Atrahasis,
  'Order the heralds to proclaim,
  To make a loud noise in the land:
  Do not revere your gods,
  Do not pray to your goddesses!
  [   ] withhold his rites!
  [   ] the flour as an offering
  [   ] to her presence
  [   ] say a prayer
  [   ] the presents]   ]
      his "hand".'
Ellil organized his assembly,
Addressed the gods his sons,
  'You are not to inflict disease on them again,
  (Even though) the people have not diminished—
      they are more than before!
  I have become restless at their noise,
  Sleep cannot overtake me because of their racket!
  Cut off food from the people,
  Let vegetation be too scant for their stomachs!
  Let Adad on high make his rain scarce,
  Let him block below, and not raise flood-water
      from the springs!
  Let the field decrease its yield,
  Let Nissaba turn away her breast,
  Let the dark fields become white,
  Let the broad countryside breed alkali
  Let earth clamp down her teats

So that no vegetation sprouts, no grain grows.
Let *ašakku* be inflicted on the people,
Let the womb be too tight to let a baby out!'
They cut off food for the people,
Vegetation . . . became too scant for their stomachs.
Adad on high made his rain scarce,
Blocked below, and did not raise flood-water from
    the springs.
The field decreased its yield,
Nissaba turned away her breast,
The dark fields became white,
The broad countryside bred alkali.
Earth clamped down her teats:
No vegetation sprouted, no grain grew.
Ašakku was inflicted on the people.
The womb was too tight to let a baby out.

v   Ea kept guard over the bolt that bars the sea,
Together with his *lahmu*-heroes.
Above, Adad made his rain scarce,
Blocked below, and did not raise flood-water from
    the springs.
The field decreased its yield,
Nissaba turned away her breast,
The dark fields became white,
The broad countryside bred alkali.
Earth clamped down her teats:
No vegetation sprouted, no grain grew.
Ašakku was inflicted on the people,
The womb was too tight to let a baby out.

(*gap of 2 lines*)

When the second year arrived
They had depleted the storehouse.
When the third year arrived
[The people's looks] were changed [by starvation].
When the fourth year arrived
Their upstanding bearing bowed,
Their well-set shoulders slouched,
People went out in public hunched over.
When the fifth year arrived,

A daughter would eye her mother coming in;
A mother would not even open her door to her
　　daughter.
A daughter would watch the scales (at the sale of
　　her) mother,
A mother would watch the scales (at the sale of her)
　　daughter.
When the sixth year arrived
They served up a daughter for a meal,
Served up a son for food.
[　　　　　　　　　　　　　　]
Only one or two households were left.
Their faces were covered with scabs (?) like malt.
People stayed alive by . . .　. . . life.
The thoughtful man Atrahasis
Kept his ear open to his master Ea.
He would speak with his god,
And his god Ea would speak with him.
He left the door of his god,
Put his bed right beside the river,
(For even) the canals were quite silent.

　　　　　　(gap of about 25 lines)

vi　When the second year arrived, they had depleted
　　　　the storehouse.
　When the third year arrived
　The people's looks were changed by starvation.
　When the fourth year arrived
　Their upstanding bearing bowed,
　Their well-set shoulders slouched,
　People went out in public hunched over.
　When the fifth year arrived,
　A daughter would eye her mother coming in;
　A mother would not even open her door to her
　　　daughter.
　A daughter would watch the scales (at the sale) of
　　　her mother,
　A mother would watch the scales (at the sale) of her
　　　daughter.
　When the sixth year arrived,

They served up a daughter for a meal,
Served up a son for food.
[   ]
Only one or two households were left.
Their faces were covered with scabs (?) like malt,
The people stayed alive by . . . . . . life.
They took a message [   ]
Entered and [   ]
The order of Atrahasis [   ]
Saying, 'How long [   ]

   (gap of about 36 lines to end of tablet)

OBV

   v   He (Ellil) was furious [with the Igigi,]
      'We, the great Anunna, all of us,
      Agreed together on [a plan].
      Anu and [Adad] were to guard [above],
      I was to guard the earth [below].
      Where Enki [went],
      He was to undo the [chain and set (us) free],
      He was to release [produce for the people].
      He was to exercise [control (?) by holding the
         balance (?)].'[34]
    Ellil made his voice heard
    And [spoke] to the vizier Nusku,
      'Have the fifty (?) *lahmu*-heroes (?) . . . fetched
        for me!
      Have them brought in to my presence!'
    The fifty (?) *lahmu*-heroes (?) were fetched for him.
    The warrior [Ellil] addressed them,
      'We, the great Anunna, [all of us],
      Agreed together on a plan.
      Anu and Adad were to guard above,
      I was to guard the earth below.
      Where you [went],
      [You were to undo the chain and set (us) free],
      [You were to release produce for the people],
      [You were to exercise control (?) by holding the
        balance (?)].'
    [   ].

The warrior Ellil [   ].

     (*gap of about 34 lines*)

vi   'Adad made his rain pour down,
    [   ] filled the pasture land
    And clouds (?) veiled [   ]
    Do not feed his people,
    And do not give Nissaba's corn, luxury for
       people, to eat.'
Then [the god (?)] grew anxious as he sat,[35]
In the gods' assembly worry gnawed at him.
[Enki (?)] grew anxious as he sat,
In the gods' assembly worry gnawed at him.

     (*3 lines fragmentary*)

[They were furious with each other], Enki and Ellil.
    'We, the great Anunna, all of us,
    Agreed together on a plan.
    Anu and Adad were to guard above,
    I was to guard the earth below.
    Where you went,
    You were to undo the chain and set (us) free!
    You were to release produce for the people!
    [You were to exercise control (?)] by holding the
      balance (?).'
[   ].
The warrior Ellil [   ]

     (*gap of 30 lines*)

vii   '[You] imposed your loads on man,
    You bestowed noise on mankind,
    You slaughtered a god together with his
      intelligence,
    You must . . . and [create a flood].
    It is indeed your power that shall be used against
      [your people!]
    You agreed to [the wrong (?)] plan!
    Have it reversed! (?)
    Let us make far-sighted Enki swear . . . an oath.'
Enki made his voice heard

And spoke to his brother gods,
  'Why should you make me swear an oath?
  Why should I use my power against my people?
  The flood that you mention to me—
  What is it? I don't even know!
  Could I give birth to a flood?
  That is Ellil's kind of work!
  Let him choose [   ]
  Let Shullat and [Hanish] march [ahead]
  [Let Erakal pull out] the mooring poles
  Let [Ninurta] march, let him make [the weirs]
    overflow.

      (gap of 2 or 3 lines to end of column)

viii   *(gap of 31 lines)*

The assembly [   ]
Do not listen to [   ]
The gods gave an explicit command.
Ellil performed a bad deed to the people.'
(*Catchline*)
Atrahasis made his voice heard
And spoke to his master,

TABLET III

OBV i   *(gap of about 10 lines)*

Atrahasis made his voice heard
And spoke to his master,
  'Indicate to me the meaning of the dream,
  [   ] let me find out its portent (?)'
Enki made his voice heard
And spoke to his servant,
  'You say, "I should find out in bed (?)".[36]
  Make sure you attend to the message I shall tell
    you!
  Wall, listen constantly to me!
  Reed hut, make sure you attend to all my words!
  Dismantle the house, build a boat,

Reject possessions, and save living things.
The boat that you build
[   ]
[   ]
Roof it like the Apsu
So that the Sun cannot see inside it!
Make upper decks and lower decks.
The tackle must be very strong,
The bitumen strong, to give strength.
I shall make rain fall on you here,
A wealth of birds, a hamper (?) of fish.'
He opened the sand clock and filled it,
He told him the sand (needed) for the Flood was
Seven nights' worth.
Atrahasis received the message.
He gathered the elders at his door.
Atrahasis made his voice heard
And spoke to the elders,
    'My god is out of favour with your god.
    Enki and [Ellil (?)] have become angry with each
        other.
    They have driven me out of [my house].
    Since I always stand in awe of Enki,
    He told (me) of this matter.
    I can no longer stay in [   ]
    I cannot set my foot on Ellil's territory (again).
    [I must go down to the Apsu and stay] with (my)
        god (?).
    This is what he told me.'

        (*gap of 4 or 5 lines to end of column*)

ii   (*gap of about 9 lines*)

The elders [   ]
The carpenter [brought his axe,]
The reed worker [brought his stone,]
[A child brought] bitumen.
The poor [fetched what was needed.]

        (*9 lines very damaged*)

Everything there was [   ]
Everything there was [   ]
Pure ones [   ]
Fat ones [   ]
He selected [and put on board.]
[The birds] that fly in the sky,
Cattle [of Shak]kan,
Wild animals (?) [   ] of open country,
[he] put on board
[   ] . . .
He invited his people [   ]
[   ] to a feast.
[   ] he put his family on board.
They were eating, they were drinking.
But he went in and out,
Could not stay still or rest on his haunches,
His heart was breaking and he was vomiting bile.
The face of the weather changed.
Adad bellowed from the clouds.
When (?) he (Atrahasis) heard his noise,
Bitumen was brought and he sealed his door.
While he was closing up his door
Adad kept bellowing from the clouds.
The winds were raging even as he went up
(And) cut through the rope, he released the boat.

iii   (*6 lines missing at beginning of column*)

Anzu was tearing at the sky with his talons,
[   ] the land,
He broke [   ]
[   ] the Flood [came out (?)].
The *kašūšu*-weapon went against the people like an
        army.
No one could see anyone else,
They could not be recognized in the catastrophe.
The Flood roared like a bull,
Like a wild ass screaming the winds [howled]
The darkness was total, there was no sun.
[   ] like white sheep.
[   ] of the Flood.

[   ]
[   ]
[   ] the noise of the Flood.
[   ]
[Anu (?)] went berserk,
[The gods (?)] ... his sons ... before him
As for Nintu the Great Mistress,
Her lips became encrusted with rime.[37]
The great gods, the Anunna,
Stayed parched and famished.
The goddess watched and wept,
Midwife of the gods, wise Mami:
   'Let daylight (?) ...
   Let it return and ...!
   However could I, in the assembly of gods,
   Have ordered such destruction with them?
   Ellil was strong enough (?) to give a wicked
     order.[38]
   Like Tiruru he ought to have cancelled that
     wicked order![39]
   I heard their cry levelled at me,
   Against myself, against my person.
   Beyond my control (?) my offspring have become
     like white sheep.[40]
   As for me, how am I to live (?) in a house of
     bereavement?
   My noise has turned to silence.
   Could I go away, up to the sky
   And live as in a cloister(?)?
   What was Anu's intention as decision-maker?
   It was his command that the gods his sons
     obeyed,
   He who did not deliberate, but sent the Flood,
   He who gathered the people to catastrophe
   [   ]

iv   (3 *lines missing at beginning of column*)

Nintu was wailing [   ]
   'Would a true father (?) have given birth to the
     [rolling (?)] sea

(So that) they could clog the river like
    dragonflies?[41]
They are washed up (?) like a raft overturned,
They are washed up like a raft overturned in open
    country!
I have seen, and wept over them!
Shall I (ever) finish weeping for them?'
She wept, she gave vent to her feelings,
Nintu wept and fuelled her passions.
The gods wept with her for the country.
She was sated with grief, she longed for beer (in
    vain).
Where she sat weeping, (there the great gods) sat
    too,
But, like sheep, could only fill their windpipes (with
    bleating).
Thirsty as they were, their lips
Discharged only the rime of famine.
For seven days and seven nights
The torrent, storm and flood came on.

(gap of about 58 lines)

v   He put down [   ],
    Provided food [   ]
    [   ]
    The gods smelt the fragrance,
    Gathered like flies over the offering.
    When they had eaten the offering,
    Nintu got up and blamed them all,
      'Whatever came over Anu who makes the
        decisions?
      Did Ellil (dare to) come for the smoke offering?
      (Those two) who did not deliberate, but sent the
        Flood,
      Gathered the people to catastrophe—
      You agreed the destruction.
      (Now) their bright faces are dark (forever).'
    Then she went up to the big flies[42]
    Which Anu had made, and (declared) before the
      gods,

'His grief is mine! My destiny goes with his!
He must deliver me from evil, and appease me!
Let me go out in the morning (?) [   ]
[   ]
vi   Let these flies be the lapis lazuli of my necklace
By which I may remember it (?) daily (?)
    [forever (?)].'
The warrior Ellil spotted the boat[43]
And was furious with the Igigi.
'We, the great Anunna, all of us,
Agreed together on an oath!
No form of life should have escaped!
How did any man survive the catastrophe?'
Anu made his voice heard
And spoke to the warrior Ellil,
'Who but Enki would do this?
He made sure that the [reed hut] disclosed the
    order.'
Enki made his voice heard
And spoke to the great gods,
'I did it, in defiance of you!
I made sure life was preserved [   ]

                 (5 *lines missing*)

Exact your punishment from the sinner.
And whoever contradicts your order

                 (12 *lines missing*)

I have given vent to my feelings!'
Ellil made his voice heard
And spoke to far-sighted Enki,
'Come, summon Nintu the womb-goddess!
Confer with each other in the assembly.'
Enki made his voice heard
And spoke to the womb-goddess Nintu,
'You are the womb-goddess who decrees destinies.[44]
        [   ] to the people.
[Let one-third of them be   ]
    [   ]
[Let another third of them be   ]

vii   In addition let there be one-third of the people,
      Among the people the woman who gives birth yet
         does
      Not give birth (successfully);
      Let there be the *pašittu*-demon among the people,
      To snatch the baby from its mother's lap.
      Establish *ugbabtu, entu, egišītu*-women:[45]
      They shall be taboo, and thus control childbirth.'

         (26 lines missing to end of column)

viii   *(8 lines missing at beginning of column)*

      How we sent the Flood.
      But a man survived the catastrophe.
      You are the counsellor of the gods;
      On your orders I created conflict.
      Let the Igigi listen to this song
      In order to praise you,
      And let them record (?) your greatness.
      I shall sing of the Flood to all people:[46]
      Listen!
      (Colophon)[47]
The End.
Third tablet,
'When the gods instead of man'
390 lines,
Total 1245
For the three tablets.
Hand of Ipiq-Aya, junior scribe.
Month Ayyar [x day],
Year Ammi-ṣaduqa was king.
A statue of himself [   ]
[   ]

NOTES TO *ATRAHASIS*

Text: Lambert and Millard 1969, Moran 1987.
When a speech in the translations breaks off because of a gap in the tablet, inverted commas are not closed so as not to imply the precise point at which the speech ends. Indentation shows, when the text resumes after a gap, whether the speech is thought to continue. The original texts have no punctuation, and since it is not always clear when a speech begins or ends even in a perfectly preserved text, the translator occasionally has to make an arbitrary decision. Words and phrases which require detailed philological argument have not been discussed: oversimplification from a scholarly point of view is inevitably the result. These remarks apply to all translations in this book. A summary of references to research on details of the text of *Atrahasis* is given by Moran 1987, to which add Wiggermann 1986 and Wilcke 1999.
OBV Enki is replaced by Ea, the later form of the name, in SBV.

1. The format of the opening line 'When . . .' may be compared with the *Epic of Creation* and with the *Theogony of Dunnu*. The meaning of this line is disputed. The translation in the original edition as 'When the gods like men' was justified by a supposed grammatical comparison with a line in II. ii, which is invalid; but it finds support in a recension of the text 1,000 years later (Lambert 1969a).
2. Play on words 'load' and 'trouble', *šupšik/šapšaqum*.
3. Or, 'The seven great Anunnaki made the Igigi . . .'
4. Land was divided for inheritance among sons in ancient Mesopotamia by casting lots. Burkert 1983, 53 has pointed out similarities with *Iliad*, XV. 187–193, Poseidon's speech to Iris telling how the earth was originally divided by lot into three domains.
5. The crucial part played by Enki's bolt and his *lahmu*-heroes is discussed in note 26.
6. For *kalakku* meaning 'excavated soil' see AHw *Nachträge*, s.v.
7. This common formulaic phrase says literally 'made/did his mouth', commonly translated 'opened his mouth'. However, it is clear from related phrases in the *Epic of Creation* and *Anzu* (see note 23 to *Anzu*) that the verb implies 'to utter', never 'to open', and 'mouth' has an extended meaning 'speech', attested in various contexts. The Akkadian phrase is alliterative, *pâšu ēpuš*.
8. The same metaphor occurs in the *Descent of Ishtar*.
9. Ennugi: a variant text has Annugal.
10. Perhaps means 'heartbeat, pulse'.
11. Perhaps a play on the words *etemmu* 'ghost' and *tēmu* 'intelligence'.
12. Moran 1970 translates: 'Let her inform him while alive of his token, And so that there be no forgetting, the ghost shall remain.' The meaning of the lines is ambiguous.
13. Wording identical to these four lines occurs in *Anzu*, I. iii.
14. Brick-making procedure is described. The brick god, Kulla, was created

by Enki who pinched off clay for the purpose, according to an incantation called 'When Anu created heaven'.

15. The brick may symbolize the prototype of man's creative ability. One of the names of the mother goddess Belet-ili is 'lapis lazuli brick', and it may be relevant that the bun-shaped 'plano-convex' brick used in early dynastic Mesopotamia resembles the bulge of pregnancy and was widely used for building despite its inappropriate shape. See Woolley/Moorey 1982, 45–6. There is no evidence to support the suggestion (Lambert and Millard 1969, 153) that a brick structure used as a birth stool is intended.

16. Verb translated 'made use of (?)' perhaps *bedû*; see AHw *Nachträge*, s.v.

17. Possibly 'crowned' or 'veiled'—the midwife covers her own head in the next episode, but the meaning is uncertain. The word occurs only in the singular.

18. The translation of the following lines largely follows Wilcke 1985a, 295 ff.

19. Possibly there is a small gap in the text here.

20. The word used for 'staff' here also means a term or recurrent period of time.

21. Or, 'She shall name Mami as their . . .'

22. Six hundred years is a round number in the sexagesimal system used by the ancient Mesopotamians. As a numerical unit, 600 was the simple noun *nēru* in Akkadian. Repetition of a number seems to occur as a literary device, e.g. in *Gilgamesh*, VI. ii. 'you dug seven and seven pits for him', or XI. 'arranged the jars seven and seven'.

23. See AHw *Nachträge*, s.v. *sillūnu*.

24. Probably refers to the concept which was prevalent in Mesopotamia of a personal god and goddess for each person.

25. 'Hand (of a god)' is a common Akkadian expression for a disease. For the verb, see AHw *Nachträge*, s.v. *šukkulu*.

26. The structure of Tablet II is difficult to see. OBV and SBV may diverge, and the point at which they overlap is uncertain. Particularly mystifying is the repeated description of six years of famine in SBV v. and vi. A fragmentary tablet from Babylon (Lambert and Millard 1969, 116 ff.) implies that Ea's *lahmu*-heroes, who were in charge of the bolt that guarded the sea, went out of control and let out fish which broke the bolt and nourished mankind (with F. Wiggermann 1986, 286, reading *làh-mi-ka/šu* instead of *šam-mi-ka/šu* 'his plants').

27. These lines were used in an incantation against drought according to a neo-Assyrian compilation (Lambert and Millard 1969, 28).

28. See AHw, s.v. *tušûm*. 'Ninefold' perhaps echoes the nine months of pregnancy and the nine days in which the brick was put down, in Tablet I. 'Thief' or, 'a benefactor', *šarrāqi* or *šarrāki*.

29. For this passage see Moran 1987, who shows why, in the flood episode, Ea/Enki had to communicate with Atrahasis by means of the reed hut, because he had been sworn to secrecy.

30. These lines refer to salination, the crystallization of salts on the topsoil when drainage of irrigation water is inadequate.

31. See Moran 1985.
32. Note the literary strategem which defies literal chronology by featuring Atrahasis as the same mortal in recurrent crises 600 years apart.
33. Or: '[Will you] cut off sickness?'
34. Literally: 'by weighing with (?) the *ašqulālu*', following AHw *Nach-träge*, s.v. *ašqulālu*; and see Glossary, s.v.
35. See Veenhof 1975–6.
36. See von Soden 1979, 32.
37. The translation takes the noun as *pulhītu* 'scab' and the verb as *arāru* 'to rot, discharge putrid liquid'.
38. See Moran 1981.
39. This reference is not understood.
40. See AHw, s.v. *ṣuppu*. Presumably means, 'like sacrificial sheep'.
41. The drowning of masses of dragonflies is alluded to also in Ut-napishtim's speech in *Gilgamesh*, X. vi.
42. The symbolism of the flies is not certain. According to Parpola 1983, 316, fly-shaped beads were used in self-flagellation by devotees of Ishtar to induce ecstasy, but he quotes no evidence. Kilmer 1987 takes them as symbolic of death and of bravery in battle. A text fragment included in Campbell Thompson 1930, plate 59, says that all the gods of Uruk turned into flies when they abandoned Uruk, so possibly there is an allusion in this passage to a previous event when the gods abandoned mankind. See also *Gilgamesh*, note 139.
43. The word used for 'boat' here, *makurru*, implies a large cargo vessel shaped like the gibbous moon.
44. At this juncture the gods replaced *lullû*, primeval man who had no natural life-span, with mortal man. Therefore the Flood marks the transition from primeval men who lived for centuries, to men whose lives decline in old age, as now. See Wilcke 1999 and George 1999.
45. These are classes of female devotees attached to temples who were not usually allowed to bear children.
46. This type of line is often found at the start of oral narrative: cf. *Gilgamesh*, *Anzu*, and *Erra and Ishum*.
47. Brief colophons also exist for the first and second tablets of *Atrahasis*. Elsewhere in this volume the translator has selected colophons arbitrarily, particularly if they are well preserved and interesting, in order to illustrate the kinds of information which they can provide.

The Epic of Gilgamesh

The *Epic of Gilgamesh* is the longest and greatest literary composition written in cuneiform Akkadian. It narrates a heroic quest for fame and immortality, pursued by a man who has an enormous capacity for friendship, for endurance and adventure, for joy and sorrow, a man of strength and weakness who loses a unique opportunity through a moment's carelessness. Our interest lies not only in the story and its characters, but also in the unique opportunity the epic provides for tracing earlier, independent folk-tales which were combined in the creation of the whole work, and we can see how the whole work in written form never became fossilized, but was constantly altered through contact with a continuing oral narrative tradition.

It is particularly difficult for the modern student of *Gilgamesh* to come to grips with the subject, for no new edition of the epic has appeared for half a century. In that time many new fragments of the epic have been discovered on a variety of archaeological sites and in museums, and our understanding of the historical background has improved very considerably. But the new information has made it increasingly apparent that we cannot often use one fragment to restore another, because each period and area had its own version of the story, so we cannot simply reconstruct a master version with variants in the way that Hebrew and Classical texts can be edited, and a new fragment may perplex us rather than elucidating an old problem. In fact, the more text fragments come to light, the harder it becomes to produce one coherent edition.

The work is classed as an epic because it features the heroic exploits of a dimly historical figure with, on the sidelines, gods and goddesses who sometimes take a part in the action, and occasionally direct mortal affairs; nevertheless, we gain an overall impression of the free will of man which can fashion its own destiny and occasionally thwart the wishes of heaven. There is no suggestion anywhere that the epic was performed or recited as part of a ceremony or ritual. The specific purpose for which it was composed is a difficult question, but the general

purpose for which the epic and its constituent stories existed in
oral form is very probably entertainment, whether in royal
courts, in private houses, around the camp-fires of desert
caravans, or on the long sea voyages between the Indus and the
head of the Arabian Gulf.

GILGAMESH IN HISTORY

We now know for certain that Gilgamesh was considered in
antiquity to be a historical character. For a long time it was not
clear whether the earlier parts of the Sumerian king list, in
which superhuman lengths of reign were attributed to all rulers,
were entirely fictional or mythical. Historical inscriptions of a
king of Kish, Enmebaragesi, who belongs to the same era, have
now come to light.

There are two different traditions concerning the parentage of
Gilgamesh. The epic itself says that one Lugalbanda was his
father, a man who is known from the Sumerian king list to have
occupied the throne of Uruk two kings before Gilgamesh and to
have been a shepherd; Sumerian epic stories about Lugalbanda
are extant. In spite of extensive and thorough excavations at
Uruk, no contemporary inscriptions are yet known for
Gilgamesh or for Lugalbanda. Precise dates cannot be given for
the lifetime of Gilgamesh, but they are generally agreed to lie
between 2800 and 2500 BC.

Another tradition of parentage for Gilgamesh comes,
curiously enough, from the king list itself, which mentions
parenthetically that the father of Gilgamesh was a *lillu* (a man
with demonic qualities), and a high priest of Kullab, which is a
part of Uruk. We could, of course, try to reconcile the two
traditions by claiming that Lugalbanda must have started life as
a *lillu*-man who became a priest at Kullab before he became king
of Uruk, but other discrepancies in the epic which cannot be
reconciled show two quite different traditions at work. Possibly
Gilgamesh conquered Uruk as an outsider, and then 'adopted' as
his father a famous ruler of the usurped dynasty. Subsequent
usurpers in ancient Mesopotamia often acted in this way. The
mother of Gilgamesh plays a part in the early episodes of the
epic; she is Ninsun, the goddess Lady Wild Cow, from whom he

inherited divinity as two-thirds of his nature. Tablets dating not long after Gilgamesh's probable lifetime show that he was regarded as a god in Mesopotamia.

The city which Gilgamesh and his father ruled is firmly identified as modern Warka in central Iraq. Excavations by German archaeologists have shown that it was enormously important in the late fourth millennium BC, with an elaborate central complex of monumental architecture. The city originally consisted of two separate towns on either side, probably, of a canal. In one town the chief, patron deity was the sky god An (or Anu); in the other it was Inanna (Ishtar) the goddess of love and war. According to traditions that emanate from Uruk, as does this epic, Inanna was the daughter of An, and the great temple which she inhabited was called Eanna, which could be translated as 'House of An (or, the sky)'. So there is a close connection between the two deities, and together they play a part at a crucial moment in the epic.

Also associated with the city of Uruk is a very early tradition of literacy, and the same is true of Shuruppak, the city of Utnapishtim: early cuneiform and pre-cuneiform clay tablets have been found on both sites. But this fact cannot be connected with the epic as written literature, for there is no evidence that any of the Gilgamesh stories were written down before about 2150 BC. The so-called 'Gilgamesh figure', a hero shown grappling masterfully with wild animals on cylinder seals and sculptures, is attested much earlier than any of the written Gilgamesh stories, earlier even than the putative existence of the hero as king of Uruk. Perhaps at times this powerful, traditional image was associated with Gilgamesh, but other associations, for instance with Nergal, Enkidu, or Shakkan, were probably also valid at different periods of extreme antiquity in Mesopotamia.

EARLY SUMERIAN STORIES FROM URUK

Around 2150 BC, there existed in written form three groups of stories about kings of Uruk. One group featured the exploits of Enmerkar, who was perhaps the grandfather of Gilgamesh. Another group featured the exploits of Lugalbanda, and a third group featured Gilgamesh. Most of the tales were very short;

they were all written in Sumerian, and some of them showed the background influence of 'contest' literature, a form of entertainment in which opposing points of view are aired, whether the merits of two deities, two people, two different animals, or two metals, for example. Such verbal contests were popular at royal courts even in medieval times, and can be found among the *Arabian Nights*.

These short stories, then, were written in Sumerian at a time when the whole land was ruled by kings of Ur in the south of Mesopotamia, a dynasty which seems to have had a special relationship with Uruk and which tried to associate its traditions with that great city. Until quite recently, it was supposed that Sumerian was the indigenous, spoken language of Ur and Uruk at that time, but we now think that this may not have been the case; it has even been suggested that Gilgamesh himself would have spoken in Akkadian, not Sumerian. Many problems concerned with the Sumerian language have yet to be solved, but it should be noted that we do not possess any evidence for groups of Sumerian stories about kings of cities other than Uruk.

The great king Shulgi, who ruled Ur from c.2150 to 2103 BC, as the second king of the third dynasty, took a keen interest in the Gilgamesh stories. He claimed that Ninsun was his own mother, and that Gilgamesh was thus his brother. His reign was a time of innovative composition, and many Sumerian hymns were written about Shulgi, who was regarded as a god during his own lifetime.

Some of the Sumerian tales about Gilgamesh were incorporated, with considerable changes, into the Akkadian epic, but at least one was not. The stories are:

1. *Gilgamesh and the halub-tree*, also known as *Gilgamesh, Enkidu, and the Netherworld*. Two versions exist in Sumerian. A part of the story was used in Tablet XII of the Akkadian epic, some time after the epic had been composed as an essentially eleven-tablet composition. In the process of adaptation, the story was changed enough that we cannot regard all of it as a direct translation, but should perhaps consider that a different version of the story, not yet attested in Sumerian sources, was used.

2. *Gilgamesh and Huwawa*, also known as *Gilgamesh and the Land of the Living*. Huwawa (Humbaba) was a monster who

guarded the pine forest. His face resembled coiled intestines, and he possessed killer rays. The Sumerian version of the story seems to be set in the Zagros mountains on the border of Elam (south-west Iran) to the east of Mesopotamia, but the Akkadian versions say distinctly that the location was Lebanon, west of Mesopotamia. There is no way in which we can reconcile the two sources; instead, they should be considered as variant versions of the same story which a flourishing oral tradition was continually changing in order to fit in with local interests and relate to the experience of particular audiences. There are many other ways in which the Sumerian story differs from the Akkadian versions, and the two known versions in Sumerian differ from each other.

3. *Gilgamesh and the Bull of Heaven*. This short Sumerian story was expanded considerably when it was incorporated into the Akkadian epic.

4. *The Death of Gilgamesh*. The Sumerian story is very fragmentary, but shows the theme of a man's quest for immortality which is denied by the gods. This is important for showing that the theme which runs right through the Akkadian epic was taken from one of the Sumerian short stories and given a new and larger setting. Both in content and in structure, the story resembles a composition known as *The Death of Ur-Nammu* (ruler of Ur 2168–2151 BC), a liturgical hymn recited in honour of the deceased monarch.

5. *The Flood*. This story seems to have been an independent tale in Sumerian. It was used not only as an episode in the final version of this epic, but was also incorporated, perhaps more effectively, into *Atrahasis*, as one method by which the gods tried to reduce overpopulation. It had no connection originally with Uruk or with Gilgamesh, and may not have been included in the Old Babylonian version of the *Epic of Gilgamesh*. The hero is a man of Shuruppak, a city not far from Uruk.

The Flood story in two of its versions contains conflicting geographical detail: the Sumerian version says that Ziusudra ended up on the island of Dilmun (Bahrain) in the Gulf, but the Akkadian story says that Ut-napishtim ended up at 'The mouth of the rivers'. Bahrain lies some 300 miles from the delta where the Tigris and Euphrates rivers flow into the sea, but we can reconcile the accounts by using a belief known from Arab tradition: that the Tigris and Euphrates flow beneath the sea and then surface in Bahrain and Failake, bringing their water to islands which are famed for their miraculous supply of sweet water.

Another problem in the story concerns the location of the mountain on which the ark eventually came to rest. No mountain is named in the Sumerian version; in spite of gaps in the text, it looks as if the sun comes out and dries up the water and the ark does not come to rest on anything but the emerging flat land. The Akkadian version names Mount Nimush, the Greek source of Berossus names Armenia, and Genesis names Mount Ararat. Now, Mount Nimush is elsewhere attested in the annals of the Assyrian king Assurnaṣirpal II in the tenth century BC, in a region that could just be described as southern Armenia, but definitely not as far north as Mount Ararat. The version with Mount Nimush may be no earlier than the date of the seventh-century text in which alone it is attested, or it could have been inspired by Assurnasirpal's famous campaign, or it could be earlier still. In any case, the two mountains which are named, Ararat in Genesis and Nimush in Akkadian *Gilgamesh*, are definitely different places.

6. *The Descent of Inanna/Ishtar to the Underworld* is known independently in Sumerian and as a shorter version in Akkadian; a translation of the latter is given in this volume. The story continued to exist independently after some of its opening lines were incorporated into *Gilgamesh*, VII. In addition, the lines in *Gilgamesh*, XII which describe Gilgamesh's attempts to persuade the great gods to help in releasing Enkidu from the Underworld closely resemble the similar episode in the Sumerian *Descent of Inanna*, where the petitioner is the goddess' vizier. The Sumerian story may originally have belonged to a group of tales about the god Dumuzi. It has no original connection either with Uruk or with the hero Gilgamesh.

7. *Gilgamesh and Agga* is a Sumerian tale of confrontation between the hero and his contemporary Agga, who was king of Kish, to the north of Uruk. It was not used in any way in the Akkadian epic.

DIFFERENT VERSIONS OF THE EPIC

It is evident from the wealth of background stories, to which the different versions of the *Epic of Gilgamesh* may be added, that in many ways the Gilgamesh literature provides ideal material for studying the formation of the epic. However, the difficulties are still enormous because the material is so fragmentary. Seldom indeed do extant fragments of different versions cover the same episodes. Some tablets were written by schoolboys whose muddles and omissions reveal their immaturity and, perhaps, the speed of dictation, rather than true textual variation. Some important episodes are still missing from all versions, and some chapters of the standard version contain a number of fragments which cannot be placed in the correct sequence with any confidence.

The Sumerian stories are now thought to be separate entities rather than forming a single epic, although it is possible that they were sometimes narrated as one series of tales. They were popular in the early second millennium but are almost certainly earlier.

The Old Babylonian tablets written in Akkadian, which date to the early second millennium, in some passages diverge fairly widely from the standard version, although there are other passages which are virtually identical. They may have formed a single, integrated epic, but this is uncertain; they definitely lacked the prologue and may have lacked the Flood story. They were found at Ur in southern Iraq; at Sippar on the Euphrates above Babylon, and at Ishchali in the kingdom of Eshnunna, east of the Tigris.

The widest geographical spread of tablets occurs in the mid- to late second millennium, but all the evidence is extremely fragmentary: an Akkadian tablet from Megiddo in Palestine, one from Emar on the Middle Euphrates (south of Carchemish), and versions in the Akkadian, Hittite, and Hurrian languages found at Hattusas, the Hittite capital in northern Anatolia. There are also some temple library tablets from the late second millennium found at Assur. These fragments do not reveal whether substantially different versions were current in written form nor whether the prologue or the Flood story had yet been incorporated.

The standard version is the best known, mainly from tablets found at Nineveh which include more than one copy of the work (each with different arrangements of tablets and columns). The palace library at Nineveh was begun by Sennacherib and completed by Assurbanipal in the first half of the seventh century BC, but there was also a library in the temple of Nabu the god of writing, and some tablets from Nimrud may have been incorporated into the Nineveh collection, since the excavator, Sir Henry Austin Layard, thought that Nimrud was a part of Nineveh. One tablet has more recently come to light from the temple of Nabu at Nimrud. Some school exercise tablets come from the site of Sultantepe near Harran, dating to the late eighth or seventh century BC.

The standard version uses and adapts some known Sumerian stories as well as others for which written forerunners are not known, such as Enkidu's seduction by Shamhat, and the aetiological story which tells why snakes shed their old skins. But it also contains other material, particularly in the first part of the epic, which may never have existed independently. With considerable skill a single work is created out of diverse elements. The methods used to stitch the pieces together are several. First, the hero Gilgamesh is present almost the entire time, although sometimes as the silent audience to another man's tale. Second, the theme of searching for fame early in the story develops into a quest for immortality in the latter part. Third, the main eleven tablets are introduced by a prologue which is repeated as an epilogue at the end. Fourth, the three dreams of Gilgamesh in Tablet IV and of Enkidu in Tablet VII are probably used to heighten tension, perhaps using wilful misinterpretation that would have been recognized as such by an audience that foresaw the approach of disaster and death. Set phrases, in particular the formulaic introduction to direct speech, also give a certain cohesion, although they are not quite standardized throughout the epic and help to betray its composite nature.

A small amount of a late version from Uruk, possibly as late as the Seleucid period, mainly covers an episode which is not yet extant in the standard version, so it is uncertain to what extent the Akkadian epic remained unchanged in its written form after the fall of Nineveh in 612 BC. Cuneiform tablets found at Ugarit and at Hattusas show that the training of scribes in cities outside the control of Babylon or of Assyria was by no means a standard one. Each court may have used local, existing written or oral material for its own purposes, adapting it to its needs. This is quite distinct from principles of scholarly scribal tradition within one particular kingdom or empire, which demanded that temple tablets be copied with scrupulous accuracy for a new library, as one of the prerogatives of conquest.

AUTHORSHIP AND COMPOSITION

Mesopotamian tradition ascribed the authorship of the seventh-century version found at Nineveh to one Sin-leqe-unnini, a master scribe and incantation-priest of the Kassite period, and it seems on the whole acceptable to treat this tradition without undue suspicion. But we shall probably never know to what extent he took a ready-formed oral narrative and just divided the text up into eleven tablets. It is recognized increasingly that a surge of literary invention, collection, and recording in Mesopotamia took place under the Kassite kings of the mid-second millennium, and that libraries were collected together in subsequent periods by copying from originals dating to that time and largely preserved in the temple libraries of Ur, Uruk, Sippar (the sun god's temple recently excavated with its library intact by Iraqi archaeologists), Nippur, and Babylon. Tablet XII, which describes Enkidu's visit to the Underworld, was appended after the prologue and epilogue had been added, perhaps during the seventh or late eighth centuries, for reasons which are still not clear. The *Odyssey* of Homer includes as a late addition a story about a man's direct contact with the Underworld, and it is possible that the *Epic of Gilgamesh*, the *Iliad*, and the *Odyssey* shared in part a common background.

This suggestion arises partly from the fact that echoes of stories from both the Greek and the Akkadian compositions are found in the *Arabian Nights*. The *Tale of Buluqiya* bears resemblances to the *Epic of Gilgamesh* which are too close to be dismissed as coincidental. The story takes place at a time when Greek was written, in other words, in pre-Islamic times. The young king Buluqiya (whose name may be a hypocoristic form of Sumerian or Hurrian Bilgamesh) sets out with a bosom friend to search for immortality, to obtain Solomon's ring (which replaces the Humbaba episode). His friend dies an untimely death at the moment when success is within their reach. Buluqiya's subsequent travels lead him through a subterranean passage (cf. *Gilgamesh*, IX. v.), reaching a kingdom where the trees have emerald leaves and ruby fruit (cf. IX. v.), and meeting a far-distant king Sakhr who has obtained immortality in a way that is impossible now for Buluqiya, by drinking from the Fountain of Life which is guarded by Al-Khiḍr (the Islamic sage for whom Atrahasis has long been recognized as forerunner). King Sakhr expounds to Buluqiya the early history of the world (cf. XI. 10–197), and then Buluqiya is spirited straight back home. The story is used to foretell the coming of Mohammed.

The story of Odysseus and Calypso in *Odyssey*, V is recognized to have some close resemblances to the episode of Gilgamesh and Siduri: the lone female plies the inconsolable hero-wanderer with drink and sends him off to a place beyond the sea reserved for a special class of honoured people. To prepare for the voyage he has to cut down and trim timbers. Atrahasis at the mouth of the rivers is replaced by Alkinoos and the blessed isle of the Phaeacians, kinsmen of the gods.

Two of the stories of Sinbad the Sailor bear close resemblances to tales in the *Odyssey*. The third voyage of Sinbad is in essence that of the Cyclops, a giant who lives on an island and eats captive sailors one by one until Sinbad blinds him with a red-hot iron, whereupon the remnant escapes as the blinded giant gropes around enraged. He hurls a rock into the sea and drowns all but two of the sailors. The fourth voyage of Sinbad can be compared with the Circe story: the sailors, captured on an island, are tempted into gluttony by magic food and driven out to the meadows like cattle by a herdsman. Only Sinbad, like Odysseus, resists temptation.

These points of contact between stories of Gilgamesh, of Odysseus, and of Sinbad and Buluqiya in the *Arabian Nights* show clearly that traditional tales were reused and adapted for different ethnic and geographical settings by ancient and medieval story-tellers, by Semites and by Greeks.

It is traditional in the Near East for desert people who travel with trading caravans to nurture the skills of the musician-poet, and we know that such people travelled with trading caravans from at least the Middle Bronze Age up until modern times. It is also traditional for ships' captains to acquire and treasure the services of musician-poets for the long voyage from Basra to India, Ceylon, and Indonesia. Under such conditions of transmission, it is no surprise to find that different versions of a favourite story contain a variety of details that cannot and should not be reconciled on the theory of a single ancestry. Instead, we may interpret different versions as displaying an endless variety due to the inventive imagination and embroidery of three or four millennia's worth of travelling raconteurs who were highly prized professionals. So extensive in duration and distance were those journeys in both ancient and medieval times, that a long story in which old folk-tales were given a new and compelling setting, skilfully recombined to create a coherent whole, was wonderful entertainment.

GILGAMESH AND KINGSHIP

Kingship was the only form of government in ancient Mesopotamia, ordained by the gods for the guidance and prosperity of people and cities, to maintain order and to protect the weak in society. Among the king's duties were military leadership, priestly functions, law-giving, and city-building. Whenever kingship broke down, so did law and order, with terrible consequences. Gilgamesh as a young king behaved badly, but this was no reason to depose him, and eventually he became wise, thanks to the gods' help through Enkidu. For the ancient Mesopotamians, *The Epic of Gilgamesh* showed that kingship must be supported even though individual kings are imperfect.

GILGAMESH

TABLET I

SBV i [Of him who] found out all things, I [shall te]ll the
land[1],
[Of him who] experienced everything, [I shall tea]ch
the whole.
He searched (?) lands (?) everywhere.
He who experienced the whole gained complete
wisdom.
He found out what was secret and uncovered what
was hidden,
He brought back a tale of times before the Flood.[2]
He had journeyed far and wide, weary and at last
resigned.
He engraved all toils on a memorial monument of
stone.
He had the wall of Uruk built, the sheepfold
Of holiest Eanna, the pure treasury.
See its wall, which is like a copper band,
Survey its battlements, which nobody else can
match,
Take the threshold, which is from time immemorial,
Approach Eanna, the home of Ishtar,
Which no future king nor any man will ever match!
Go up on to the wall of Uruk and walk around!
Inspect the foundation platform and scrutinize the
brickwork!
Testify that its bricks are baked bricks,
And that the Seven Counsellors must have laid its
foundations![3]
One square mile is city, one square mile is orchards,
one square mile is claypits, as well as the open
ground of Ishtar's temple.
Three square miles and the open ground comprise
Uruk.

Look for the copper tablet-box,
Undo its bronze lock,
Open the door to its secret,
Lift out the lapis lazuli tablet and read it,
The story of that man, Gilgamesh, who went
    through all kinds of sufferings.
He was superior to other kings, a warrior lord of
    great stature,[4]
A hero born of Uruk, a goring wild bull.
He marches at the front as leader,
He goes behind, the support of his brothers,
A strong net, the protection of his men,
The raging flood-wave, which can destroy even a
    stone wall.
Son of Lugalbanda, Gilgamesh, perfect in strength,
Son of the lofty cow, the wild cow Ninsun.
He is Gilgamesh, perfect in splendour,[5]
Who opened up passes in the mountains,
Who could dig pits even in the mountainside,
Who crossed the ocean, the broad seas, as far as the
    sunrise.
Who inspected the edges of the world, kept
    searching for eternal life,
Who reached Ut-napishtim the far-distant, by force.
Who restored to their rightful place cult centres (?)
    which the Flood had ruined.[6]
There is nobody among the kings of teeming
    humanity
Who can compare with him,
Who can say 'I am king' beside Gilgamesh.
Gilgamesh (was) named from birth for fame.
ii Two-thirds of him was divine, and one-third mortal.
Belet-ili designed the shape of his body,[7]
Made his form perfect, [   ]
[   ] was proud [   ]
[   ]
[   ]

In Uruk the Sheepfold he would walk about,
Show himself superior, his head held high like a
    wild bull.

He had no rival, and at his *pukku*[8]

His weapons would rise up, his comrades have to
     rise up.

The young men of Uruk became dejected in their
     private [quarters (?)].

Gilgamesh would not leave any son alone for his
     father.

Day and night his [behaviour (?)] was overbearing.

He was the shepherd (?) [   ]

He was their shepherd (?) yet [   ]

Powerful, superb, [knowledgeable and expert],

Gilgamesh would not leave [young girls alone],

The daughters of warriors, the brides of young
     men.

The gods often heard their complaints.

The gods of heaven [   ] the lord of Uruk.
     'Did [Aruru (?)] create such a rampant wild bull?
     Is there no rival? At the *pukku*
     His weapons rise up, his comrades have to rise
        up.
     Gilgamesh will not leave any son alone for his
        father.
     Day and night his [behaviour (?)] is overbearing.
     He is the shepherd of Uruk the Sheepfold,
     He is their shepherd, yet [   ]
     Powerful, superb, knowledgeable [and expert],
     Gilgamesh will not leave young girls [alone],
     The daughters of warriors, the brides of young
        men.
     Anu often hears their complaints.'

They called upon great Aruru:
     'You, Aruru, you created [mankind (?)]!
     Now create someone for him, to match (?) the
        ardour (?) of his energies![9]
     Let them be regular rivals, and let Uruk be
        allowed peace!'

When Aruru heard this, she created inside herself
     the word (?) of Anu.[10]

Aruru washed her hands, pinched off a piece of clay,
     cast it out into open country.

She created a [primitive man], Enkidu the warrior:
  offspring of silence (?), sky-bolt of Ninurta.[10]
His whole body was shaggy with hair, he was
  furnished with tresses like a woman,
His locks of hair grew luxuriant like grain.
He knew neither people nor country; he was
  dressed as cattle are.
With gazelles he eats vegetation,
With cattle he quenches his thirst at the watering
  place.
With wild beasts he presses forward for water.
A hunter, a brigand,[11]
Came face to face with him beside the watering
  place.
He saw him on three successive days beside the
  watering place.
The hunter looked at him, and was dumbstruck to
  see him.
In perplexity (?) he went back into his house
And was afraid, stayed mute, was silent,
And was ill at ease, his face worried.
[   ] the grief in his innermost being.
His face was like that of a long-distance traveller.[12]

iii The hunter made his voice heard and spoke, he said
       to his father,
     'Father, there was a young man who came [from
       the mountain (?)],
     [On the land] he was strong, he was powerful.
     His strength was very hard, like a sky-bolt of
       Anu.[13]
     He walks about on the mountain all the time,
     All the time he eats vegetation with cattle,
     All the time he puts his feet in (the water) at the
       watering place.
     I am too frightened to approach him.
     He kept filling in the pits that I dug [   ],
     He kept pulling out the traps that I laid.
     He kept helping cattle, wild beasts of open
       country, to escape my grasp.
     He will not allow me to work [in open country].'

His father spoke to him, to the hunter,
  '[   ] Uruk, Gilgamesh.
  [   ] his open country.
  [His strength is very hard, like a sky-bolt of Anu]
  [Go, set] your face [towards Uruk].
  [   ] the strength of a man,
  [   ] lead (her) forth, and
  [   ] the strong man.
  When he approaches the cattle at the watering
      place,
  She must take off her clothes and reveal her
      attractions.
  He will see her and go close to her.
  Then his cattle, who have grown up in open
      country with him, will become alien to him.'
[He listened] to the advice of his father [   ].
The hunter went off [to see Gilgamesh (?)].
He took the road, set [his face] towards Uruk,
Entered the presence (?) of Gilgamesh [   ]:
  'There was a young man who [came from the
      mountain (?)],
  On the land he was strong, he was powerful.
  His strength is very hard, like a sky-bolt of Anu.
  He walks about on the mountain all the time,
  All the time he eats vegetation with cattle,
  All the time he puts his feet in (the water) at the
      watering place.
  I am too frightened to approach him.
  He kept filling in the pits that I dug,
  He kept pulling out the traps that I laid.
  He kept helping cattle, wild beasts of open
      country, to escape my grasp.
  He did not allow me to work in the open
      country.'
Gilgamesh spoke to him, to the hunter,
  'Go, hunter, lead forth the harlot Shamhat,[14]
  And when he approaches the cattle at the
      watering place,
  She must take off her clothes and reveal her
      attractions.

He will see her and go close to her.
Then his cattle, who have grown up in open
    country with him, will become alien to him.'
The hunter went; he led forth the harlot Shamhat
    with him,
And they took the road, they made the journey.
In three days they reached the appointed place.
Hunter and harlot sat down in their hiding
    place (?).
For one day, then a second, they sat at the watering
    place.
Then cattle arrived at the watering place; they drank.

iv Then wild beasts arrived at the water; they satisfied
    their need.
And he, Enkidu, whose origin is the mountain,
(Who) eats vegetation with gazelles,
Drinks (at) the watering place with cattle,
Satisfied his need for water with wild beasts.
Shamhat looked at the primitive man,
The murderous youth from the depths of open
    country.
   'Here he is, Shamhat, bare your bosom,
Open your legs and let him take in your
    attractions!
Do not pull away, take wind of him!
He will see you and come close to you.
Spread open your garments, and let him lie upon
    you,
Do for him, the primitive man, as women do.
Then his cattle, who have grown up in open
    country with him, will become alien to him.
His love-making he will lavish upon you!'
Shamhat loosened her undergarments, opened her
    legs and he took in her attractions.
She did not pull away. She took wind of him,
Spread open her garments, and he lay upon her.[15]
She did for him, the primitive man, as women do.
His love-making he lavished upon her.
For six days and seven nights Enkidu was aroused
    and poured himself into Shamhat.

When he was sated with her charms,
He set his face towards the open country of his
    cattle.
The gazelles saw Enkidu and scattered,
The cattle of open country kept away from his
    body.
For Enkidu had stripped (?); his body was too clean.
His legs, which used to keep pace with (?) his cattle,
    were at a standstill.
Enkidu had been diminished, he could not run as
    before.
Yet he had acquired judgement (?), had become
    wiser.
He turned back (?), he sat at the harlot's feet.
The harlot was looking at his expression,
And he listened attentively to what the harlot said.
The harlot spoke to him, to Enkidu,
    'You have become [profound] Enkidu, you have
        become like a god.
    Why should you roam open country with wild
        beasts?
    Come, let me take you into Uruk the Sheepfold,
    To the pure house, the dwelling of Anu and
        Ishtar,
    Where Gilgamesh is perfect in strength,
    And is like a wild bull, more powerful than (any
        of) the people.'
She spoke to him, and her speech was acceptable.
Knowing his own mind (now), he would seek for a
    friend.
Enkidu spoke to her, to the harlot,
    'Come, Shamhat; invite me
    To the pure house, the holy dwelling of Anu and
        Ishtar,
    Where Gilgamesh is perfect in strength,
    And is like a wild bull, more powerful than (any
        of) the people.
    Let me challenge him, and [   ]
v   (By saying:) "In Uruk I shall be the strongest!"
    I shall go in and alter destiny:

One who was born in open country has
    [superior(?)] strength!'
Shamhat answered,
    'Come on, let us go forth, and let me please you!
    [   ] there are, I know.
Go, Enkidu, into Uruk the Sheepfold
Where young men are girded with sashes
And every day is a feast day,
Where the drums are beaten
And girls (?) [show off] (their) figures,
Adorned with joy and full of happiness.
In bed at night great men [   ]
O Enkidu! You who [know nothing (?)] of life!
Let me show you Gilgamesh, a man of joy and
    woe!
Look at him, observe his face,
He is beautiful in manhood, dignified,
His whole body is charged with seductive charm.
He is more powerful in strength of arms than
    you!
He does not sleep by day or night.
O Enkidu, change your plan for punishing him!
Shamash loves Gilgamesh,
And Anu, Ellil, and Ea made him wise!
Before you came from the mountains,
Gilgamesh was dreaming about you in Uruk.
Gilgamesh arose and described a dream, he told it
    to his mother,[16]
"Mother, I saw a dream in the night.
There were stars in the sky for me.
And (something) like a sky-bolt of Anu kept
    falling upon me!
I tried to lift it up, but it was too heavy for me.
I tried to turn it over, but I couldn't budge it.
The country(men) of Uruk were standing over
    [it].[17]
[The countrymen had gathered (?)] over it,
The men crowded over it,
The young men massed over it,
They kissed its feet like very young children.

I loved it as a wife, doted on it,
[I carried it], laid it at your feet,
You treated it as equal to me."
[The wise mother of Gilgamesh], all-knowing,
   understood,
She spoke to her lord.
[The wise wild cow Ninsun] all-knowing,
   understood,
She spoke to Gilgamesh,
"[When there were] stars in the sky for you,
And something like a sky-bolt of Anu kept falling
   upon you,
You tried to lift it up, but it was too heavy for you,
You tried to turn it over, but you couldn't budge
   it,
[You carried it], laid it at my feet,
I treated it as equal to you,
And you loved it as a wife, and doted on it:

vi   (It means) a strong partner shall come to you,
   one who can save the life of a friend,
He will be the most powerful in strength of arms
   in the land.
His strength will be as great as that of a sky-bolt
   of Anu.
You will love him as a wife, you will dote upon
   him.
[And he will always] keep you safe (?).
[That is the meaning] of your dream."[18]
Gilgamesh spoke to her, to his mother.
"Mother, I have had a second dream.
An axe was thrown down in the street (?) of
   Uruk the Sheepfold and they gathered over it,
The country(men) of Uruk stood over it.
The land gathered together over it,
The men massed over it.
[I carried it], laid it at your feet.
I loved it as a wife, doted upon it.
And you treated it as equal to me."
The wise mother of Gilgamesh, all-knowing,
   understood, she spoke to her son.

The wise wild cow Ninsun, all-knowing,
    understood, she spoke to Gilgamesh,
"The copper axe which you saw is a man.
You will love it as a wife, you will dote upon it,
And I shall treat it as equal to you.
A strong partner will come to you, one who can
    save the life of a comrade.
He will be the most powerful in strength of arms
    in the land.
His strength will be as great as that of a sky-bolt
    of Anu."
Gilgamesh spoke to his mother,
"Let it fall, then, according to the word of Ellil
    the great counsellor.
I shall gain a friend to advise me."
Ninsun retold his dreams.'
Thus Shamhat heard the dreams of Gilgamesh and
    told them to Enkidu.
'[The dreams mean that you will lo]ve one
    another.

TABLET II

(II. i not extant; gap of about 45 lines)

ii Enkidu was seated before her in Tirannu
   [   ] tears
   [   ] trusted Mulliltu

    (gap of a few lines)

Why [   ]
They were consulting together by
    themselves [   ]
At his decision [   ]
Who understood in his heart [   ]
Which Shamhat [   ]
One garment [   ]
And a second garment which [   ]
She held him (by the hand (?)) and like
    gods [   ]

To the shepherds' hut [   ]
The shepherds were gathered around him
Of their own accord, and by themselves—
   'The young man—how like Gilgamesh in build,
   Mature in build, as sturdy (?) as battlements.
   Why was he born in the mountains?
   He is just as powerful in strength of arms as a
      sky-bolt of Anu!'
They put food in front of him; [   ]
They put drink in front of him; [   ]
Enkidu would not eat the food; he narrowed his
      eyes and stared.

     (*gap of a few lines*)

[   ]   [   ]
He slew wolves and [   ]
[   ] the herdsmen [   ]
Enkidu[   ] a herdsman [   ]
[   ] you stayed at home [   ]
[   ] Uruk the Sheepfold [   ]

     (*gap*)

[He stood] in the street of Uruk [the Sheepfold]
[   ] the strong [   ]
He barred the way [of Gilgamesh]
The country of Uruk was standing around him,
The country gathered together over him,
The men massed (?) over him,
The young men crowded over him,
Kissed his feet as if he were a toddler.
When the young man [   ]
The bed was laid at night for Ishhara
And for godlike Gilgamesh an equal match was
      found.
Enkidu blocked his access at the door of the father-
    in-law's house,
He would not allow Gilgamesh to enter.
They grappled at the door of the father-in-law's house,
Wrestled in the street, in the public square. [19]
Doorframes shook, walls quaked.

iii   (*about 37 lines missing*)

'He was the most powerful in strength of arms in
   the land,
His strength was as great as that of a sky-bolt of
   Anu,
A build as sturdy as battlements [   ].'
The [wise] mother of Gilgamesh, [all-knowing (?)],
Spoke [to her son].
The wild cow Ninsun [spoke to Gilgamesh],
   'My son, [   ]
   Bitterly [   ]
iv [   ]
Seized [   ]·
He brought up to his door [   ]
Bitterly he was weeping [   ]
   'Enkidu had no [   ]
   His hair is allowed to hang loose [   ]·
   He was born in open country, and who can
      prevail over him?'
Enkidu stood, listened to him speaking,
Pondered, and then sat down, began to cry.
His eyes grew dim with tears.
His arms slackened, his strength [( )]
(Then) they grasped one another,
And embraced and held (?) hands.
[Gilgamesh made his voice heard and spoke],
He said [to] Enkidu,
   '[Why are your eyes] filled [with tears]?

        (*about 29 lines missing*)

v   'Ellil has destined him to keep the Pine Forest
        safe,[20]
   To be the terror of people.
   Humbaba, whose shout is the flood-weapon,
      whose utterance is Fire, and whose breath is
      Death,
   Can hear for a distance of sixty leagues
      through (?) the . . . of the forest, so who can
      penetrate his forest?[21]

Ellil has destined him to keep the Pine Forest
safe, to be the terror of people:
Debility would seize anyone who penetrated his
forest.'
Gilgamesh spoke to him, to Enkidu,
'Are you saying that [   ]?

(gap of about 34 lines)

vi [   ]
Gilgamesh [made his] voice heard [and spoke to
Enkidu],
'My friend, are there not [   ]²²
Are there no children (?) [   ]?'
Enkidu made his voice heard and [spoke to
Gilgamesh],
'My friend, were we to go to him, [   ]
Humbaba [   ]'
Gilgamesh made his voice heard [and spoke to
Enkidu],
'My friend, we really should [   ]

(gap of a few lines)

They sat and pondered on [   ]
'We made a *hassinnu*-axe [   ]
A *pāšu*-axe with a whole talent of [bronze for
each half (?)]
Their swords weighed a whole talent
each; [   ]
Their belts weighed a whole talent each; their
belts [   ]
(new break) ... (new break) ... [   ]²³
Listen to me, young men
Young men of Uruk who know [   ]
I am adamant: I shall take the road [to Humbaba].
I shall face unknown opposition, [I shall ride
along an unknown] road.
Give me your blessing, since I [have decided (?)]
on the course,
That I may enter the city-gate of Uruk [again in
future (?)]

And [celebrate] the New Year Festival once again
  in [future] years (?),[24]
And take part in the New Year Festival in years
  [to come] (?).
Let the New Year Festival be performed, let joy
  [resound],   ]
  Let *illuru*-cries ring out in [   ].'[25]
Enkidu gave advice to the elders,
The young men of Uruk [   ]
  'Tell him not to go to the [Pine] Forest,
  That journey is not to be undertaken! A
  man [   ]
  The guardian of the Pine [Forest   ]

   (*gap of a few lines*)

The great counsellors of Uruk rose up
And gave an opinion to [Gilgamesh]:
  'You are [still young (?), Gilgamesh, you are
  impetuous to [   ],
  But you do not know what you will
  find [   ]
  Humbaba, whose shout is the flood-weapon,
  Whose utterance is Fire and whose breath is Death,
  Can hear for up to sixty leagues the sounds
  of his forest.
  Whoever goes down to his forest
  [   ] or two.
  Who, even among the Igigi, can face him?
  Ellil destined him to keep the Pine Forest safe, to
  be the terror of people.'
Gilgamesh listened to the speech of the great
  counsellors.

   (*gap of a few lines*)

TABLET III

i [   ]
  Do not trust entirely, Gilgamesh, in your own
  strength.

When you have looked long enough, trust to
   your first blow.
He who leads the way will save his comrade.
He who knows the paths, he will (?) guard his
   friend.
Let Enkidu go in front of you,
He knows the way of the Pine Forest.
He can look at the fight and instruct in the battle.
Let Enkidu guard the friend, keep the comrade
   safe,
Bring him back safe in person for brides,[26]
So that we in our assembly may rely on you as
   king,
And that you in turn as king may rely on us
   again.'
Gilgamesh made his voice heard and spoke,
He said to Enkidu,
   'Come, my friend, let us go to the great palace,
   To Ninsun, the great queen.
   Ninsun is wise, all-knowing, she understands,
   She will set the steps of good advice at our feet.'
They grasped each other by the hand,
And Gilgamesh and Enkidu went to the great palace,
To Ninsun the great queen.
Gilgamesh rose up and entered into [   ].
   'Ninsun, I am adamant. [I shall take]
   The distant path to where [Humbaba lives].
   [I shall face] unknown [opposition],
   [I shall ride along] an unknown [road][27]
   Until the day when, having travelled far and
      wide,
   I finally reach the Pine Forest,
   Until I slay ferocious Humbaba,
   And exterminate from the land Something Evil,
      which Shamash hates.[28]

            (*about 5 lines missing*)

   [   ] into your presence.'
[Ninsun] paid attention [to all the words]
Of Gilgamesh, her son.

ii   Ninsun entered her chamber.
     [   ] soap-plant.
     [She put on a garment (?)], adornment of her body,
     [Put on toggle-pins (?),] adornment of her breast,
     [   ], wore her crown on her head.
     [   ] . . .
     [   ] she went up on to the roof.
     She came before Shamash, made a smoke-offering,
     Made a *surqinnu*-offering before Shamash and
          raised her arms:
          'Why did you single out my son Gilgamesh (and)
               impose a restless spirit on him?
          Now you have affected him and he will take[29]
          The distant path to where Humbaba lives.
          He faces an unknown struggle,
          He will ride along an unknown road
          Until the day when, having travelled far and
               wide,
          He finally reaches the Pine Forest,
          Until he slays ferocious Humbaba,
          And exterminates from the land Something Evil
               which you hate.
          On the day when you [   ] at the side
               of [   ],
          May Aya, the daughter-in-law, not be too fearful
               of you to commend him to you.
          Entrust him (?) to the night watchmen,
          [   ] whip [   ]

               (*gap of about 13 lines*)

               (*column iii fragmentary*
                    See Supplement 2, p. 340)

iv   (*gap of about 13 lines*)

     [   ] Gilgamesh [   ]
     She extinguished the smoke-offering
          and [   ].
     She called Enkidu to her and gave her decision.
          'Enkidu, you are a strong man, though not from
               my womb.

Now, your offspring [shall be dedicated to
    Shamash (?)] with the oblates of Gilgamesh:[30]
Priestesses, devotees, and votaresses.'
She placed symbols around Enkidu's neck, (saying)
'Priestesses have accepted the orphan,
The daughters of gods have adopted a foundling.
I hereby take Enkidu to be my son.
Gilgamesh shall accept Enkidu [as his brother].'

   (*3 lines fragmentary*)

[   ] to the Pine Forest
Whether a month (?) [or   ]
Whether a year (?) [or   ].'

   (*gap of about 4 lines*)[31]

   (*A damaged fragment indicates that Gilgamesh
   and Enkidu make offerings of juniper and incense
   at a shrine. A door of pine is mentioned, perhaps
   promised to Ellil in return for success against
   Humbaba*)

v   (*this gap and the next gap represent about
   27 lines*)

'[Let Enkidu] guard the friend, [keep the comrade
    safe.]
[Let him bring him back safe in person] for brides,
So that we in our assembly may rely on you as
    king,
And that you in turn as king may rely on us
    again.'
Enkidu made his voice heard and spoke,
He said to [Gilgamesh],
 'My friend, turn back [   ]
 A journey that is not [   ]

   (*gap*)

vi   (*See Supplement 3, p. 341*)

TABLET IV

i   (*gap of about 5 lines?*)

At twenty leagues they ate their ration.[32]
At thirty leagues they stopped for the night.
Fifty leagues they travelled during the day.
The distance (took from) the new moon to the full
    moon, then three days more: they came to
    Lebanon.
(There) they dug a pit in front of Shamash.
They [refilled their waterskins (?)].
Gilgamesh went up on to the mountain,
And made his flour-offering to [   ]:[33]
  'O mountain, bring me a dream, a favourable
    one!'
Enkidu arranged it (?) for him, for Gilgamesh.
A dust-devil passed by, and he/it
    fixed (?) [   ]
He made him lie down inside the circle
    and [   ]
[   ] like wild barley [   ]
    blood (?) [   ].[34]
Gilgamesh sat with his chin on his knees.
Sleep, which spills out over people, overcame him.
In the middle watch he finished his sleep.
He rose up and said to his friend,
  'My friend, didn't you call me? Then why am I
    awake?
  Didn't you touch me? Why am I so upset?
  Didn't a god pass by? Then why is my flesh so
    feeble?
  My friend, [I had a dream (?)]
  And the dream that I had was extremely
    upsetting.
  At the foot of the mountain [   ]
  [   ] fell/hit [   ].
  We were like flies (?) [   ].'
[He who] was born in open country, and [   ]
Enkidu explained the dream to his friend.

'My friend, your dream is favourable.
The dream is very significant [   ]
My friend, the mountain which you
    saw [(   )] (means:)
We shall seize Humbaba, sl[ay him],
And cast his corpse on to waste ground.
At the light of dawn we shall hear the favourable
    word of Shamash.'
At twenty leagues they ate their ration.
At thirty leagues they stopped for the night.
(There) they dug a pit in front of Shamash.[35]
Gilgamesh went up on to [the mountain]
And made his flour-offering to [   ]
    'O mountain, bring me a dream, a favourable
        one!'
Enkidu arranged it for him, for Gilgamesh.

> (*gap into which the following may be
> restored:*)

(A dust devil passed by, and he/it fixed [   ]
He made him lie down inside the circle and [   ]
[   ] like wild barley [   ]
Gilgamesh sat with his chin on his knees.
Sleep, which spills out over people, overcame him.
In the middle watch he finished his sleep,
He rose up and said to his friend,
    'My friend, didn't you call me? Then why am I
        awake?
    Didn't you touch me? Why am I so upset?
    Didn't a god pass by? Then why is my flesh so
        feeble?
    My friend, I had a second (?) dream,
    And the dream that I had was extremely
        upsetting.)

> (*The contents of the second dream are not
> preserved*)

ii   (*about 20 lines missing*)

    'My friend, this [is the explanation of your
        dream (?)]

Humbaba like [   ]
Until light flared up (?) [   ]
We shall place on top of him (?) [   ]
We were furious [at (?)] Humbaba [(   )]
[   ] we stood over him.
And in the morning the word of Shamash was
    favourable.'
At twenty leagues they ate their ration.
At thirty leagues they stopped for the night.
Fifty leagues they travelled during the day.
(There) they dug a pit in front of Shamash.
They refilled (?) [their waterskins (?)],
Gilgamesh went up on to [the mountain],
And made his flour-offering to [   ]:

iii   'O mountain, bring me a dream, a favourable
          one!'
Enkidu arranged it for him, for Gilgamesh.
A dust-devil passed by, and he/it fixed [   ]
He made him lie down inside the circle
    and [   ]
[   ] like wild barley [   ]
Gilgamesh sat with his chin on his knees.
Sleep, which spills out over people, overcame him.
In the middle watch he finished his sleep.
He rose up and said to his friend,
    'My friend, didn't you call me? Then why am I
        awake?
    Didn't you touch me? Why am I so upset?
    Didn't a god pass by? Then why is my flesh so
        feeble?
    My friend, I had a third dream,[36]
    And the dream that I had was extremely
        upsetting.
    Heaven cried out, earth groaned.
    Day grew silent, darkness emerged,
    Lightning flashed, fire broke out.
    [Flames] crackled, death rained down.[37]
    (Then) sparks were dimmed, and the fire was
        extinguished.
    [The coals which] kept falling turned to embers.

[Let us go back] down to open country where we
    can get advice.'
Enkidu listened, and made him accept his dream; he
    spoke to Gilgamesh,

      (interpretation of third dream missing)[38]

      (gap of about 23 lines)

iv?   *(About 6 lines of 45 partly preserved)*

'[One alone cannot (?)   ]*[39]*
[They are strangers (?)   ]
It is a slippery path, and [one] does
    not [   ] But two [   ]
Two ... [   ]
A three-stranded cord [is hardest to break (?)]
A strong lion [cannot prevail over (?) two of its
    own cubs.]

      (Column v not extant; gap of about 45 lines)

vi   *(gap of about 15 lines)*

Enkidu made his voice heard and spoke; he said to
    Gilgamesh,
    '[How (?)] can I go down into [the Pine Forest?]
    Or open up the path, when my arms are
     paralysed (?) ?'
Gilgamesh made his voice heard and spoke; he said
    to Enkidu,
    'Why, my friend, do we [talk (?)] like cowards?
    We can cross all the mountains [   ]
    [   ] to our face, before (?) we have
     cut down [pines (?)]
    My friend, experienced in conflict, who
     has [   ] battle,
    You have rubbed yourself with plants so you
     need not fear death.
    You shall have a double mantle of radiance
     like ...
    Your shout shall be as loud as a kettledrum.
    Paralysis shall leave your arms, and impotence
     shall leave your loins.

Hold my hand, my friend, let us set off!
Your heart shall soon burn (?) for conflict; forget
    death and [think only of] life (?).
Man is strong, prepared to fight, responsible.
He who goes in front (and) guards his (friend's)
    body, shall keep the comrade safe.
They shall have established fame for their
    [future (?)].'
[   ] they arrived together.
[   ] of their words, they stood.
(*Catchline*)
They stood and admired (?) the forest.

TABLET V

SBV i They stood at the edge of the forest,
       Gazed and gazed at the height of the pines,
       Gazed and gazed at the entrance to the pines,
       Where Humbaba made tracks as he went to and fro.
       The paths were well trodden and the road was
           excellent.
       They beheld the Pine Mountain, dwelling-place of
           gods, shrine of Irnini.
       The pines held up their luxuriance even on the face
           of the mountain.
       Their shade was good, filling one with happiness.
       Undergrowth burgeoned, entangling the forest.

       (*8 fragmentary lines, then gap*)

       (*They entered the forest and found
       Humbaba*)[40]

LV   Humbaba made his voice heard and spoke; he said
           to Gilgamesh,
       'The fool Gilgamesh (and (?)) the brutish man
           ought to ask themselves, why have you come
           to see me?[41]
       Your [friend] Enkidu is small fry who does not
           know his own father!

You are so very small that I regard you as I do a
   turtle or a tortoise
Which does not suck its mother's milk, so I do
   not approach you.
[Even if I] were to kill (?) you, would I satisfy
   my stomach?
[Why,   ], Gilgamesh, have you let (him)
   reach me,
[   ] ...
So I shall bite [through your/his] windpipe and
   neck, Gilgamesh,
And leave [your/his body] for birds of the forest,
   roaring (lions), birds of prey and scavengers.'
Gilgamesh made his voice heard and spoke; he said
   to Enkidu,
   'My friend, Humbaba has changed his mood
   And ... has come upon him [   ]⁴²
   And my heart [trembles lest he   ]
      suddenly!'
Enkidu made his voice heard and spoke; he said to
   Gilgamesh,
   'My friend, why do you talk like a coward?
   And your speech was feeble (?), and you tried to
      hide (?).
   Now, my friend, he has drawn you out (?)
   With the (blow)pipe of the coppersmith for
      heating (?)
   To count back each league swollen (?) with the
      heat (?), each league of cold,
   To dispatch the flood-weapon, to lash with the
      whip!
   Don't retrace your footsteps! Don't turn back!
   [   ] Make your blows harder!

         (*gap of a few lines (?)*)

SBV   His (Gilgamesh's) tears flowed before
          Shamash [( )]⁴³
       'Remember what you said in Uruk!
       Stand there (?) and listen to me! (?)'
       [Shamash] heard the words

Of Gilgamesh, scion of Uruk, [and said],
  'As soon as a loud voice from the sky calls down
    to him,[44]
  Rush, stand up to him, let him not [enter the
    forest (?)],
  Let him not go down to the wood,
    nor [   ].
  [Humbaba] will [not] be clothed in seven cloaks,[45]
  He will be wearing [only one]; six are taken
    off (?).
  Like a charging wild bull which
    pierces [   ]
  He shouts only once, but fills one with terror.
  The guardian of the forests will shout [   ]
  [   ]
  Humbaba like [   ] will shout.

        (*gap of uncertain length*)

ii As soon as the swords [   ]
    [   ] from the sheaths [   ]
    Streaked with verdigris (?) [   ][46]
    Dagger, sword [   ]
    One [   ]
    They wore [   ]
    Humbaba [made his voice heard and spoke (?)]
      'He will not go (?) [   ]
      He will not go (?) [   ]

          (*7 lines illegible*)

    May Ellil [   ].'
    Enkidu [made] his voice heard [and spoke],
    [He addressed his speech (?)] to Humbaba,
      'One alone (?) [cannot   ]
      They are strangers (?) [   ]
      It is a slippery path, and [one] does not
    [but two   ]
      Two . . . [   ]
      A three-stranded cord [is hardest to break (?)]
      A strong lion [cannot prevail over (?)] two of its
        own cubs.

(*3 broken lines, then gap of uncertain length,
then 2 broken lines*)

LV He struck (?) (his) head (?), and matched
    him [   ]
They stirred up the ground with the heels of their
    feet,[47]
Sirara and Lebanon were split apart at their
    gyrations,
White clouds grew black,
Death dropped down over them like a fog.
Shamash summoned up great tempests against
    Humbaba,
South Wind, North Wind, East Wind, West Wind,
    Moaning Wind,
Gale, *šaparziqqu*-Wind, *imhullu*-Wind, . . .-Wind
Asakku, Wintry Wind, Tempest, Whirlwind,
Thirteen winds rose up at him and Humbaba's face
    grew dark.[48]
He could not charge forwards, he could not run
    backwards.
Thus the weapons of Gilgamesh succeeded against
    Humbaba.
Humbaba gasped for breath, he addressed
    Gilgamesh,
    'You are young, Gilgamesh; your mother gave
    birth to you,
    And you are the offspring of [   ]
    You rose (?) at the command of Shamash, Lord of
    the Mountain
    And you are the scion of Uruk, king Gilgamesh.
    [   ] Gilgamesh [   ]
    [   ]
    Gilgamesh [   ]
    I shall make (them) grow luxuriantly for you
    in [   ]
    As many trees as you [   ]
    I shall keep for you myrtle wood, [   ]
    Timbers to be the pride [of your palace (?)].'
Enkidu made his voice heard and spoke; he said to
    Gilgamesh,

'[My friend], don't listen to [the words] of
Humbaba.

(*3 broken lines, gap of about 15 lines*)

iii 'You have found out the nature of my forest, the
nature [of my dwelling]
And (now) you know all their . . .-s.
I should have taken you (and) slain you at the
entrance to my forest's growth,
I should have given your flesh to be eaten by the
birds of the forest, roaring (lions), birds of
prey, and scavengers.
But now, Enkidu, it is in your power (?) to . . .,
So tell Gilgamesh to spare my life (?)!'
Enkidu made his voice heard and spoke; he said to
Gilgamesh,
'My friend, finish him off, slay him, grind him
up, that [I may survive]
Humbaba the guardian of the [Pine] Forest!
Finish him off, slay him, grind him up that [I
may survive]
Humbaba, the guardian of the forest.
(Do it) before the leader Ellil hears, [(   )]
[Lest (?)] the gods (?) be filled with fury at
us [(   )]
Ellil in Nippur, Shamash in [Sippar].
Set up an eternal [memorial]
To [tell] how Gilgamesh [slew] Humbaba!'
Humbaba listened, and [   ]

(*gap of about 20 lines*)

iv (*gap of about 24 lines*)

'You sit like a shepherd [   ]
And just like . . . [   ]
Now, Enkidu, thus settle (?) your own
release (?)[49]
And tell Gilgamesh that he may save his life.'
Enkidu made his voice heard and spoke; he said [to
Gilgamesh],
'My friend, [finish off] Humbaba, the guardian of

the Pine Forest, [finish him off], slay him [and
    grind him up, that I may survive].
(Do it) before the leader Ellil
    hears, [   ]
Lest (?) the gods (?) be filled with fury at
    us [   ].
Ellil in Nippur, Shamash in Sippar. [Set up an
    eternal memorial]
To tell how Gilgamesh [slew (?)] Humbaba.'
Humbaba listened and [   ]

v   (*gap of about 13 lines*)

'Neither one of them shall outlive
His friend! Gilgamesh and Enkidu shall never
    become (?) old men (?).'⁵⁰
Enkidu made his voice heard and spoke; he said to
    Gilgamesh,
'My friend, I talk to you but you don't listen to
    me!

          (*2 broken lines*)

[   ] of his friend.
[   ] at his side.
[   ]
[   ] until he pulled out the entrails.
[   ] he/it springs away.
[   ] sharpens (?) teeth
[   ] abundance (?) fell on to the mountain.
[   ] abundance (?) fell on to the mountain.

          (*8 lines missing to end of column*)

vi   (*gap of about 22 lines*)

[   ] their dark patch (?) of verdigris.
Gilgamesh was cutting down the trees; Enkidu kept
    tugging at the stumps.
Enkidu made his voice heard and spoke; he said to
    Gilgamesh,
'My friend, I have had a fully mature pine cut
    down,

The crown of which butted against the sky.
I made a door six poles high and two poles wide,
Its doorpost is a cubit . . ., its lower and upper
    hinges are (made) from a single [   ].
Let the Euphrates carry [it] to Nippur;
    Nippur [   ].
[   ].'

They tied together a raft, they put down [   ]
Enkidu embarked [   ]
And Gilgamesh [   ] the head of Humbaba.
(*Catchline*)
He washed [his filthy] hair, [he cleaned his gear]
(*Colophon*)
Fifth tablet, series [of Gilgamesh]

TABLET VI

SBV i He washed his filthy hair, he cleaned his gear,
Shook out his locks over his back,
Threw away his dirty clothes and put on fresh ones.
He clothed himself in robes and tied on a sash.
Gilgamesh put his crown on his head
And Ishtar the princess raised her eyes to the
    beauty of Gilgamesh.
    'Come to me, Gilgamesh, and be my lover!
    Bestow on me the gift of your fruit!
    You can be my husband, and I can be your
        wife.[51]
    I shall have a chariot of lapis lazuli and gold
        harnessed for you,
    With wheels of gold, and horns of *elmēšu*-stone[52]
    You shall harness *ūmu*-demons as great mules!
    Enter into our house through the fragrance of
        pine!
    When you enter our house
    The wonderfully-wrought threshold shall kiss
        your feet![53]
    Kings, nobles, princes shall bow down beneath
        you.

The verdure (?) of mountain and country shall
    bring you produce,[54]
Your goats shall bear triplets, your ewes twins,
Your loaded donkey shall outpace the mule.
Your horses shall run proud at the chariot,
[Your ox] shall be unrivalled at the yoke.'
Gilgamesh made his voice heard and spoke,
He said to Ishtar the princess,
    'What could I give you if I possessed you?
I would give you body oil and garments,
I would give you food and sustenance.
Could I provide you with bread fit for gods?
Could I provide you with ale fit for kings?
[   ]
Could I heap up [   ]
[   ] a robe?
[if] I possess you?
[You would be   ] ice,
A draughty door that can't keep out winds and
    gusts,
A palace that [rejects (?)] its own warriors (?),

ii   An elephant which [   ] its covering
Bitumen which [stains (?)] its carrier,
A waterskin which [soaks (?)] its carrier,
A juggernaut (?) which [smashes (?)] a stone
    wall,[55]
A battering ram which destroys [   ] of
    war,
A shoe which bites into [the foot] of its wearer.
Which of your lovers [lasted] forever?
Which of your masterful paramours went to
    heaven?
Come, let me [describe (?)] your lovers to you!
He of the sheep (?) [... ... ...]
    knew him:
For Dumuzi the lover of your youth
You decreed that he should keep weeping year
    after year.
You loved the colourful *allallu*-bird,[56]
But you hit him and broke his wing.

He stays in the woods crying "My wing!"
You loved the lion, whose strength is complete,[57]
But you dug seven and seven pits for him.[58]
You loved the horse, so trustworthy in battle,
But you decreed the whip, goad, and lash for him,
You decreed that he should gallop seven leagues
(non-stop),
You decreed that he should be overwrought and
thirsty,
You decreed endless weeping for his mother
Sililu.
You loved the shepherd, herdsman, and chief
shepherd
Who was always heaping up the glowing ashes
for you,
And cooked ewe-lambs for you every day.[59]
But you hit him and turned him into a wolf,
His own herd-boys hunt him down
And his dogs tear at his haunches.[60]
You loved Ishullanu, your father's gardener,
Who was always bringing you baskets of dates.
They brightened your table every day;
You lifted your eyes to him and went to him
"My own Ishullanu, let us enjoy your strength,
So put out your hand and touch our vulva!"

iii   But Ishullanu said to you,
"Me? What do you want of me?
Did my mother not bake for me, and did I not
eat?
What I eat (with you) would be loaves of
dishonour and disgrace,
Rushes would be my only covering against the
cold."
You listened as he said this,
And you hit him, turned him into a frog (?),
Left him to stay amid the fruits of his labours.
But the pole (?) goes up no more, [his] bucket
goes down no more.[61]
And how about me? You will love me and then
[treat me] just like them!'

When Ishtar heard this,
Ishtar was furious, and [went up] to heaven.
Ishtar went up and wept before her father Anu,
Her tears flowed before her mother Antu.
>'Father, Gilgamesh has shamed me again and
>   again!
>Gilgamesh spelt out to me my dishonour,
>My dishonour and my disgrace.'
Anu made his voice heard and spoke,
He said to the princess Ishtar,
>'Why (?) didn't you accuse Gilgamesh the king
>   for yourself,
>Since Gilgamesh spelt out your dishonour,
>Your dishonour and your disgrace?'
Ishtar made her voice heard and spoke,
She said to her father Anu,
>'Father, please give me the Bull of Heaven, and
>   let me strike Gilgamesh down!
>Let me . . . Gilgamesh in his dwelling!
>If you don't give me the Bull of Heaven,
>I shall strike (?) [   ]
>I shall set my face towards the infernal regions,
>I shall raise up the dead, and they will eat the
>   living,[62]
>I shall make the dead outnumber the living!'
Anu made his voice heard and spoke,
He said to the princess Ishtar,
>'On no account should you request the Bull of
>   Heaven from me!
>There would be seven years of chaff in the land
>   of Uruk,
>You would gather chalk (?) [instead of gems (?)],
>You would raise (?) grass (?) [instead of . . . (?)].'
Ishtar made her voice heard and spoke,
She said to her father Anu,
>'I have heaped up a store [of grain in Uruk (?)],
>I have ensured the production of [   ],
>[   ] years of chaff.
>[   ] has been gathered.
>[   ] grass.

[   ] for him.

(*gap of one or more lines*)

[   ] of the Bull of Heaven [   ].'

iv   Anu listened to Ishtar speaking,
And he put the Bull of Heaven's reins in her hands.
Ishtar [took hold] and directed it.
When it arrived in the land of Uruk
It [   ]
It went down to the river, and seven [   ]
    river [   ].
At the snorting of the Bull of Heaven a chasm
    opened up, and one hundred young men of
    Uruk fell into it,
Two hundred young men, three hundred young
    men.
At its second snorting another chasm opened up,
    and another hundred young men of Uruk fell
    into it,
Two hundred young men, three hundred young
    men fell into it.
At its third snorting a chasm opened up,
And Enkidu fell into it.
But Enkidu leapt out. He seized the Bull of Heaven
    by the horns.
The Bull of Heaven blew spittle into his face,
With its thick tail it whipped up its dung.
Enkidu made his voice heard and spoke,
He said to Gilgamesh,
    'My friend, we were too arrogant [when we killed
      Humbaba].
    How can we give recompense [for our action]?
    My friend, I have seen [   ]
    And my strength [   ]
    Let me pull out [   ]
    [   ]
    Let me seize [   ]
    Let me [   ]
    In [   ]
    And plunge your sword [   ]

In between the base of the horns and the neck
tendons.'
Enkidu spun round [to] the Bull of Heaven,
And seized it by its thick tail,
And [   ]

v   Then Gilgamesh, like a but[cher (?)] heroic
and [   ]
Plunged his sword in between the base of the horns
and the neck tendons.
When they had struck down the Bull of Heaven
they pulled out its innards,
Set them before Shamash,
Backed away and prostrated themselves before
Shamash.
Then the two brothers sat down.
Ishtar went up on to the wall of Uruk the Sheepfold.
She was contorted with rage, she hurled down
curses,
'That man Gilgamesh who reviled me has killed
the Bull of Heaven!'
Enkidu listened to Ishtar saying this,
And he pulled out the Bull of Heaven's shoulder
and slapped it into her face:
'If I could only get at you as that does,
I would do the same to you myself,
I would hang its intestines on your arms!'[63]
Ishtar gathered the crimped courtesans,
Prostitutes and harlots.[64]
She arranged for weeping over the Bull of Heaven's
shoulder.
Gilgamesh called craftsmen, all the armourers,
And the craftsmen admired the thickness of its
horns.
Thirty minas of lapis lazuli was (needed for) each of
their pouring ends,[65]
Two minas of gold (?) (was needed for) each of their
sheathings.[66]
Six kor of oil was the capacity of both.[67]
He dedicated (them) for anointing his god
Lugalbanda,[68]

Took them in and hung them on his bed (where he
    slept) as head of the family.[69]
In the Euphrates they washed their hands
And held hands and came
Riding through the main street of Uruk.
The people of Uruk gathered and gazed at them.

vi Gilgamesh addressed a word to [his] retainers,
    'Who is finest among the young men?
    Who is proudest among the males?'
    'Gilgamesh is finest among the young men!
    Gilgamesh is proudest among the males!
    [   ] we knew in our anger
    There is nobody like him who can please
      her [   ].
    [   ]'
Gilgamesh made merry in his palace.
Then they lay down, the young men were lying in
    bed for the night,
And Enkidu lay down and had a dream.
Enkidu got up and described the dream,
He said to his friend,
(*Catchline*)
    'My friend, why are the great gods consulting
      together?

TABLET VII

i   'My friend, why are the great gods consulting
      together?

      (*gap of about 20 lines, which may partly be
      filled in essence from a Hittite version,
      which is given here*)[70]

Then daylight came. [And] Enkidu said to
    Gilgamesh,
    'O my brother, what a dream [I saw] last night!
    Anu, Ellil, Ea, and heavenly Shamash [were in
      the assembly].
    And Anu said to Ellil, "As they have slain the
      Bull of Heaven,

So too they have slain Huwawa, who [guarded]
    the mountains pla[nted] with pines.''
And Anu said, ''One of them [must die].''
Ellil replied: ''Let Enkidu die, but let Gilgamesh
    not die.''
Then heavenly Shamash said to valiant Ellil,
''Was it not according to your word that they
    slew the Bull of Heaven and Huwawa? Should
    now innocent Enkidu die?''
But Ellil turned in anger to heavenly Shamash,
    saying,
''(The fact is), you accompanied them daily, like
    one of their comrades.'' '
Enkidu lay down before Gilgamesh, his tears
    flowing like streams.
'O my brother, my brother is so dear to me.
But they are taking me from my brother.'
And: 'I shall sit among the dead, I shall [   ]
    the threshold of the dead;
Never again [shall I see] my dear brother with
    my own eyes.'

        (*end of Hittite insertion*)

Enkidu made his [voice heard and spoke],
He said to [his friend Gilgamesh],
    'Come, [   ]
    In [   ]
    The door [   ]
    Because [   ]

        (*3 broken lines*)

ii?   Enkidu lifted up [   ]
    He discussed [   ] with the door.
    'Door, don't [you] remember the words?
    Are not . . . . . . [   ]?
    I selected the timber for you over twenty leagues,
    Until I had found a fully mature pine.
    There is no other wood like yours!
    Your height is six poles, your width two poles,[71]

Your doorpost, your lower and upper hinge (?)
    are made [from a single tree.]
I made you, I carried you to Nippur [   ]
Be aware, door, that this was a favour to you,
And this was a good deed done for you [   ]
I myself raised the axe, I cut you down,
Loaded you myself on to the raft, [   ]
I myself [   ] temple of Shamash
[   ]
I myself set (you) up in his gate [   ]
[   ]
I myself [   ]
And in Uruk [   ]

    (*2 broken lines*)

Now, door, it was I who made you,
I who carried you to Nippur.
But the king who shall arise after me shall go
    through you,
Gilgamesh shall [go through] your portals
And change (?) my name, and put on his own
    name!'[72]
He tore out (?) [the door (?) and]
    hurled (?) [   ].
He kept listening to his words, [   ] straight
    away[73]
Gilgamesh kept listening to the words of his friend
    Enkidu, and his tears flowed.
Gilgamesh made his voice heard and spoke; he said
    to Enkidu [   ],
    'You, who used to be reasonable, [now speak]
    otherwise!
Why, my friend, did your heart speak
    otherwise (?).
The dream was very precious, and the warning
    awful; your lips buzzed like flies (?)!
The warning was awful, the dream was precious.
They have left a legacy of grieving for next year.
The dream has left a legacy of grief for next year.
[I shall go] and offer prayers to the great gods,

I shall search out [your goddess (?)], look for
   your god,
[   ] the father of the gods.
To Ellil the counsellor, father of the
   gods [   ].
I shall make a statue of you with countless
   gold [   ]'[74]
[The words] he spoke were not like [   ],
[What] he said did not go back, did not [alter (?)]
[The   ] that he cast (?) did not go back, he did not
   erase. [   ]
[   ] to the people [   ]. At the first light
   of morning
Enkidu [raised] his head, wept before Shamash,
His tears flowed before the rays of the Sun.
   'I hereby beseech you, Shamash, because my fate
      is different (?),
   [Because] the hunter, the brigand,
   Did not let me attain as much as my friend,
   Let the hunter never attain as much as his
      friend!
   Make his advantage vanish, make his strength
      less!
   [   ] his share from your presence,
   Let [   ] not enter, let it go out through the
      window!'
When he had cursed the hunter as much as he
   wanted,
He decided to curse the harlot too.
   'Come, Shamhat, I shall fix a fate for you!
   [Curses (?)] shall not cease for ever and ever.
   I shall curse you with a great curse![75]
   Straight away my curses shall rise up against
      you!
   You shall never make your house voluptuous
      again,
   You shall not release [   ] of your
      young bulls,
   You shall not let them into the girls' rooms.
   Filth shall impregnate your lovely lap (?),

iii

The drunkard shall soak your party dress with
    vomit,
[   ] fingers (?),
[Your cosmetic paint (?) shall be] the potter's
    lump of clay (?),
You shall never obtain the best cosmetic [oil (?),]
Bright silver, people's affluence, shall not
    accumulate in your house,
The [   ] of your [   ] shall
    be your porch,
The crossroads (?) shall be your only sitting place,
Waste ground your only lying place, the shade of
    a city wall your only sitting place.[76]
Thorns and spikes shall skin your feet,
The drunkard and the thirsty shall slap your
    cheek,[76]
[   ] shall shout out against you.
The builder shall never plaster the [walls (?) of
    your house,][77]
Owls will nest [in your roof beams (?),]
Feasting shall never take place in your house,

    (about 4 broken lines)

Because you defiled me when I was pure,
Because you seduced me in the open country when
    I was pure.'
Shamash heard the utterance of his mouth.
Immediately a loud voice called down to him from
    the sky:
'Enkidu, why are you cursing my harlot Shamhat,
Who fed you on food fit for gods,
Gave you ale to drink, fit for kings,
Clothed you with a great robe,
Then provided you with Gilgamesh for a fine partner?
And now Gilgamesh, the friend who is a brother
    to you
Will lay you to rest on a great bed
And lay you to rest on a bed of loving care,
And let you stay in a restful dwelling, the
    dwelling on the left.[78]

Princes of the earth will kiss your feet.
He will make the people of Uruk weep for you,
    mourn for you,
Will fill the proud people with woe,
And he himself will neglect his appearance after
    you(r death).
Clothed only in a lionskin, he will roam the open
    country.'
Enkidu listened to the speech of Shamash the
    warrior.
[His anger abated (?)]; his heart became quiet.

(about 2 lines missing)

iv   'Come, Shamhat, I shall change your fate!
My utterance, which cursed you, shall bless you
    instead.
Governors and princes shall love you,
The single-league man shall smite his thigh (for
    you),
The double-league man shall shake out his locks
    (for you).
The herdsman shall not hold back for you, he
    shall undo his belt for you.
He shall give you ivory, lapis lazuli, and gold,
Rings (and) brooches (?) shall be presents for you.
Rain shall pour down for him (?), his storage jars
    shall be heaped full.
The diviner shall lead you into the palace (?) of
    the gods.
Because of you, the mother of seven, the
    honoured wife, shall be deserted.'[79]
Then Enkidu [wept (?)], for he was sick at heart.
[   ] he lay down alone.
He spoke what was in his mind to his friend.
'Listen again, my friend! I had a dream in the
    night.
The sky called out, the earth replied,
I was standing in between them.
There was a young man, whose face was
    obscured.

His face was like that of an Anzu-bird.
He had the paws of a lion, he had the claws of an
    eagle.
He seized me by my locks, using great force
    against me.
I hit him, and he jumped like a *keppū*-toy,[80]
He hit me and forced me down like an
    [onager (?)],
Like a wild bull he trampled on me,
He squeezed my whole body.
(I cried out:) "Save me, my friend, don't desert
    me!"
But you were afraid, and did not [help me (?)],
You [   ].

    (*3 broken lines*)

[He hit me and] turned me into a dove.
[   ] my arms, like a bird.
He seized me, drove me down to the dark house,
    dwelling of Erkalla's god,[81]
To the house which those who enter cannot leave,
On the road where travelling is one way only,
To the house where those who stay are deprived
    of light,
Where dust is their food, and clay their bread.
They are clothed, like birds, with feathers,
And they see no light, and they dwell in
    darkness.
Over the door [and the bolt, dust has settled.]
I looked at the house that I had entered,
And crowns were heaped up.
I [   ] those with crowns who had
    ruled the land from time immemorial,
[Priests (?) of] Anu and Ellil regularly set out
    cooked meats,
Set out baked (bread), set out cold water from
    waterskins.
In the house of dust that I had entered
Dwelt the *enu* and *lagaru*-priests,
Dwelt the *isippu* and *lumahhu*-priests,

Dwelt the *gudapsû*-priests of the great gods,
Dwelt Etana, dwelt Shakkan[82]
Dwelt Ereshkigal, the Queen of Earth.
Belet-ṣeri, the scribe of Earth, was kneeling before
    her.
She was holding [a tablet] and kept reading aloud
    to her.
She raised her head and looked at me:
"[Who (?)   ] brought this man?"

   (*gap of about 50 lines for column v*)

vi   (*gap of about 2 lines*)

[   ] experienced all kinds of troubles,
Remember me, my friend, and do not forget what
    I went through.
My friend saw an in[describable] dream.'
From the day he saw the dream, his [strength] was
    finished.
Enkidu lay there the first day, then [a second day.]
[The illness] of Enkidu, as he lay in bed, [grew
    worse, his flesh weaker.]
A third day and a fourth day, the [illness] of
    [Enkidu grew worse, his flesh weaker (?),]
A fifth, sixth and seventh day, eighth, ninth [and
    tenth.]
The illness of Enkidu [grew worse, his flesh
    weaker (?)].
An eleventh and twelfth day [his illness grew worse,
    his flesh weaker.]
Enkidu, as he lay in bed, [   ]
Gilgamesh cried out and [   ]
 'My friend is cursing me, [   ]
 Because in the midst of [   ][83]
 I was afraid of the fight [   ]
 My friend, who [was so strong (?)] in the fight,
     [cursed me (?)]
 I, in [   ]

  (*gap of up to 30 lines*)

TABLET VIII

i When the first light of dawn appeared[84]
Gilgamesh said to his friend,
    'Enkidu, my friend, your mother a gazelle,
    And your father a wild donkey sired you,
    Their milk was from onagers; they reared (?)
        you,
    And cattle made you familiar with all the
        pastures.
    Enkidu's paths [led to] the Pine Forest.
    They shall weep for you night and day, never fall
        silent,[85]
    Weep for you, the elders of the broad city, of
        Uruk the Sheepfold.
    The summit will bless (us) after our death,
    They shall weep for you, the [   ]s of the
        mountains,
    They shall mourn [   ]
    [The open country as if it were your father], the
        field as if it were your mother.[86]
    They shall weep for you, [myrtle (?)], cypress,
        and pine,
    In the midst of which we armed ourselves (?) in
        our fury.
    They shall weep for you, the bear, hyena,
        leopard, tiger, stag, cheetah,
    Lion, wild bulls, deer, mountain goat, cattle, and
        other wild beasts of open country.
    It shall weep for you, the holy river Ulaya, along
        whose bank
    We used to walk so proudly.
    It shall weep for you, the pure Euphrates,
    With whose water in waterskins we used to
        refresh ourselves.
    They shall weep for you, the young men of the
        broad city, of Uruk the Sheepfold,
    Who watched the fighting when we struck down
        the Bull of Heaven.

He shall weep for you, the ploughman at [his
    plough (?)]
Who extols your name with sweet Alala.
He shall weep for you, [   ] of the
    broad city, of Uruk the Sheepfold,
Who will extol your name in the first . . .
He shall weep for you, the shepherd, the
    herdsman (?),
Who used to make (?) the beer mixture (?) for
    your mouth.
She shall weep for you, [the wet-nurse (?)]
Who used to put butter on your lower parts.
He (?) shall weep for you, the elder (?)
Who used to put ale to your mouth.
She shall weep for you, the harlot [   ]
By whom you were anointed with perfumed oil.
They shall weep for you, [parents]-in-
    law
Who [comfort (?)] the wife . . . of your loins (?)
They shall weep for you, the young men, [like
    brothers (?)]
They shall weep for you and tear out (?) their
    hair over you.
For you, Enkidu, I, (like ?) your mother, your
    father,
Will weep on your (*lit.* his) plains [   ]

ii   Listen to me, young men, listen to me!
Listen to me, elders of Uruk, listen to me!
I myself must weep for Enkidu my friend,
Mourn bitterly, like a wailing woman.
As for the axe at my side, spur to my arm,
The sword in my belt, the shield for my front,
My festival clothes, my manly sash:
Evil [Fate (?)] rose up and robbed me of them.
My friend was the hunted mule, wild ass of the
    mountains, leopard of open country.
Enkidu the strong man was the hunted wild ass of
    [the mountains, leopard of open country].[87]
We who met, and scaled the mountain,
Seized the Bull of Heaven and slew it,

Demolished Humbaba the mighty one of the Pine
  Forest,
Now, what is the sleep that has taken hold of
  you?
Turn to me, you! You aren't listening to me!
But he cannot lift his head.
I touch his heart, but it does not beat at all.'[88]
He covered his friend's face like a daughter-in-
  law.[89]
He circled over him like an eagle,
Like a lioness whose cubs are [trapped] in a pit,[90]
He paced back and forth.
He (?) tore out and spoilt (?) well-curled hair,
He stripped off and threw away finery as if it were
  taboo.[91]
When the first light of dawn appeared, Gilgamesh
  sent out a shout through the land.
The smith, the [   ], the coppersmith,
  the silversmith, the jeweller (were summoned).
He made [a likeness (?)] of his friend, he fashioned
  a statue of his friend.[92]
The four limbs of the friend were [made of   ],
  his chest was of lapis lazuli,
His (?) skin was of gold [   ]

  (*gap of about 12 lines*)

iii   '[I will lay you to rest] on a bed [of loving care][93]
       And will let you stay [in a restful dwelling, a
         dwelling of the left].
       Princes of the earth [will kiss your feet].
       I will make the people [of Uruk] weep for you,
         [mourn for you].
       [I will fill] the proud people with sorrow for
         you.
       And I myself will neglect my appearance after
         you(r death)
       Clad only in a lionskin, I will roam the open
         country.'
When the first light of dawn appeared
Gilgamesh arose and [went to his treasury],

He undid its fastenings
And looked at the treasure.
He brought out carnelian, flint, alabaster,

[   ] kept making (?)
[|] for his friend
[   ] ditto
[   ] minas of gold for his friend ditto
[   ] minas of gold for his friend ditto
[   ] minas of gold for his friend ditto
[   ] minas of gold for his friend ditto
[   ] in which thirty minas of gold were held.
[   ] ditto
[   ] their [   ] ditto
[   ] their thickness ditto
[   ] their (?) [   ] ditto
[   ] large
[   ] ditto
[   ] of his waist
[   ] ditto
[   ] ditto
[   ] ditto
[   ] ditto

(*A new fragment of about 73 lines, perhaps from col. iv,
lists burial goods, animal sacrifices, and items offered to
individual deities, after displaying to Shamash. They
include: various weapons with handles of gold and ivory;
fattened oxen are sacrificed and the meat taken to the
rulers of the Underworld; a wooden item for Ishtar; an
item for Namraṣit; a flask of lapis lazuli for Ereshkigal
queen of the Underworld; a carnelian flute for Dumuzi; a
chair and sceptre of lapis lazuli for Namtar, vizier of the
Underworld; an item for Hushbisha, consort of Namtar; a
silver bracelet for Qassu-ṭabat the sweeper of Erishkigal;
an item of alabaster inlaid with lapis and carnelian,
decorated with a picture of the Pine Forest, for Nin-
shuluhha the cleaner of the house; a double-edged dagger
with a lapis haft, decorated with a picture of the*

Euphrates river, for Bibbu the slaughterer of the Underworld; an item with an alabaster back for . . . the scapegoat (?)[96] *of the Underworld; one further item made with lapis lazuli and carnelian. Each item is displayed to Shamash, and each deity is asked to welcome Enkidu and to walk at his side in the Underworld, so that Enkidu be not sick at heart.)*

v   *(gap of about 20 lines)*

        '[   ] their names [   ]
        [   ] the judge of the Anunnaki [   ]'
    When [Gilgamesh (?)] heard this,
    He . . . [   ].
    When the first light of dawn appeared, Gilgamesh
        opened [   ],
    Set out a great table of *elammakku*-wood,[97]
    And filled a carnelian bowl with honey,
    Filled a lapis lazuli bowl with butter.
    [   ] he decorated and displayed it to
        Shamash.

        (gap of 1 line to end of column)

vi   *(gap of up to 45 lines for column vi)*

TABLET IX

i Gilgamesh mourned bitterly for Enkidu his friend,
    And roamed open country.
        'Shall I die too? Am I not like Enkidu?
        Grief has entered my innermost being,
        I am afraid of Death, and so I roam open
            country.[98]
        I shall take the road and go quickly
        To see Ut-napishtim, son of Ubara-Tutu.
        (When) I reached the mountain passes at night,
        I saw lions and was afraid.

I raised my head, I prayed to Sin.
My prayers went to Sin, the [light (?)] of the
    gods.
"[   ], keep me safe!"'
[He   ] went to sleep, awoke at a dream
[And   ] was glad to be alive (?).
He took up an axe to his side
Drew the sword [from] his belt.
Like an arrow he fell among them,
Struck [   ], shattered the [   ].
Then [   ] of midday (?)
He threw down/gave [   ]
He carved out [   ]
The name of the first [   ]
The name of the second [   ]

       *(6 lines fragmentary, then about 7 lines
       missing)*

ii   The name (?) of the mountain [is (?)] Mashu.
When he reached the mountain Mashu
Which daily guards the coming out [of Shamash]—
Their upper parts [touch (?)] the sky's foundation,
Below, their breasts reach Arallu.[99]
They guard its gate, Scorpion-men[100]
Whose aura is frightful, and whose glance is death.
Their terrifying mantles of radiance drape the
    mountains.
They guard the sun at dawn and dusk—
Gilgamesh looked at them, and fear and terror
    clouded his face.
He took the initiative and gestured to them in
    greeting.
A Scorpion-man shouted to his woman,
    'Someone has come to us. His body is the flesh of
      gods.'
The Scorpion-man's woman answered him,
    'Two-thirds of him is divine, and one-third of
      him mortal.'
The Scorpion-man, the male, shouted,

Addressed his words to [Gilgamesh, the flesh of (?)]
   gods.
  '[Who are you, that comes to us on (?)] a distant
    journey?
  [   ] to my presence
  [   ] whose crossing is difficult
  [   ] let me learn your [   ]
  [   ] placed
  [   ] let me learn your [   ]

      (*gap of about 12 lines*)

iii   (*gap of 2 lines*)

  'Concerning Ut-napishtim, my father [   ]
  Who stood in the gods' assembly and sought out
    eternal life.
  Death and Life [   ].'
The Scorpion-man made his voice heard and spoke,
He said to Gilgamesh,
  'It is impossible, Gilgamesh, [   ]
  Nobody has passed through the mountain's
    inaccessible tract.
  For even after twelve leagues [   ]
  The darkness is too dense, there is no [light.]
  To the dawn [   ]
  To the dusk [   ]
  To the dusk [   ]
  They sent out [   ]

      (*5 lines fragmentary, then 16 lines missing*)

iv   (*gap of about 18 lines*)

  In grief [   ]
  By cold and heat [my face is weathered (?)]
  In exhaustion [   ]
  Now, you [   ].'
The Scorpion-man [made his voice heard and
    spoke],
[He said to] Gilgamesh the [   ],
  'Go, Gilgamesh, [   ]
  Mashu [   ]

Mountains [   ]
Safely (?) [   ]
The main gate of the land of [   ].'
Gilgamesh [listened to the Scorpion-man],
To the words of [the guardian of the gate (?)].
The path (of ?) Shamash [   ]
When he had achieved one league
The darkness was dense, there was no light,
It was impossible [for him to see] ahead or behind.
When he had achieved two leagues

v   (*gap of about 8 lines*)

[When he had achieved] four leagues, [he hurried
        on (?)];[101]
[The darkness was] still dense, [there was no light],
It was impossible [for him to see ahead or behind].
[When he had achieved] five leagues, [he hurried
        on (?)];
[The darkness was] still dense, [there was no light],
It was impossible [for him to see ahead or behind].
When [he had achieved six] leagues, [he hurried
        on (?)];
The darkness was still dense, [there was no light],
It was impossible [for him to see ahead or behind].
When he had achieved seven leagues, [he hurried
        on (?)];
The darkness was still dense, [there was] no [light],
It was impossible for him [to see] ahead or behind.
When he had achieved eight leagues, he hurried on;
The darkness was still dense, there was no light,
It was [impossible for him to see] ahead or behind.
[When he had achieved] nine leagues, the north
        wind [   ][102]
[   ] his face
[But the darkness was still dense, there was no]
        light,[103]
[It was impossible for him to see] ahead or behind.
[When he had] achieved [ten leagues]
[   ] came close.
[   ] leagues.

[he] came out in front of the sun.
[   ] brightness was everywhere.
All kinds of [thorny, prickly], spiky bushes were
      visible, blossoming with gemstones.[104]
Carnelian bore fruit
Hanging in clusters, lovely to look at,
Lapis lazuli bore foliage,
Bore fruit, and was delightful to view.

vi   (*gap of about 24 lines*)

[   ] pine
Its fronds of banded agate [   ]
Sea-*laruššu* [   ] of *sāsu*-stone[105]
Like brambles and thorn bushes [of] . . .-stone,
Carob trees [of] (green) *abašmû*-stone,
Šubû-stone, haematite [   ]
Riches and wealth [   ]
Like [   ] turquoise
Which [   ] the sea.
[   ]
As Gilgamesh walked around [at   ]
He raised [his eyes   ]
(*Catchline*)
Siduri [the alewife] who lives down by the sea

TABLET X

i Siduri the alewife, who lives down by the sea,[106]
Lives and [   ].
Vat-stands are made for her, [fermentation-vats] are
      made for her,[107]
Covered by a covering and [   ].[108]
Gilgamesh was pacing around and [   ]
Clad only in a (lion)skin [   ]
He had the flesh of gods upon [his body],
But grief was in [his innermost being].
His face was like that of a long-distance traveller.
The alewife looked at him from a distance.
She pondered in her heart, and [spoke] a word

To herself, and she [advised herself]:
 'Perhaps this man is an assassin.
 Is he going somewhere in [   ]?'
The alewife looked at him and locked [her door],
She locked her door, locked it [with a bolt].
Then he, Gilgamesh, noticed [   ]
Raised his chin and [   ]
Gilgamesh spoke to her, to the alewife;
 'Alewife, why did you look at me [and lock] your
  door,
 Lock your door, [lock it] with a bolt?
 I will smash the door, I will shatter [the bolt]!¹⁰⁹
 [   ] of mine
 [   ] open country.
 [Gilg]amesh
 [   ] door
 [   ]
 [   ]
 [al]ewife

   (3 broken lines)

 [We destroyed Humbaba, who lived in the] Pine
  Forest.
 [We killed] lions at the mountain passes.'
[The alewife] spoke to him, to Gilgamesh,
 '[If you are truly Gilgamesh], that struck down
  the Guardian,
 [Destroyed] Humbaba, who lived in the Pine
  Forest,
 Killed lions at the mountain [passes],
 [Seized the Bull of Heaven who came down from
  the sky, struck him down],
 [Why are your cheeks wasted], your face dejected,
 [Your heart so wretched, your appearance worn]
  out,
 [And grief] in your innermost being?
 Your face is like that of a long-distance traveller,
 Your face is weathered by [cold and heat . . .],
 [Clad only in a lionskin] you roam open country.'
[Gilgamesh spoke to her, to Siduri the alewife],

'[How could my cheeks not be wasted, nor my
    face dejected],
[Nor my heart wretched, nor my appearance
    worn out],
[Nor grief in my innermost being],
[Nor my face like that of a long-distance
    traveller],

ii   [Nor my face weathered by cold and heat . . .],
[Nor roaming open country, clad only in a
    lionskin?]
[My friend whom I love so much, who
    experienced every hardship with me],
[Enkidu, whom I love so much, who experienced
    every hardship with me—]
[The fate of mortals conquered him!] Six days
    [and seven nights I wept over him],
[I did not allow him to] be buried, [until a worm
    fell out of his nose].
[I was frightened and   ].
I am afraid of Death, [and so I roam open
    country].
The words of my friend [weigh upon me].
[I roam open country] for long distances; the
    words of my friend Enkidu weigh upon me.[110]
I roam open country on long journeys.
[How, O how] could I stay silent, how, O how
    could I keep quiet [   ]?
My friend whom I love has turned to clay:
    Enkidu my friend whom I love [has turned to
    clay].
Am I not like him? Must I lie down too,
Never to rise, ever again?'
Gilgamesh spoke to her, to the alewife,
    'Now, alewife, which is the way to
    Ut-napishtim?[111]
Give me directions (?), [whatever they are]; give
    me directions (?).
If it is possible, I shall cross the sea;
If it is impossible I shall roam open country
    again.'

The alewife spoke to him, to Gilgamesh,
  'There has never been a ferry of any kind,
    Gilgamesh,
  And nobody from time immemorial has crossed
    the sea.
  Shamash the warrior is the only one who has
    crossed the sea: apart from Shamash, nobody
    has crossed the sea.
  The crossing is difficult, the way of it very
    difficult,
  And in between are lethal waters which bar the
    way ahead.[112]
  Wherever, then, could you cross the sea,
    Gilgamesh?
  And once you reached the lethal waters, what
    would you do?
  (Yet) there is, Gilgamesh, a boatman of Ut-
    napishtim, Ur-shanabi,
  He—the "things of stone" identify him (?)—will
    be trimming a young pine in the forest.[113]
  Go, and let him see your face.
  If it is possible, cross with him. If it is impossible,
    retreat back.'
When Gilgamesh heard this
He took up an axe to his side,
Drew the sword from his belt,
Stole up and drove them off,[114]
Like an arrow he fell among them.
In the midst of the forest the noise resounded (?).
Ur-shanabi looked and drew (?) his sword (?),
Took up an axe and [crept up on (?)] him.
Then he, Gilgamesh, hit him on the head,[115]
Seized his arms and [   ] of his chest.
And the "things of stone" [   ] the boat,
Which do not [   ] lethal [waters]
[   ] broad [sea (?)]
In the waters [   ] held back.
He smashed [them and   ] to the river.
[   ] the boat
And [   ] on the bank.

[Gilgamesh spoke to him, to Ur-shanabi] the
    boatman,
  '[   ] I shall enter
  [   ] to you.'
iii Ur-shanabi spoke to him, to Gilgamesh,
    'Why are your cheeks wasted, your face dejected,
    Your heart so wretched, your appearance worn
      out,
    And grief in your innermost being?
    Your face is like that of a long-distance traveller.
    Your face is weathered by cold and heat [ ]
    Clad only in a lionskin, you roam open country.'
  Gilgamesh spoke to him, to Ur-shanabi the
      boatman,
    'How could my cheeks not be wasted, nor my
      face dejected,
    Nor my heart wretched, nor my appearance worn
      out,
    Nor grief in my innermost being,
    Nor my face like that of a long-distance traveller,
    Nor my face weathered by wind and heat [   ]
    Nor roaming open country clad only in a
      lionskin?
    My friend was the hunted mule, wild ass of the
      mountain, leopard of open country,
    Enkidu my friend was the hunted mule, wild ass
      of the mountain, leopard of open country.
    We who met, and scaled the mountain,
    Seized the Bull of Heaven and slew it,
    Demolished Humbaba who dwelt in the Pine
      Forest,
    Killed lions in the passes of the mountains,
    My friend whom I love so much, who
      experienced every hardship with me,
    Enkidu my friend whom I love so much, who
      experienced every hardship with me—
    The fate of mortals conquered him!
    For six days and seven nights I wept over him: I
      did not allow him to be buried
    Until a worm fell out of his nose.

I was frightened and [   ].
I am afraid of Death, and so I roam open country.
The words of my friend weigh upon me.
I roam open country for long distances; the words
    of Enkidu my friend weigh upon me.
I roam open country on long journeys.
How, O how could I stay silent, how, O how
    could I keep quiet?
My friend whom I love has turned to clay:
    Enkidu my friend whom I love has turned to
    clay.
Am I not like him? Must I lie down too,
Never to rise, ever again?'
Gilgamesh spoke to him, to Ur-shanabi the boatman,
    'Now, Ur-shanabi, which is the way to
    Ut-napishtim?
Give me directions (?), whatever they are; give
    me directions (?).
If it is possible, I shall cross the sea;
If it is impossible, I shall roam open country
    again.'
Ur-shanabi spoke to him, to Gilgamesh,
    'Your own hands, Gilgamesh, have
    hindered [   ],
You have smashed the "things of stone", you
    have [   ].
The "things of stone" are smashed, and their
    strings (?) are pulled out.
Take up an axe, Gilgamesh, to your side,
Go down to the forest, [cut] three hundred poles
    each thirty metres (long).
Trim (them) and put "knobs" (on them); then
    bring them to me (?) [at the boat (?)]'[116]
When Gilgamesh heard this,
He took up an axe to his side, drew a sword from
    his belt,
Went down to the forest and [cut] three hundred
    poles each thirty metres (long).
He trimmed (them) and put "knobs" (on them): he
    brought them [to Ur-shanabi at the boat (?)]

And Gilgamesh and Ur-shanabi embarked [in the
     boat(s)]
They cast off the *magillu*-boat and sailed away.[117]
(After) a journey of a new moon and a full moon,
     on the third day [   ]
Ur-shanabi reached the lethal waters.

iv Ur-shanabi spoke to him, to Gilgamesh,
     'Stay clear, Gilgamesh, take one pole at a time,
     Don't let the lethal water wet your hand!
       [Hold (?)] the knob!
     Take a second, a third, then a fourth pole,
       Gilgamesh.
     Take a fifth, a sixth, then a seventh pole,
       Gilgamesh.
     Take an eighth, a ninth, then a tenth pole,
       Gilgamesh.
     Take an eleventh, a twelfth pole, Gilgamesh.'
Within seven hundred and twenty metres (?)
       Gilgamesh had used up the poles.
Then he undid his belt, [   ]
Gilgamesh stripped himself; [   ]
With his arms he lifted up (?) the thwart (?).
Ut-napishtim was looking on from a distance,
Pondered and spoke to himself,
Took counsel with himself:
     'Why are the [things of stone(?)] broken,
     And the wrong gear aboard [ ]?
     Surely it can't be my man coming on? And on
       the right [   ].
     I am looking, but I can't make [it out],
     I am looking, but [   ]
     I am looking, [   ]

          (*gap of about 20 lines*)

[Ut-napishtim spoke to him, to Gilgamesh],
     ['Why are your cheeks wasted, your face
       dejected],
     [Your heart so wretched, your appearance worn
       out],

[And grief in your innermost being]?
[Your face is like that of a long-distance
    traveller].
[Your face is weathered by cold and heat . . .]
[Clad only in a lionskin you roam open
    country].'[118]

[Gilgamesh spoke to him, to Ut-napishtim],
    ['How would my cheeks not be wasted, nor my
      face dejected],

v   [Nor my heart wretched, nor] my appearance
      [worn out],
    [Nor grief in] my innermost being,
    [Nor] my face like [that of a long-distance
      traveller],
    [Nor] my face [weathered by cold and heat . . .]
    [Nor] roaming open country [clad only in a
      lionskin]?

My friend was the hunted mule, wild ass of the
    mountain, leopard of open country,
Enkidu my friend was the hunted mule, wild ass
    of the mountain, leopard of open country.[119]
We who met and scaled the mountain,
Seized the Bull of Heaven and slew it,
Demolished Humbaba who dwelt in the Pine
    Forest,
Killed lions in the passes of the mountains,
My friend whom I love so much, who
    experienced every hardship with me,
Enkidu my friend whom I love so much, who
    experienced every hardship with me—
The fate of mortals conquered him! For six days
    and seven nights I wept over him,
I did not allow him to be buried
Until a worm fell out of his nose.
I was frightened [   ]. I am afraid of
    Death, [and so I roam open country].
I roam open country for long distances;
The words of my friend weigh upon me.
The words of Enkidu my friend weigh upon me.
I roam the open country on long journeys.

How, O how could I stay silent, how, O how
   could I keep quiet?
My friend whom I love has turned to clay:
   Enkidu my friend whom I love has turned to
   clay.
Am I not like him? Must I lie down too,
   Never to rise, ever again?'
Gilgamesh spoke to him, to Ut-napishtim,
   'So I thought I would go to see Ut-napishtim the
   far-distant, of whom people speak.
I searched, went through all countries,
Passed through and through difficult lands,
And crossed to and fro all seas.
My face never had enough of sweet sleep,
My fibre was filled with grief.
I made myself over-anxious by lack of sleep.
What did I gain from my toils?
I did not make a good impression (?) on the
   alewife, for my clothes were finished.
I killed a bear, hyena, lion, leopard, tiger, deer,
   mountain goat, cattle, and other wild beasts of
   open country.
I ate meat from them, I spread out their skins.
Let her door be bolted against grief with pitch and
   bitumen!
Because of me, games are spoiled [   ],
My own misfortunes (?) have reduced me to
   misery (?).'
Ut-napishtim spoke to him, to Gilgamesh,
   'Why do you prolong grief, Gilgamesh?
Since [the gods made you] from the flesh of gods
   and mankind,
Since [the gods] made you like your father and
   mother,
[Death is inevitable (?)] at some time, both for
   Gilgamesh and for a fool,
But a throne is set down [for you (?)] in the
   assembly [   ].
To a fool is given dregs instead of butter,
Rubbish and sweepings which like [   ]

Clothed in a loincloth (?) like [   ]
Like a belt [   ]
Because he has no [sense (?)]
Has no word of advice [   ].'
vi   Gilgamesh raised his head,

        (*2 broken lines*)

[   ] Sin and Bel (?) [   ]
[   ] Sin, Bel [   ]
[   ] are manifest (?) and the gods [   ]
[   ] untiring [   ]
From the front of [   ]
As for you, plan (?) and [   ]
Your partnership [   ]
If Gilgamesh cares for (?) the temple of the gods
He will [   ] the holy shrines
[   ] gods [   ].

        (*3 broken lines*)

[   ] mankind,
[   ] they took to his fate.
[Why (?)] have you exerted yourself? What have
    you achieved (?)?
You have made yourself weary for lack of sleep,
You only fill your flesh with grief,
You only bring the distant days (of reckoning)
    closer.
Mankind's fame is cut down like reeds in a
    reed-bed.
A fine young man, a fine girl,
[   ] of Death.
Nobody sees Death,
Nobody sees the face of Death,
Nobody hears the voice of Death.
Savage Death just cuts mankind down.
Sometimes we build a house, sometimes we make
    a nest,[120]
But then brothers divide it upon inheritance.
Sometimes there is hostility in [the land],
But then the river rises and brings flood-water.

Dragonflies drift on the river,[121]
Their faces look upon the face of the Sun,
(But then) suddenly there is nothing.
The sleeping (?) and the dead are just like each
    other,
Death's picture cannot be drawn.
The primitive man (is as any) young man (?).
    When they blessed me,
The Anunnaki, the great gods, assembled;
Mammitum who creates fate decreed destinies
    with them.
They appointed death and life.
They did not mark out days for death,
But they did so for life.'

TABLET XI

i Gilgamesh spoke to him, to Ut-napishtim the
        far-distant,
    'I look at you, Ut-napishtim
    And your limbs are no different—you are just
        like me.
    Indeed, you are not at all different—you are just
        like me.
    I feel the urge to prove myself against you (?), to
        pick a fight (?)
    [   ] you lie on your back.
    [   ] how you came to stand in the gods'
        assembly and sought eternal life?'
Ut-napishtim spoke to him, to Gilgamesh,
    'Let me reveal to you a closely guarded matter,
        Gilgamesh,
    And let me tell you the secret of the gods.
    Shuruppak is a city that you yourself know,
    Situated [on the bank of] the Euphrates.
    That city was already old when the gods within it
    Decided that the great gods should make a flood.
    There was Anu their father,
    Warrior Ellil their counsellor,

Ninurta was their chamberlain,
Ennugi their canal-controller.
Far-sighted Ea swore the oath (of secrecy) with
    them,[122]
So he repeated their speech to a reed hut,
"Reed hut, reed hut, brick wall, brick wall,
Listen, reed hut, and pay attention, brick wall:
(This is the message:)
Man of Shuruppak, son of Ubara-Tutu,
Dismantle your house, build a boat.
Leave possessions, search out living things.
Reject chattels and save lives!
Put aboard the seed of all living things, into the
    boat.
The boat that you are to build
Shall have her dimensions in proportion,
Her width and length shall be in harmony,
Roof her like the Apsu."
I realized and spoke to my master Ea,
"I have paid attention to the words that you
    spoke in this way,
My master, and I shall act upon them.
But how can I explain myself to the city, the men
    and the elders?"
Ea made his voice heard and spoke,
He said to me, his servant,
"You shall speak to them thus:
"I think that Ellil has rejected me,
And so I cannot stay in your city,
And I cannot set foot on Ellil's land again.
I must go down to the Apsu and stay with my
    master Ea.
Then he will shower abundance upon you,
A wealth of fowl, a treasure of fish.
[   ] prosperity, a harvest,
In the morning cakes/"darkness",[123]
In the evening a rain of wheat/"heaviness" he
    will shower upon you." "
When the first light of dawn appeared
The country gathered about me.

The carpenter brought his axe,
The reed-worker brought his stone,
The young men [   ]
[   ] oakum (?)[124]
Children carried the bitumen,
The poor fetched what was needed [   ].

ii   On the fifth day I laid down her form.[125]
One acre was her circumference, ten poles each
    the height of her walls,
Her top edge was likewise ten poles all round.
I laid down her structure, drew it out,
Gave her six decks,
Divided her into seven.
Her middle I divided into nine,
Drove the water pegs into her middle.
I saw to the paddles and put down what was
    needed:
Three *sar* of bitumen I poured into the kiln,[126]
Three *sar* of pitch I poured into the inside.
Three *sar* of oil they fetched, the workmen who
    carried the baskets.
Not counting the *sar* of oil which the dust (?)
    soaked up,
The boatman stowed away two more *sar* of oil.
At the [   ] I slaughtered oxen.
I sacrificed sheep every day.
I gave the workmen ale and beer to drink,
Oil and wine as if they were river water
They made a feast, like the New Year's Day
    festival.
When the sun [rose (?)] I provided hand oil.
[When] the sun went down the boat was
    complete.
[The launching was (?)] very difficult;
Launching rollers had to be fetched (from) above
    (to) below.
Two-thirds of it [stood clear of the water
    line (?)].[127]
I loaded her with everything there was,
Loaded her with all the silver,

Loaded her with all the gold
Loaded her with all the seed of living things, all
    of them.
I put on board the boat all my kith and kin.
Put on board cattle from open country, wild
    beasts from open country, all kinds of
    craftsmen.
Shamash had fixed the hour:
"In the morning cakes/"darkness",
In the evening a rain of wheat/"heaviness"
(I) shall shower down:
Enter into the boat and shut your door!"
That hour arrived;
In the morning cakes/"darkness", in the evening
    a rain of wheat/"heaviness" showered down.
I saw the shape of the storm,
The storm was terrifying to see.
I went aboard the boat and closed the door.
To seal the boat I handed over the (floating)
    palace with her cargo to Puzur-Amurru the
    boatman.[128]
When the first light of dawn appeared,
A black cloud came up from the base of the sky.
Adad kept rumbling inside it.
Shullat and Hanish were marching ahead,
Marched as chamberlains (over) (?) mountain and
    country.[129]
Erakal pulled out the mooring (?) poles,
Ninurta marched on and made the weir(s)
    overflow.
The Anunnaki had to carry torches,
They lit up the land with their brightness.
The calm before the Storm-god came over the
    sky,
Everything light turned to darkness.
[   ]

iii   On the first day the tempest [rose up],
Blew swiftly and [brought (?) the flood-weapon],
Like a battle force [the destructive *kašūšu*-
    weapon] passed over [the people]

No man could see his fellow,
Nor could people be distinguished from the
    sky.[130]
Even the gods were afraid of the flood-weapon.
They withdrew; they went up to the heaven of
    Anu.[131]
The gods cowered, like dogs crouched by an
    outside wall.
Ishtar screamed like a woman giving birth;
The Mistress of the Gods, sweet of voice, was
    wailing,
"Has that time really returned to clay,
Because I spoke evil in the gods' assembly?
How could I have spoken such evil in the gods'
    assembly?
I should have (?) ordered a battle to destroy my
    people;[132]
I myself gave birth (to them), they are my own
    people,
Yet they fill the sea like fish spawn!"
The gods of the Anunnaki were weeping with
    her.
The gods, humbled, sat there weeping.
Their lips were closed and covered with scab.[133]
For six days and [seven (?)] nights
The wind blew, flood and tempest overwhelmed
    the land;
When the seventh day arrived the tempest, flood
    and onslaught
Which had struggled like a woman in labour,
    blew themselves out (?).
The sea became calm, the *imhullu*-wind grew
    quiet, the flood held back.
I looked at the weather; silence reigned,[134]
For all mankind had returned to clay.
The flood-plain was flat as a roof.
I opened a porthole and light fell on my cheeks.
I bent down, then sat. I wept.
My tears ran down my cheeks.
I looked for banks, for limits to the sea.

Areas of land were emerging everywhere (?).
The boat had come to rest on Mount Nimush.
The mountain Nimush held the boat fast and did
   not let it budge.[135]
The first and second day the mountain Nimush
   held the boat fast and did not let it budge.
The third and fourth day the mountain Nimush
   held the boat fast and did not let it budge.
The fifth and sixth day the mountain Nimush
   held the boat fast and did not let it budge.
When the seventh day arrived,
I put out and released a dove.
The dove went; it came back,
For no perching place was visible to it, and it
   turned round.
I put out and released a swallow.
The swallow went; it came back,
For no perching place was visible to it, and it
   turned round.
I put out and released a raven.[136]
The raven went, and saw the waters receding.
And it ate, preened (?), lifted its tail and did not
   turn round.
Then I put (everything ?) out to the four winds,
   and I made a sacrifice,
Set out a *surqinnu*-offering upon the mountain
   peak,
Arranged the jars seven and seven;[137]
Into the bottom of them I poured (essences of ?)
   reeds, pine, and myrtle.[138]
The gods smelt the fragrance,
The gods smelt the pleasant fragrance,
The gods like flies gathered over the sacrifice.
As soon as the Mistress of the Gods arrived
iv   She raised the great flies which Anu had made to
   please her:[139]
"Behold, O gods, I shall never forget (the
   significance of) my lapis lazuli necklace,
I shall remember these times, and I shall never
   forget.

Let other gods come to the *surqinnu*-offering
But let Ellil not come to the *surqinnu*-offering,
Because he did not consult before imposing the
    flood,
And consigned my people to destruction!"
As soon as Ellil arrived[140]
He saw the boat. Ellil was furious,
Filled with anger at the Igigi gods.
"What sort of life survived? No man should have
    lived through the destruction!"[141]
Ninurta made his voice heard and spoke,
He said to the warrior Ellil,
"Who other than Ea would have done such a
    thing?
For Ea can do everything!"
Ea made his voice heard and spoke,
He said to the warrior Ellil,
"You are the sage of the gods, warrior,
So how, O how, could you fail to consult, and
    impose the flood?
Punish the sinner for his sin, punish the criminal
    for his crime,
But ease off, let work not cease; be patient, let
    not [   ]
Instead of your imposing a flood, let a lion come
    up and diminish the people.
Instead of your imposing a flood, let a wolf come
    up and diminish the people.
Instead of your imposing a flood, let famine be
    imposed and [lessen] the land.
Instead of your imposing a flood, let Erra rise up
    and savage the people.
I did not disclose the secret of the great gods,
I just showed Atrahasis a dream, and thus he
    heard the secret of the gods."
Now the advice (that prevailed) was his advice.
Ellil came up into the boat,
And seized my hand and led me up.
He led up my woman and made her kneel down
    at my side.

He touched our foreheads, stood between us,
   blessed us:
"Until now Ut-napishtim was mortal,
But henceforth Ut-napishtim and his woman shall
   be as we gods are.
Ut-napishtim shall dwell far off at the mouth of
   the rivers."
They took me and made me dwell far off, at the
   mouth of the rivers.
So now, who can gather the gods on your behalf,
   (Gilgamesh),
That you too may find eternal life which you
   seek?
For a start, you must not sleep for six days and
   seven nights.'
As soon as he was sitting, (his head?) between his
   knees,
Sleep breathed over him like a fog.
Ut-napishtim spoke to her, to his wife,
   'Look at the young man who wants eternal life!
Sleep breathes over him like a fog!'
His wife spoke to him, to Ut-napishtim the
   far-distant,
   'Touch him, and let the man wake up.
Let him go back in peace the way he came,
Go back to his country through the great gate,
   through which he once left.'
Ut-napishtim spoke to her, to his wife,
   'Man behaves badly: he will behave badly
   towards you.
v   For a start, bake a daily portion for him, put it
   each time by his head,
And mark on the wall the days that he sleeps.'
She baked a daily portion for him, put it each time
   by his head,
And marked on the wall for him the days that he
   slept.
His first day's portion was dried out,
The second was going bad, the third was soggy,
The fourth had white mould on (?)

The fifth had discoloured,
The sixth was stinking (?),
The seventh—at that moment he touched him and
　　the man woke up.
Gilgamesh spoke to him, to Ut-napishtim the
　　far-distant,
　'No sooner had sleep come upon me
　Than you touched me, straight away, and roused
　　me!'
Ut-napishtim spoke to him, to Gilgamesh,
　'[Look (?), Gil]gamesh, count your daily portions,
　[That the number of days you slept] may be
　　proved to you.
　Your [first] day's ration [is dried out],
　The second is going bad, the third is soggy,
　The fourth has white mould on (?),
　The fifth has discoloured, the sixth is stinking (?),
　[The seventh—] at that moment you woke up.'
Gilgamesh spoke to him, to Ut-napishtim the
　　far-distant,
　'How, O how could I have done it, Ut-napishtim?
　　Wherever can I go?
　The Snatchers have blocked my [routes (?)]:
　Death is waiting in my bedroom,
　And wherever I set my foot, Death is there too.'
Ut-napishtim spoke to him, to Ur-shanabi the
　　boatman,
　'Ur-shanabi, the quay will cast you out, the ferry
　　will reject you.
　Be deprived of her side, at whose side you once
　　went. [142]
　The man whom you led: filthy hair fetters his
　　body,
　Skins have ruined the beauty of his flesh.
　Take him, Ur-shanabi, bring him to a wash-bowl,
　And let him wash in water his filthy hair, as
　　clean as possible (?).
　Let him throw away his skins, and let the sea
　　carry them off.
　Let his body be soaked (until it is) fresh.

Put a new headband on his head.
Have him wear a robe as a proud garment
Until he comes to his city,
Until he reaches his journey's end.
The garment shall not discolour, but stay
    absolutely new.'
Ur-shanabi took him and brought him to a
    wash-bowl,
And he washed in water his filthy hair, as clean as
    possible (?).
He threw away his skins, and the sea carried them
    off.
His body was soaked (until it was) fresh.
He put a new headband on his head.
He wore a robe as a proud garment
Until he came to his city,
Until he reached his journey's end.
The garment would not discolour, and stayed
    absolutely new.
Gilgamesh and Ur-shanabi embarked on the boat.
They cast off the *magillu*-boat and sailed away.
His wife spoke to him, to Ut-napishtim the
    far-distant,
    'Gilgamesh came, weary, striving,
    What will you give him to take back to his
        country?'
And Gilgamesh out there raised the pole,
He brought the boat near the shore.
Ut-napishtim spoke to him, to Gilgamesh,
vi   'Gilgamesh, you came, weary, striving,
    What can I give you to take back to your
        country?
    Let me reveal a closely guarded matter,
        Gilgamesh,
    And let me tell you the secret of the gods.
    There is a plant whose root is like camel-thorn,
    Whose thorn, like a rose's, will spike [your
        hands].
    If you yourself can win that plant, you will find
        [rejuvenation (?)].'[143]

When Gilgamesh heard this, he opened the pipe,
He tied heavy stones to his feet.
They dragged him down into the Apsu, and [he saw
the plant].
He took the plant himself: it spiked [his hands].
He cut the heavy stones from his feet.
The sea threw him up on to its shore.
Gilgamesh spoke to him, to Ur-shanabi the
boatman,
  'Ur-shanabi, this plant is a plant to cure a crisis!
  With it a man may win the breath of life.
  I shall take it back to Uruk the Sheepfold; I shall
    give it to an elder to eat, and so try out the
    plant.
  Its name (shall be): "An old man grows into a
    young man".
  I too shall eat (it) and turn into the young man
    that I once was.'
At twenty leagues they ate their ration.
At thirty leagues they stopped for the night.
Gilgamesh saw a pool whose water was cool,
And went down into the water and washed.
A snake smelt the fragrance of the plant.
It came up silently and carried off the plant.
As it took it away, it shed its scaly skin.[144]
Thereupon Gilgamesh sat down and wept.
His tears flowed over his cheeks.
[He spoke to (?)] Ur-shanabi the boatman,
  'For what purpose (?), Ur-shanabi, have my arms
    grown weary?
  For what purpose (?) was the blood inside me so
    red (?)?
  I did not gain an advantage for myself,
  I have given the advantage to the "lion of the
    ground".[145]
  Now the current will carry (?) twenty leagues
    away.
  While I was opening the pipe, [arranging (?)] the
    gear (?),
  I found (?) a door-thong (?) which must have

been set there as an omen for me. I shall give
up.
And I have left the boat on the shore.'
At twenty leagues they ate their ration.
At thirty leagues they stopped for the night.
They reached Uruk the Sheepfold.
Gilgamesh spoke to him, to Ur-shanabi the
boatman,
'Go up on to the wall of Uruk, Ur-shanabi, and
walk around,[146]
Inspect the foundation platform and scrutinize the
brickwork! Testify that its bricks are baked
bricks,
And that the Seven Counsellors must have laid its
foundations!
One square mile is city, one square mile is
orchards, one square mile is claypits, as well as
the open ground of Ishtar's temple.
Three square miles and the open ground comprise
Uruk.'
(*Catchline*)
'If only I had left the *pukku* in the carpenter's
house today!'

TABLET XII[147]

i   'If only I had left the *pukku* in the carpenter's
house today![148]
[I would have left (?)] the carpenter's wife like
the mother who bore me,
[I would have left (?)] the carpenter's daughter
like my little sister.
Today the *pukku* fell into the Earth[149]
And my *mekkû* fell into the Earth.'
Enkidu [asked] Gilgamesh,
'My lord, what did you weep for, and your heart
[grow sad]?[150]
I shall bring up the *pukku* from the Earth today,
I shall bring up the *mekkû* from the Earth.'

Gilgamesh [said to] Enkidu,
  'If you [go down] to the Earth,[151]
  [You must follow] my instructions.
  [You must not put on] a clean garment,
  For they will recognize that you are a stranger.
  You must not be anointed with perfumed oil from
      an ointment jar,
  For they will gather around you at the smell of
      it.
  You must not toss a throw-stick into the Earth,
  For those who are hit by the throw-stick will
      encircle you.
  You must not raise a club in your hands,
  For ghosts will flit around you.
  You must not put shoes on your feet
  Lest you make a noise in the Earth.
  You must not kiss the wife you love,
  You must not hit the wife you hate,
  You must not kiss the son you love,
  You must not hit the son you hate,
  For the Earth's outcry will seize you.
  She who sleeps and sleeps, the mother of Ninazu
      who sleeps—[152]
  Her pure shoulders are not covered with a
      garment,
  Her breasts are not pendulous like an ointment
      jar in a *šappatu*-basin.'[153]

ii He [did not follow his lord's instructions.]
  He put on a clean garment,
  So they recognized that he was a stranger.
  He was anointed with perfumed oil from an
      ointment jar
  So they gathered around him at the smell of it.
  He tossed a throw-stick into the Earth,
  So those who were hit by the throw-stick encircled
      him.
  He raised a club in his hands,
  So ghosts flitted around (him).
  He put shoes on his feet,
  He made a noise in the Earth.

He kissed the wife he loved,
He hit the wife he hated,
He kissed he son he loved,
He hit the son he hated,
(And) the Earth's outcry did seize him.
She who sleeps and sleeps, the mother of Ninazu
who sleeps—[154]
Her pure shoulders were not covered with a
garment,
Her breasts were not pendulous like an ointment jar
in a *šikkatu*-basin.

iii   When Enkidu [tried] to go up again out of the
Earth,
Namtar did not seize him, nor did Asakku seize
him: the Earth seized him.
The croucher, Ukur the merciless, did not seize
him: the Earth seized him.
He did not fall in a fight among males: the Earth
seized him.
Then the son of Ninsun [went] and wept for his
servant Enkidu.
He went off on his own to Ekur, Ellil's temple.[155]
   'Father Ellil, today the *pukku* fell into the Earth,
   And my *mekkû* fell into the Earth,
   And the Earth seized Enkidu, who went down to
   bring them up.
   Namtar did not seize him, nor did Asakku seize
   him: the Earth seized him.
   The croucher, Ukur the merciless, did not seize
   him: the Earth seized him.
   He did not fall in a fight among males: the Earth
   seized him.'
Father Ellil answered him not a word, so he went
off alone to Sin's temple.[156]
   'Father Sin, today the *pukku* fell into the Earth,
   My *mekkû* fell into the Earth.
   The Earth seized Enkidu, who went down to bring
   them up.
   Namtar did not seize him, nor did Asakku seize
   him: the Earth seized him.

The croucher, Ukur the merciless, did not seize
him: the Earth seized him.
He did not fall in a fight among males: the Earth
seized him.'
Father Sin answered him not a word, so he went off
alone to Ea's temple.
'Father Ea, today the *pukku* fell into the Earth,
And my *mekkû* fell into the Earth,
And the Earth seized Enkidu, who went down to
bring them up.
Namtar did not seize him, nor did Asakku-demon
seize him: the Earth seized him.
The croucher, Ukur the merciless, did not seize
him: the Earth seized him.
He did not fall in a fight among males: the Earth
seized him.'
Father Ea answered him,
He spoke to the warrior [Ukur],[157]
'Warlike young man Ukur [   ]
You must open up a hole in the Earth now (?),[158]
So that the spirit [of Enkidu can come out of the
Earth like a gust of wind].
[And return (?)] to his brother [Gilgamesh].'[159]
The warlike young man Ukur [   ]
Opened up a hole in the Earth then (?),[158]
And the spirit of Enkidu came out of the Earth like
a gust of wind.[160]
They hugged and kissed (?),
They discussed, they agonized.
iv   'Tell me, my friend, tell me, my friend,
Tell me Earth's conditions that you found!'
'I can't tell you, my friend, I can't tell you!
If I tell you Earth's conditions that I found,
You must sit (and) weep!
I would sit and weep!
[Your wife (?),] whom you touched, and your
heart was glad,
Vermin eat [like (?)] an old [garment].
[Your son (?) whom] you touched, and your heart
was glad,

[Sits in a crevice (?)] full of dust.
"Woe" she said, and grovelled in the dust.[161]
"Woe" he said, and grovelled in the dust.
I saw [the father of one (?) whom you (once)
    saw (?)][162]
Covered [   ]
He weeps bitterly over it (?).
I saw [the father of two (?) whom you (once)
    saw (?)]
He eats bread [sitting on two bricks (?)]
I saw [the father of three (?) whom you (once)
    saw (?)]
He drinks water [from a waterskin]
I saw [the father of four (?) whom] you (once)
    saw
[   ] his heart is glad with a team of four!
I saw [the father of five (?) whom] you (once)
    saw:
Like a first-rate scribe he is open-handed,
Enters the palace [as a matter of course].
I saw [the father of six (?) whom] you (once) saw

(*gap of about 6 lines*)

v   Like a fine emblem [   ]
     Like [   ]

(*gap of about 25 lines*)

I saw him, whom you saw at the poles
    [of   ][163]
Now he cries for his mother as he tears out the
    pegs.
I saw him, whom you saw [die] a sudden death:
vi   He lies in bed and drinks pure water.
I saw him, whom you saw killed in battle:
His father and mother honour him and his wife
    weeps over him.
I saw him, whose corpse you saw abandoned in
    the open country:
His ghost does not sleep in the Earth.

> I saw him whom you saw, whose ghost has
>   nobody to supply it:[164]
> He feeds on dregs from dishes, and bits of bread
>   that lie abandoned in the streets.'[165]

(*Colophon*)

Tablet 12, 'Of him who found out all things'
[   ] written, inspected.

   (*break*)

NOTES TO *GILGAMESH*

Text: see Tigay 1982 for bibliography.

The translation is made up from many clay tablet fragments. Most of them date from the eighth century BC onwards, and many of them were found at Nineveh. They are all SBV unless otherwise indicated, namely in Tablet V which is LV from Uruk. Some tablets contain 6 columns (3 to a side) but others have only 2 or 4 columns (1 or 2 to a side). The number of lines of text per column varies between about 33 and 75, with the exception of final columns, which may contain far fewer lines than the previous columns, depending on how well the scribe judged the surface area available for his text. There is great variation of column length even within six-column tablets from Nineveh. Among the versions, the text is differently divided, both as to columns and as to individual tablets. Thus, for instance, Tablet IV, column vi in one version may only overlap to a small extent with Tablet IV, column vi in another version, and a single site like Nineveh may have yielded up more than one version; Tablet VI has much shorter columns in the second half than in the first. Therefore, to estimate accurately the length of gaps, where a disjointed text is made up of fragments, is extremely difficult and sometimes impossible. For the purposes of this book, a rule-of-thumb has been adopted: gaps are reckoned at forty-five lines per column except in the case of Tablets III and IX, and parts of V, for which the reckoning is thirty-five lines per column. Thus the line numbers given for gaps are intended only as a very rough guide, and may in some instances prove to be misleading. Column numbers are taken as far as possible from a single well-preserved tablet if several versions exist with columns divided at different points, as is the case with Tablet XI. A full edition of the Akkadian text is being prepared by A. George and I. Finkel.

1. Opening lines following Kwasman 1999. The opening is of a type characteristic of oral narrative. Cf. the opening lines of *Anzu* and *Erra and Ishum*.
2. Probably refers to Ut-napishtim's story in Tablet XI.
3. This sentence is taken as an oath clause with suppressed apodosis. 'The Seven Counsellors' probably refers to the Seven Sages who brought

skills and crafts to mankind. Baked bricks were only used for top-quality work; unbaked mud bricks were commonly used.

4. An Old Babylonian version of the epic began at this point. See note 14 to OBV *Gilgamesh*.

5. The Hittite version attributes Gilgamesh's superior form to both the sun-god and to the storm-god, and refers to Gilgamesh as 'gods' in the plural; this may be a Phoenician usage. See note 11 on *Nergal and Ereshkigal*.

6. Or, 'ordinances', or 'forms of life' rather than 'cult centres'. See Moran 1977 and Lambert 1979.

7. In a Hittite version of *Gilgamesh*, he is described as a giant, 11 cubits (about 5 m.) tall (Friedrich 1929).

8. Or, 'When he was alerted', *puqqu*, rather than 'at his *pukku*'. If the latter, it refers to the game of *pukku* and *mekkû*, variously interpreted as 'drum and drumstick', 'hoop and driving-stick', and as a hockey-type of game played at weddings and having significance for fertility. The two objects are elsewhere used to describe the clash of battle, and are one of Ishtar's toys or games. Orphans, widows, and young girls are affected by its use, for which they lament and cry out against injustice.

9. The word translated here as 'someone' and as 'word' is a pun in Akkadian: *zikru*, 'name, speech, order' and *zikru/zikaru*, 'male, man'.

10. The three metaphorical words used to describe Enkidu: 'word(?) of Anu', 'sky-bolt of Ninurta/Anu', 'axe', all may be puns on terms for cult personnel of uncertain sexual affinities who were found particularly in Uruk, associated with Ishtar's cult: *zikru/sekru*, *kiṣru/kezru*, and *haṣṣinnu/assinnu* (Kilmer 1982 + SMD).

11. The Hittite version names the hunter as Shangashush.

12. It has been suggested that Gilgamesh or Enkidu, rather than the hunter, is the subject of these lines, which are repeated in Tablet X with Gilgamesh as the subject.

13. Perhaps means meteoric iron.

14. Shamhat is used as personal name here; it means 'voluptuous woman, prostitute', in particular as a type of cultic devotee of Ishtar in Uruk.

15. Pun: 'over her open country'/'over her back', both *ṣēru*. The joke could be conveyed in English as 'hilly flanks'. Intercourse from the rear is well attested on ancient representations from Mesopotamia. See RlA, s.v. *Heilige Hochzeit*, §14, p. 266.

16. OBV (Pennsylvania tablet) joins the story at this point.

17. This rhetorical group of four lines corresponds to a single line in OBV.

18. Or: 'Your dream [was favourable and very significant].'

19. In the month of Ab a wrestling contest always took place, and the month was dedicated to Gilgamesh.

20. The usual translation of *erēnu* as 'cedar' is almost certainly wrong. The main grounds for a translation as 'pine' are: that roof-beams thus named in texts have been excavated and analysed invariably as pine, and that the wood was obtained in antiquity not only from the Lebanon mountains, but also from the Zagros and the Amanus ranges, where cedars do

not grow. The Akkadian word may have covered a different and wider range of trees than the English word 'pine'.

21. The word translated 'leagues' is a double hour. The Mesopotamians divided the day into 12 hours corresponding to our 24, and they calculated distances according to the time a journey would take rather than its linear measurement.

22. 'My friend': the relationship of Enkidu and Gilgamesh as friends of equal status contrasts with their roles as servant and master in the Sumerian stories.

23. 'New break' is a comment made by a scribe copying the text from a damaged tablet.

24. The word for the New Year's Festival, *akītu*, meant any major city festival at early periods, but by the time the Nineveh tablets were written, it would have acquired the specific meaning given here. During the festival, the king's officials would swear an oath of allegiance for the coming year, and the king, if not abroad, probably took part, representing a god in a ceremony of sacred marriage with a priestess.

25. *illuru* is an exclamation rather like 'Halleluyah'.

26. Pun perhaps: 'brides/graves', *hīrtu*, *hīratu* 'bride', *hirītu* 'grave', both with plural *hirāti*.

27. Or, restore as in II. vi: 'Give me your blessing, since I [have decided] on the course, That I may enter the city gate of Uruk [again in future(?)], And [celebrate] the New Year Festival once again in [future years(?)], and take part...'

28. Something Evil is the name of a demon (see Glossary, s.v. *Demons*).

29. In the Sumerian story of *Gilgamesh and Huwawa*, Gilgamesh is not inspired by the sun-god to set forth, but has to persuade the sun-god to help him.

30. CAD takes *atmuka* as 'I discussed your case' rather than 'your offspring'.

31. It appears from plate 13 of Campbell-Thompson 1930 that the two fragments from Nineveh, K 3423 + Rm 579 and K 9885 ended column iv at different points in the text.

32. The placing of fragments and the sequence of events is still uncertain. This translation assumes that the sequence: journey—introduction to dream—dream—interpretation of dream, occurs three times. A three-dream sequence also occurs in Tablets I and (?)VII. The relationship of the tablets from Assur, LKU 39 and 40, to the Ninevite version is not clear. It has been suggested that this expedition reflects campaigns to the west by Sargon of Agade or by third dynasty rulers at Ur, in the late third millennium. In the Sumerian story of Gilgamesh and Huwawa, citizens of Uruk accompany the two heroes; but they journey alone together in this Akkadian version. In the Hittite version they travel along the Euphrates to the Pine Forest (Otten 1958).

33. This echoes the instructions from the elders of Uruk to Gilgamesh before he sets out in OBV. The actions, of digging a well and making an offering of flour, are reminiscent of a ritual carried out in open country to pacify the demons and ghosts that haunted the countryside (Ebeli·

1931, 83). There was also an incantation called 'Well of Gilgamesh' which was recited before a new well was dug (CAD, B, 336a).

34. 'Wild barley', literally 'mountain barley'.

35. The expected line 'They refilled(?) [their water-skins]' is omitted. It is possible that the missing line was doubled up and fitted into the damaged second half of the line.

36. Omens including dreams were frequently sought in a series of three deliberately for assurance and confirmation.

37. Or: '[Clouds] billowed'.

38. Presumably the interpretation was bad. Possibly at roughly this point in the story the missing episode should be placed, to which Gilgamesh refers in VII. vi. and IX. i. See note 83 below. Column iv presumably contained an episode in which Enkidu became paralysed; and column v may describe the search for and discovery of special healing herbs, as referred to in vi; but Enkidu was not healed immediately.

39. These lines contain proverbial expressions to illustrate the truth that 'two are stronger than one'. In the Sumerian tale *Gilgamesh and Huwawa* a similar speech containing proverbs is made by Gilgamesh to Enkidu. Comparison has been made with Ecclesiastes 4: 9–12: 'Two are better than one because they have a good reward for their labour. For if they fall, the one will lift up his fellow; but woe to him that is alone when he falleth, for he hath not another to help him up. Again, if two lie together, then they have heat; but how can one be warm alone? And if one prevail against him, two shall withstand him; and a three-fold cord is not quickly broken.' For other echoes of *Gilgamesh* in Ecclesiastes, see OBV, notes 17 and 26.

40. The Hittite and Sumerian versions at about this point show that Humbaba was alerted to impending danger by the noise of pines crashing down. Several of the passages in this tablet are taken from LV and may be different from SBV, which is not extant for most of this episode (von Weiher 1988).

41. The word used for 'fool' is *lillu*, and may be a scathing and punning reference to the tradition in which Gilgamesh's father was a *lillu* of Kullab; see Introduction, p. 40.

42. Or, 'He has lifted up a crossbeam', reading the damaged noun as *binītu*.

43. The placing of this fragment is very uncertain. It comes apparently from a different recension to other Nineveh tablets of this epic. The text of Tablets IV and V may not have been divided per tablet in the same way in each recension. In the Sumerian version, Gilgamesh's prayer to Shamash for help is answered by Shamash giving him the winds as weapons.

44. Line restored from VII. iii. 34.

45. Alliteration on the letters HLP; compare *Epic of Creation*, note 18.

46. Reading *[sungin]nu* rather than *[habalgin]nu*, "iron", which would not be appropriate in a Bronze Age text.

47. Tentatively taking the verb as *behāšu*, 'stirred', rather than *bêšu*, '(the earth) divided'. George 1987 has suggested that this passage gives an aetiology for the Rift Valley (Beqa'a) in Lebanon. Pun: Sirara/Saria,

'Mt. Hermon' and *sâru*, 'to dance, 'gyrate'. Saria/Sirara was known to the ancient Mesopotamians as 'Pine Mountain'.

48. The Sumerian story has seven winds, the Hittite version eight.
49. Tentatively reading *kikaša*, 'thus'.
50. Reading *kibrû*, 'old man' rather than *kibru*, 'bank'. These two lines may represent the dying Humbaba's curse.
51. Ereshkigal's proposal to Nergal in *Nergal and Ereshkigal* is expressed in identical terms.
52. The 'horns' of a chariot are probably the yoke terminals, which are made of alabaster on Egyptian New Kingdom chariots, and in Middle Bronze Age tablets from Mari. *elmēšu*-stone: a lustrous, precious, semi-mythical stone, possibly amber, often used with rock crystal.
53. The adjective *arattû*, 'wonderfully wrought', originally meant 'made in Aratta', an unlocated land to the east of Mesopotamia, famous for craftsmanship in the Early Dynastic period.
54. 'Verdure': taking the signs as *lul-lub-di*, very tentatively interpreted as a variant form of *lullumti*.
55. 'Juggernaut', or 'a limestone block', but that makes poor sense. The word used, *pīlu*, can be interpreted as a phonetic variation on the word for an elephant, *pīru*, which occurred three lines previously.
56. *allallu*-bird: possibly a roller. Its cry *kappī*, 'my wing', may be onomatopoeic for a general bird cry, since the Anzu bird makes a similar cry, 'wing to wing', in *Anzu*, ii.
57. Variant gives a spoonerism, *migir*, 'contentment' for *gimir*, 'complete'.
58. Repetition of a number apparently for emphasis, with or without 'and', seems to be a rhetorical device. See note 22 to *Atrahasis*.
59. A variant text has 'offerings' for 'ewe-lambs'.
60. This metamorphosis has been compared to the Greek myth of Actaeon.
61. Presumably a reference to shaduf irrigation.
62. Ishtar makes this threat to the doorkeeper of the Underworld in the *Descent of Ishtar*; and Ereshkigal makes the same threat in *Nergal and Ereshkigal*, for Namtar to relay to the goddess. It has been compared to *Odyssey*, XII. 374, in which Helios threatened Zeus that he would give light to the Underworld.
63. Presumably as trophies of victory. This line may allude to a cult practice.
64. These are cultic devotees of Ishtar.
65. Thirty minas is about 15 kg., 2 minas about 1 kg. Lapis lazuli was one of the most highly prized gemstones in ancient Mesopotamia. It was obtained from mountains in north-east Afghanistan.
66. Reading *šinnû manê* with AHw.
67. Six kor is about 1,800 litres.
68. Lugalbanda was Gilgamesh's father. This line implies that Gilgamesh kept a statue or statuette of him in his bedroom where he anointed it regularly. In certain parts of the Near East at certain periods, deceased ancestors were referred to as gods. Cf. note 74 below.
69. Pun: 'Took them in' *erēbu Š*/ 'Made a vessel of a horn-end' *šarāmu D*.
70. The Hittite version is given following R. Stefanini, JNES 28, 1969.

71. Six poles: there is a 'light' and a 'heavy' measure for this, so either about 36 m. or 54 m. is the English equivalent.

72. Could also be read *linaqqir*, 'cut away (my name)', rather than *linakkir*, 'change'.

73. Literally 'fast and early'.

74. Statues were made to stand in temples, representing their originals by standing constantly in the gods' presence; or they were made for distinguished people at their death to be the recipients of funerary rites, particularly anointing. Cf. note 68 above.

75. The identical phrase in *Descent of Ishtar* is used for Ereshkigal's curse of Good-Looks.

76. Identical curses are found in the *Descent of Ishtar*.

77. Or, restore 'roof'; both walls and roofs of mud brick houses have to be replastered very frequently.

78. 'The dwelling on the left': a parallel is found in the myth of the hero Er, son of Armenius, which Socrates related at the end of Plato's *Republic*. When the souls of men were judged at death, the just ascended to heaven via an opening on the right of the judges, and the unjust descended to the lower regions via an opening on the left.

79. The word used means a first wife, literally 'chosen one'. Upon the death of such a wife, a man was often obliged to marry the widow of a relative.

80. The old interpretation of *keppū* as a skipping rope was based on a misinterpretation of a glyptic scene, and should be abandoned. It may be a whipping-top (a spinning top lashed into faster gyrations with a cord), which is shown in action at Carchemish on a mural sculpture in relief of the early first millennium. (SMD)

81. Almost identical to the opening passage in *Descent of Ishtar*.

82. No myths yet uncovered account for the presence in the Underworld of either Etana the king of Kish or Shakkan the cattle-god. For Shakkan rather than Sumuqan see Cagni 1969, 158.

83. This may be a reference to an incident which is referred to again in IX. i, and which may have been related fully in a still missing episode in IV, or later, in between the slaying of Humbaba and of the Bull of Heaven. A possible reconstruction is: Gilgamesh and Enkidu were attacked by lions at night in the mountain passes on their way to the Pine Forest. Gilgamesh was afraid and prayed to Sin; Enkidu killed the lions and reproached Gilgamesh; and when they slept, Enkidu had a dream portending his own death. In VII. vi. and IX. i. Gilgamesh interpreted the episode to mean that his cowardice caused Enkidu's death.

84. Much of Tablet VIII is known from a school text which contains schoolboy errors. This opening stock line, which recurs in Tablet XI, has been compared to the stock line in the *Odyssey*: 'As soon as rosy-fingered dawn appeared'.

85. 'They shall weep for you' is repeated with the word for 'ditto' in subsequent lines.

86. Restored from Craig 1895–7, I, 60, a religious text which appears to quote this line.

87. Dittos are used in one version where this phrase is repeated in subsequent lines.
88. This line has been compared with *Iliad*, XVIII. 317, when Achilles puts his hands on the breast of the dead Patroklos.
89. It is not certain where the speech ends, since different versions vary the person of the verbs in subsequent lines.
90. The simile has been compared with *Iliad*, XVIII. 318: 'As a deep-bearded lion, whose whelps some stag-hunter has snatched away out of a deep wood; and the lion coming afterwards grieves and ranges through many glens . . .'
91. According to information from variants, this passage is corrupt.
92. A late composition found at Sultantepe takes the form of a letter written by Gilgamesh to another king and mentions a lump of gold weighing 30 minas (about 15 kg.) for the statue(?) of Enkidu, as well as blocks of jasper and lapis lazuli (Gurney 1957).
93. Partly restored from VII. i.
94. This part of the text probably describes the precious materials used to make a composite statue of Enkidu. Statues of deceased kings and high officials have been found in temples and palaces, but not in graves.
95. Grave goods were 'shown' to Shamash before they were placed in the grave with the body (McGinnis 1987). The procedure is that of the *taklimtu* ritual of lying-in-state.
96. The word *mašhaltappû*, translated as 'scapegoat', is problematic. George (1999) restores the name of a deity in apposition to the scapegoat as [Dumuzi]-abzu; a translation *mašhaltappû*-priest may be preferable.
97. *elammaku* was a highly prized timber imported from Syria.
98. Or, 'I fear a death (in which) I must roam open country.' If the dead were restless they were thought to haunt desert country and cause harm.
99. Similar but variant wording is found in Sargon II of Assyria's letter to the gods describing his eighth campaign, line 19 (Thureau-Dangin 1912).
100. It is not certain whether there was a single pair of scorpion people or many of them.
101. It was suggested by Gressmann 1926 that this episode is based on a two-mile rock tunnel near the source of the Tigris, which is described by Lehmann-Haupt 1910. An episode similar to this is found in several stories in the *Arabian Nights*.
102. Dittos are used when this phrase is repeated in subsequent lines.
103. This is the approximate sense of the line, but there are unresolved difficulties in the text.
104. Reading *PAP a-[ša-gi eṭ-ṭe-t]i gi-iṣ-ṣi . . .* For the suggestion that the jewel garden was in Bahrein, see During Caspars 1983, but compare the description given by Lehmann-Haupt for the luscious vegetation at the mouth of the Tigris tunnel. It is almost certainly misguided to try to identify such semi-mythological settings with precision.

105. The Akkadian words are used here for gemstones that have not been identified.

106. The profession 'ale-wife', female seller of beer, is well known from its occurrence in several laws in the Code of Hammurabi and the Edicts of Ammi-saduqa which concern long-distance trade in the early second millennium BC. She seems to have lived outside the normal protection of male members of a family, and to have served beer, the staple drink of ancient Mesopotamia, to travellers. Her supplies were provided by the palace that sponsored her. An Akkadian list describes Siduri as 'Ishtar of wisdom'. The whole episode has been compared to the story of Calypso in *Odyssey*, V; see Introduction, p. 48.

107. In the Hittite version the fermentation vats are made of gold (Friedrich 1930). Possibly 'gold' should also be restored here in the Akkadian text.

108. It has been suggested that the name Calypso is a translation of the Akkadian 'cover', but with an incomplete context, the suggestion is far from secure.

109. Gilgamesh's threat is identical to that of Ishtar in *Ishtar's Descent*.

110. This may refer to the reproach or curse of Enkidu which he presumably made during the episode of killing lions. See note 83. The ditto sign is used instead of 'weigh upon me'.

111. In the Hittite version Ut-napishtim is called Ulluya, and a Hurrian fragment has Ullush.

112. 'Lethal waters': literally 'waters of death'. This phrase has been connected with the Classical view that the Underworld was encircled by a river, which is also found in some Akkadian texts (see Glossary, s.v. Hubur). However, Gilgamesh is journeying not to the Underworld, but to the Mouth of the Rivers. There seem to have been two different traditions about the Underworld, with and without a surrounding river.

113. 'Things of stone': meaning uncertain. 'Anchors' or 'stone stern-poles' have been suggested. According to OBV they bring Ur-shanabi safely over the lethal water. 'Identify him': possibly '(are) with him' rather than '(are) his mark of identification'. 'A young pine': probably timber stripped for poles. The previous translation, as some kind of snake, is definitely wrong (AHw, s.v. *urnu*).

114. It is unclear whom Gilgamesh drove away. The text may be corrupt here. An almost identical passage occurs in SBV *Nergal and Ereshkigal*.

115. Or, 'And he (Ur-shanabi) hit him, Gilgamesh, on the head'.

116. Perhaps the knobs are devices to help prevent the lethal water touching Gilgamesh. The poles seem to replace the 'things of stone' in that function. For the readings of numbers in this passage, see Powell 1982, 93–4.

117. The *magillu* was a mythical boat and fabulous creature, connected with the semi-mythical lands Magan and Meluhha. It was 'defeated' by Ninurta, who displayed it as a trophy. See Cooper 1978, 148.

118. This is the accepted restoration, although, of course, Ut-napishtim would not have seen Gilgamesh on his wanderings overland.

119. Ditto sign is used for the repeat in the second half of the line.

120. Following AHw, s.v. *matīma* as 'sometimes', the phrase is not taken as

an interrogative; and 'make a nest' (CAD, s.v. *qanānu*) is preferred to 'seal' (*kanāku* with an emendation of the text, Lambert 1980a).

121. This natural phenomenon is also mentioned in *Atrahasis*; see note 41 to that text.

122. See note 29 to *Atrahasis*.

123. These lines are loaded with double meanings and puns. The puns are indicated in the translation: *kukku*, 'a kind of cake' and *kukkû*, 'darkness'; *kibtu*, 'wheat' and *kibittu*, 'heaviness'.

124. 'Oakum': tentatively reading *pitilta*, literally 'palm-bast'.

125. The ancient Mesopotamians were builders of rafts and reed boats for use on rivers, not builders of timber-frame vessels. The ark as described here seems to be a tub of 'quffah' type, which consists mainly of a framework of reed matting liberally coated with bitumen and oil to make it waterproof, fitted inside with benches and supporting poles. See also note 43 to *Atrahasis*.

126. Three sar is about 24,000 gallons.

127. 'Had to be fetched': see Gurney 1979; and for the Plimsoll line effect, SMD.

128. No boatman occurs in *Atrahasis*, and we do not meet Puzur-Amurru elsewhere in *Gilgamesh*. However, his naming on this occasion suggests the possibility of a missing tradition in which he played a more important role.

129. Or, 'Mountain and Country marched as chamberlains'.

130. Or, 'in the rain'. See George 1985b, an interpretation that relies on variant texts attempting to express exactly the same notion.

131. The Mesopotamians thought that there were three heavens: upper, middle, and lower. The upper was the domain of Anu.

132. Or, 'Did I order a catastrophe to destroy my people?'

133. The text is corrupt, possibly because the word for 'scab, rime', *pulhītu*, had fallen out of common usage and was 'reinterpreted'. See note 37 to *Atrahasis*.

134. The same phrase 'silence reigned' occurs in *Anzu*, I. iii. after Anzu flew off with the Tablet of Destinies.

135. For Nimush, previously read Niṣir, see Lambert 1986. The place has been identified with Pir Omar Gudrun, north of Suleimaniyah, northeast of Kirkuk; called Kinipa by the Lullu/Lullubu people, and a very impressive peak (Speiser 1926–7).

136. The text says 'my raven' where the writing is syllabic; the logograms in the preceding lines could be read as 'my dove' and 'my swallow'.

137. For repetition of numbers perhaps as a rhetorical device, see note 22 on *Atrahasis*.

138. 'Into the bottom of them': or, 'beneath them', but there is evidence elsewhere that libations were poured *into* such jars.

139. See note 42 to *Atrahasis*. If the flies refer to a past event, it may be better to translate: 'Behold, O gods, I ought never to have forgotten.'

140. The Hittite version has Kumarbi instead of Ellil here.

141. Or, 'Some sort of life survived!'

142. Possibly refers to Ur-shanabi's boat.

143. These instructions are clearly abbreviated, since they omit most of the information that Gilgamesh needed in order to act as he did.

144. Or, 'As it went back'. This episode is an aetiological story explaining why snakes can shed their old skins.

145. This expression may mean 'chameleon' (Sjöberg 1984) but presumably refers to the snake here.

146. This passage adapts the opening lines of *Gilgamesh* to Ur-shanabi's visit, thus forming an epilogue, to which the short Tablet XII is clearly an addition.

147. The Sumerian tale on which this Akkadian tablet seems to be mainly based had 303 lines. This Akkadian version does not begin until line 172 of it. Some lines give a very close translation of the Sumerian; other lines are more free of its influence in wording, and some are expanded or additional to the Sumerian. The Sumerian account begins by describing primeval times when a single *halub*-tree grew beside the Euphrates. Inanna planted it in her temple garden. It housed a snake and the Anzu-bird. Gilgamesh cut it down to make a chair and bed for Inanna, and a *pukku* and *mekkû* for himself. The latter accidentally fell into the Underworld while still new. Gilgamesh lamented their loss, and *Gilgamesh*, XII begins half-way through his speech of lament. Thus the opening to XII cannot be understood without knowledge of an independent Sumerian tale (Shaffer 1963).

148. For possible meanings of *pukku* and *mekkû* see note 8.

149. 'Earth' is a name for the Underworld.

150. 'My lord': at this point the relationship between Gilgamesh and Enkidu is that of master and servant, as in the Sumerian stories of Gilgamesh, whereas in the rest of the Akkadian epic they are equal comrades. However, later in this tablet Gilgamesh is called Enkidu's brother.

151. This implies that Enkidu has not yet died, thus contradicting Tablet VII.

152. Ereshkigal is meant.

153. The precise nature of the simile is uncertain; perhaps the pot was kept in the oil storage jar as a scoop; its shape or its bobbing motion may be crucial to the imagery.

154. The following seven lines are not represented in the Sumerian story.

155. The following episode is similar to the Sumerian *Descent of Inanna*, when her vizier Nin-shubur appeals to the great gods to rescue her from the Underworld.

156. The following seven lines are not represented in the Sumerian story.

157. Ukur is elsewhere referred to as the ghost of Nergal, king of the Underworld.

158. The precise function of the Akkadian particle *luman* translated 'now(?)' and 'then(?)' here, is not certain.

159. Another suggested restoration is: 'That he might tell the ways of the Underworld to his brother' (Jensen 1906).

160. This episode has been compared with *Iliad*, XXIII, when Achilles dreams that Patroklos' ghost visits him, and they try in vain to embrace; and with Odysseus' attempt to hug his mother's ghost in *Odyssey*, XI. ⌐ there is little doubt that Gilgamesh and Enkidu succeed in em┴

The ghosts of Enkidu and of Patroklos are both compared to a gust of wind.

161. These two lines are identical in Akkadian, and correspond to a single line of Sumerian, so dittography is possible. It is also possible to take them as an interjection by Gilgamesh.

162. One Sumerian version seems to give the following sequence in the form of question-and-answer, e.g. 'Did you see the man with one son? Did you see him? How was he?' 'He . . .' and so on. It is difficult to interpret the Akkadian as a direct translation. The common translation, 'Did you see . . ?' 'I saw (him)' ignores the subjunctive ending on 'you saw'. Some translators interpret the second Sumerian 'Did you see?' as 'I saw', although the verbal form is identical and ambiguous.

163. These two lines may describe the crushing to death of a man while helping to launch a ship, rather than by falling from a mast, which is scarcely appropriate to the ships of that time and area. The Sumerian version has a different order of lines from here onwards.

164. In a ritual text (Ebeling 1931, 132–3) Gilgamesh as judge of the Underworld is invoked to placate such spirits: 'Incantation. You, ghost belonging to nobody, who have nobody to bury you or speak your name, whose name nobody knows . . . before Shamash, Gilgamesh, the Anunnaki, (and) the ghost(s) of my family you hereby receive a present, you are honoured with a gift.'

165. One Sumerian version ends: 'Did you see my stillborn children who never knew life? Did you see them? How are they?' 'They play at a gold and silver table laden with butter and honey.' 'Did you see him who was set on fire? Did you see him? How was he?' 'His ghost is not there. His smoke went up to the sky.'

GILGAMESH (OLD BABYLONIAN VERSION)

Tablet I not extant

TABLET II

i   Gilgamesh got up and described the dream;[1]
He spoke to his mother,
   'Mother, in the middle of (?) the night
   I was feeling lusty and walking around
   Among the young men.
   The stars of heaven gathered (?) to me,
   And a decoy (?) from Anum fell on to me.[2]
   I tried to lift it, but it was too heavy for me.
   I tried to budge it, but I could not budge it.
   The land of Uruk gathered around it,
   The young men kissed its feet,
   I took responsibility (?) for it,
   They loaded it on to me,
   I lifted it and brought it to you.'
The mother of Gilgamesh, she who knows all
     things,
Spoke to Gilgamesh,
   'I imagine, Gilgamesh, it is your match.
   It was born in the open country
   And a mountain reared it.
   You saw it and you were glad,[3]
   The young men kissed its feet,
   You embraced it
   And brought it to me.'
He went back to sleep and saw a second (dream),
Got up, told his mother,
   '[Mother,] I saw a second one.
   [   ] in the street

Of spacious Uruk
An axe was thrown down,
And they gathered around it.
The axe looked somehow strange.
I saw it and I was glad.
I loved it as a wife.
And I doted on it.
I took it and placed it
At my side.'[4]

The mother of Gilgamesh, she who knows all
    things,
Spoke to Gilgamesh,

(gap of 22 lines)

ii   'Because I will treat him as equal to you.'
Gilgamesh described the dream.
Enkidu stayed with the harlot.[5]
They made love together.
He forgot the open country where he was born.
For six days and seven nights,
Enkidu was aroused,
And poured himself into Shamkat (?)
The harlot made her voice heard
And spoke to Enkidu,
    'I am looking at you, Enkidu, you are godlike.
    Why do you go around open country
    With wild beasts?
    Come with me, let me take you
    Into spacious Uruk,
    To the pure house, Anum's dwelling.
    Enkidu, get up, let me lead you
    To Eanna, Anum's dwelling,
    Where [Gilgamesh, perfectly (?)] made (?),
    And you [   ].
    You will love him as yourself.
    Come on, get up from the ground.
    No more (?) sex (?).'
He listened to her speech, agreed with her
    command;
The woman's (?) suggestions

Penetrated his heart.
She took off her garments,
Clothed him in one,
Dressed herself
In a second garment,
Took his hand,
Like a goddess (?) led him[6]
To a shepherd's hut
Where there was a sheep-pen.
The shepherds gathered over him

(gap of 4 or 5 lines)

iii   He used to suck the milk
Of wild animals.
They put food in front of him.
He narrowed his eyes, and looked,
Then stared.
Enkidu knew nothing
Of eating bread,
Of drinking beer.
He had never learned.
The harlot made her voice heard
And spoke to Enkidu,
    'Eat the food, Enkidu,
    The symbol of life.
    Drink the beer, destiny of the land.'[7]
Enkidu ate the bread
Until he had had enough.
He drank the beer,
Seven whole jars,
Relaxed, felt joyful.
His heart rejoiced,
His face beamed,
He smeared himself with [   ].
His body was hairy.
He anointed himself with oil
And became like any man,
Put on clothes.
He was like a warrior,[8]
Took his weapon,

Fought with lions.
The shepherds could rest at night;
He beat off wolves,
Drove off lions.
The older (?) herdsmen lay down;
Enkidu was their guard,
A man awake.
One young man
Spoke to [   ]

(*gap of about 23 lines to end of column*)

iv   (*gap of about 17 lines at beginning of
       column*)

He made merry.
He raised his eyes
And saw the man,
Said to the harlot,
  'Shamkat, bring the man here!
  Why has he come?
  Let me call him by name.'
The harlot called the man.
He went up to him and spoke to him,
  'Young man, where are you hurrying?
  What is the cause of your exertion?'
The young man made his voice heard
And spoke to Enkidu,
  'They have invited me to the houses of fathers-
    in-law,
  —It is the people's destiny—
  For choosing daughters-in-law.
  I fill the table of ceremonies[9]
  With delightful food of the father-in-law's city.
  For the king of spacious Uruk,
  Open the ... of people for bridegrooms![10]
  For Gilgamesh the king of spacious Uruk,
  Open the ... of people for bridegrooms!
  He will impregnate the destined wife,
  He first,
  The husband afterwards.

It was ordered by the counsel of Anum
And destined for him
When his umbilical cord was severed.'
At the word of the young man
His face went livid.

(*gap of about 12 lines*)

v   (*gap*)

Enkidu went in front
And Shamkat behind him.
He entered into spacious Uruk,
And men gathered about him.
He stood in the street
Of spacious Uruk
And people gathered
And talked about him.
  'He is just like Gilgamesh in form,
  Shorter in shape,
  Very strong (?) bones (?).
  [Mountains (?)] gave (him) birth (?).
  He used to eat [   ]
  He used to suck
  The milk of wild animals.
  In Uruk sacrifices will be constant,
  Young men will purify themselves.
  The *lušānum*-instrument plays
  For the young man who looks so upright!'[11]
  A match is found at last
  For godlike Gilgamesh!'
The bed was made
For Ishhara,
And Gilgamesh, (who) every night
Had met the girls,
Came away,
For [Enkidu] stood (?) in the street,
Barred the path
Of Gilgamesh.

(*gap*)

vi   Lusty [   ]
     Gilgamesh [   ]
     Upon [   ]
     He was in a rage, [   ]
     [Enkidu] got up
     In front of him
     And they confronted each other in the country's
         main square.
     Enkidu blocked the door
     With his foot,
     Did not let Gilgamesh enter.
     Like bulls they grappled
     And crouched.
     They demolished the doorframe;
     The wall shook.
     Gilgamesh and Enkidu
     Grappled
     And crouched like bulls.
     They demolished the doorframe;
     The wall shook.
     Gilgamesh went down (?),
     His foot on the ground.
     His rage subsided
     And he turned away.
     When he had turned away
     Enkidu spoke to him,
     To Gilgamesh,
       'Your mother bore you
       To be unique,
       The wild cow of the Sheepfold,[12]
       Ninsun,[13]
       Raised your head above death (?).
       Ellil decreed for you
       Kingship over people.'
     (*Colophon*)
     Second tablet of 'He was superior to [other
        kings].'[14]

TABLET III

i   (*about 10 lines missing, 8 fragmentary*)
They kissed each other
And made friends.

(*Fragmentary or broken away to end of
column*)

ii   (*About 12 lines missing*)

'A rival [   ]
Set for him, and [   ]
The mourners [   ]
The mother of [Gilgamesh (?)   ]

(*about 10 lines missing*)

[His eyes filled] with tears,
He felt [furious]
And [dreadfully] tormented.
Enkidu's [eyes] filled with tears,
[He felt] furious
And [dreadfully] tormented.
[Gilgamesh] lowered (?) his face,
[Said] to Enkidu,
  '[Why] are your eyes
  Filled with tears?
  You are furious,
  You are [dreadfully] tormented.'
[Enkidu] made [his voice heard]
And spoke to Gilgamesh,
  'Howls of grief, my friend,
  Have made my neck muscles stand out,
  My arms are weak
  And my strength is feeble.'
Gilgamesh made his voice heard
And spoke to Enkidu,

iii   (*about 4 lines missing*)

Smiting Huwawa [   ]
    ₁   ] shall I slay

And [   ] shall I destroy!
[I shall cut down] pines
[   ] the forest.

   (*2 lines fragmentary*)

Enkidu made his voice heard
And spoke to Gilgamesh,
   'It was dark (?), my friend, on the mountain,
   When I used to go with the cattle.
   The forest extended (?) for sixty leagues in each
      direction.
   Who can penetrate to its depths?
   Huwawa's shout is the flood-weapon,
   His utterance is Fire,[15]
   His breath is Death.
   Why do you want
   To do this?
   Huwawa's home
   Is an impossible challenge!
Gilgamesh made his voice heard
And spoke to Enkidu,
   '[My friend (?)] let me go up to its mountain,
   [Let me set off to the] forest (?)!

   (*3 lines fragmentary*)

   The dwelling of [Huwawa]
   An axe [   ]
   You [   ]
   I shall [   ].'
Enkidu made his voice heard
And spoke to Gilgamesh,
   'How can we go
   To the Pine Forest?
   Its guardian is Wer [   ]
   He is strong, he never sleeps.
   Huwawa [   ] Wer,
   Adad [   ]
   He [   ]

iv   To keep the Pine Forest safe,
          [   ] seven terrors.'
          Gilgamesh made his voice heard
          And spoke to [Enkidu],
                'Who can go up to heaven, my friend?
                Only the gods dwell (?) with Shamash forever.[16]
                Mankind can number his days.
                Whatever he may achieve, it is only wind.[17]
                Do you fear death on this occasion?
                Where is the strength of your heroic nature?
                Let me go in front of you,
                And your voice call out: "Go close, don't be
                    afraid!"
                If I should fall, I shall have won fame.
                People will say, "Gilgamesh grappled in combat
                With ferocious Huwawa.
                He was (nobly ?) born." But you grew up in
                    open country;
                (When) a lion sprang at you, you knew
                    everything,

                    (*4 lines fragmentary*)

                You said this to me, you made me furious.
                I shall set [to work]
                And cut down pines,
                Ensure fame that will last forever.
                [Come], my friend, I shall . . . to the forge.
                They will cast (?) [weapons] in our presence.'
          They held hands and . . . to the forge.
          The craftsmen sat, gave it thought,
          Cast large *pāšum*-axes,
          Cast *haṣṣinnum*-axes three talents each,
          Cast great swords,
          Blades two talents each,
          Rivets at their sides, thirty minas each,
          Gold [   ]s of the swords, thirty minas each.
          Gilgamesh and Enkidu contributed ten talents each.
          The main gates (?) of Uruk (?) [   ]
          [   ] listened and the men assembled
          Made merry in the street of spacious Uruk.

Gilgamesh [   ] his merry-making.
[The elders of] spacious [Uruk]
Sat [   ] before him.
[Gilgamesh] spoke [to them, saying],
    '[   ] of spacious [Uruk]

    (*one or more lines missing*)

v   Let me see the god (?) who speaks,
    Whose name the lands ever echo (?)!
    Let me conquer him in the Pine Forest
    And give the country cause to hear
    How powerful Uruk's scion is!
    Let me set to work and cut down pines,
    Ensure fame that will last forever!'
The elders of spacious Uruk
Spoke in turn to Gilgamesh,
    'Your courage, Gilgamesh, leads you to
        foolhardiness.[18]
    You do not know what you are trying to do.
    We hear that Huwawa's looks are alien:
    Who could face his weapons?
    The forest extends (?) for sixty (?) leagues in each
        direction.
    Who can penetrate to its depths?
    Huwawa's shout is the flood-weapon,
    His utterance is Fire, his breath is Death.
    Why do you want to do this?
    Huwawa's home is an impossible challenge!'
Gilgamesh listened to the speech of his advisers,
And looked and smiled (?) at his friend.
    'So my friend, should [I too speak] thus?
    Should I be afraid of him and [   ]

        (*about 8 lines missing*)

    Your god [   ] you,
    Let him make you take the road
    To the quay of spacious Uruk.'
Gilgamesh was crouching (?) down [   ]
And the words he spoke [   ]
    'I shall indeed go! Shamash [   ]

> There let me keep my life safe!
> Bring me back to the quay in [safety (?)],
> Place protection [over me (?)].'

Gilgamesh called out and [   ]
His command [   ]

(about 6 lines missing)

vi   Tears ran down Gilgamesh's [cheeks].
> '[   ] the journey that I never made?
> Does my god not know its course?
> Must I live in security [forever (?)]?
> [   ] in joy of heart?
> Must I be satisfied by a home with your manly
>   charms?
> [   ] on thrones?'
> [   ] his equipment
> [   ] great daggers
> [   ] bow and quiver.
> [   ] they put their hands.

He took a *pāšum*-axe,
[He   ] his quiver,
[A bow] of Anshan design,[19]
[   ] his sword in his belt.
The men made ready (?) to go,
[   ] brought close to Gilgamesh.
> 'Whenever will you be brought back to Uruk?'
The elders blessed him,
Gave Gilgamesh advice for the journey,
> 'Do not rely, Gilgamesh, on your own strength.
> Keep your eyes sharp and guard yourself!
> Let Enkidu walk ahead of you;
> Watch the path, keep to the road.
> He knows the entrances to the forest,
> Every trick of Huwawa.
> He in the lead will keep a comrade safe.
> His eyes must be sharp, and he will guard you!
> Shamash will let you win your triumph!
> May your eyes gain the experience of your
>   mouth's utterance.
> May he open up the closed path for you,

May he prepare the way for your tracks,
May he prepare the mountain for your feet,
May he bring you the things that please you
At night! May Lugalbanda stand by you
In your triumph!
Win your triumph as easily as children (?).[20]
Wash your feet
In the river of Huwawa, as you intend.
Dig a pit when you stop for the night.[21]
Make sure there is always water in your
   waterskin.
You must libate cool water for Shamash
And you must recall Lugalbanda.'[22]
Enkidu made his voice heard, spoke to Gilgamesh,
   '[   ], make the journey.
   Don't be afraid, watch me.
   [   ] his dwelling is dark.
   They will go off on [the road to] Huwawa
   [   ] order them to return.

     (*about 4 lines missing*)

   [   ] let them go with me
   [   ] to you.'
[The] men gladly
[Listened] to his saying this.
The young men [   ]
   'Go, Gilgamesh, [   ]
   May your god go [with you],
   May he let you win [your triumph.]'
Gilgamesh and [Enkidu]

    (*2 lines fragmentary*)[23]

     TABLET IV(?)

Enkidu [spoke] to him, to Gilgamesh,[24]
   'Slay him! [   ] your gods (?)

    (*2 lines fragmentary*)

Gilgamesh (?) [   ] to Enkidu [   ]

'Now [   ]
The mantles of radiance are lost in the forest,
The mantles of radiance are lost, the rays have
    darkened to . . .'
Enkidu spoke to him, to Gilgamesh,
    'My friend, catch a bird and where do its
        fledglings go?
    Let's look for the mantles of radiance afterwards.
    Just as fledglings, they are flitting about in the
        forest!
    Go back: slay him, and slay his servant [   ].'
Gilgamesh listened to the speech of his companion;
Took the axe in his hand,
Drew the sword from his belt.
Gilgamesh slew him at the neck;
Enkidu his friend struck at (?) the heart.
At the third [blow] he fell.
Everything [   ]
Huwawa the guardian he slew, to the ground.
At two [   ]
With him he slew [   ]
The forests [   ]
He slew (?) [   ] of the forest,
At whose shout Saria and Lebanon [   ]
[   ] the mountains
[   ] all the mountain peaks.
He slew the [   ] of pines;
The broken [   ] returned.
The net [   ] the sword
[   ]
The dwelling of the Enunaki, [   ].
Gilgamesh cleaved the trees, Enkidu dug out the
    stumps.
[Enkidu made his voice heard and] spoke to
    Gilgamesh,
    '[   ] the Pine Forest
    [   ] has changed.

        (*break*)

Tablets V to IX(?) not extant

TABLET X(?)

i   *(at least 15 lines missing)*[25]

'[   ] of their hides, he eats meat.
[   ] Euphrates, Gilgamesh, which never
    existed,
Whenever the winds chase (?) the water.'
Shamash was worried, bent down to (?) him,
Spoke to Gilgamesh,
    'Gilgamesh, where do you roam?
    You will not find the (eternal) life that you seek.'
Gilgamesh spoke to him, to the warrior Shamash,
    'While I go roaming (?) in the open country
    Sleeplessness (?) is less common (?) within the
        Earth.
    So should I sleep for all the years?
    Rather let my eyes see the sun, and let me have
        my fill of light!
    Darkness is empty; how much is light in
        comparison?
    Will a dead man see the sun's rays ever
        again (?)?'

ii   *(gap of uncertain length)*

'He experienced all troubles with me;
Enkidu, whom I love so much,
Experienced all troubles with me.
He suffered the fate of mankind.
Day and night I wept over him,
Did not allow him to be buried—
Would that my friend could rise up at my
    voice!—
Seven days and seven nights
Until a worm fell from his nose.
Since his death I have not found eternal life.
I keep wandering like a bandit in the open
    country.
Now that I have found you, alewife,

        May I not find the death I dread.'
The alewife spoke to him, to Gilgamesh,
iii   'Gilgamesh, where do you roam?
      You will not find the eternal life you seek.
      When the gods created mankind
      They appointed death for mankind,
      Kept eternal life in their own hands.
      So, Gilgamesh, let your stomach be full,
      Day and night enjoy yourself in every way,
      Every day arrange for pleasures.
      Day and night, dance and play,
      Wear fresh clothes.
      Keep your head washed, bathe in water,
      Appreciate the child who holds your hand,
      Let your wife enjoy herself in your lap.[26]
      This is the work [   ][27]
      [   ]
      That which the living [   ]'
Gilgamesh spoke to her, to the alewife,
      'What are you saying, alewife? [   ]
      My heart is grieving for my friend:
      What are you saying, alewife?
      My heart is grieving for Enkidu [   ].
      You live, alewife, on the edge of the sea;
      You see all kinds of [   ] there.
      Show me a track [   ]
      If it is possible, [let me cross] the sea.'
The alewife spoke to him, to Gilgamesh,
      'There is nobody, Gilgamesh, like you
      Who travels [   ]

        (gap)

iv   He kept breaking them in his fury.
     He turned and stood over him.
     Sur-sunabu looked into his eyes,
     Sur-sunabu spoke to him, to Gilgamesh,
        'Tell me what your name is!
        I am Sur-sunabu, belonging to Uta-na'ishtim the
          far-distant.'
     Gilgamesh spoke to him, to Sur-sunabu,

'Gilgamesh is my name,
I who came from Uruk, Eanni,
I who travelled across (?) mountains,
A distant journey (from ?) the East.
Now, I have seen your face, Sur-sunabu:
Show me Uta-na'ishtim the far-distant.'
Sur-sunabu spoke to him, to Gilgamesh,
'[I will show you Uta-na'ishtim the far-]distant.
[   ] you will ride in a boat.
I will bring you to [the place where . . .] sprang
up.
Where (?) they will gather and deliberate, both of
them.
He will speak a word to him.'
Sur-sunabu spoke to him, to Gilgamesh,
'The "things of stone", Gilgamesh, bring me
across
So that I do not touch the lethal water:
But in your fury you broke them!
The "things of stone" with me were intended to
bring me across.
Take an axe, Gilgamesh, in your hand,
And cut three hundred poles each thirty metres
(long).
[   ] arrange ropes.

(gap to end of tablet)

Tablets XI(?) and XII(?) not extant

NOTES TO *GILGAMESH* (OLD BABYLONIAN VERSION)

Four OBV tablets are translated here. They are known as the Pennsylvania (see
von Soden 1981), Yale (see Tigay 1982, 281–3), Ishchali (Greengus 1979, pl.
92), and Meissner (Millard 1964) tablets, and occur in that order. The various
tablets of the OBV do not overlap, but the Pennsylvania and Yale tablets were
probably written by the same scribe, and Tigay 1977, 215–18 has argued that
the epic already formed an integrated whole. Lines tend to be much short
than on SBV tablets, probably owing to the narrow columns into which tal

were divided at that period; studies of metre, notably von Soden 1981, join up some lines to form a single line of metre.

Pennsylvania Tablet

The beginning of an Old Babylonian version of the Akkadian epic is not yet attested. This tablet forms the second in the series, and the colophon at the end of it gives the opening lines as 'He was superior to other...', which corresponds to line 27 of SBV, and shows that this OBV did not contain the prologue and epilogue. The exact number of lines per column is not known, so that the estimates given are uncertain. They are based on the assumption of a sixty-line column.

1. The logogram which stands for the name of Gilgamesh is an abbreviation, and it could be read as a shortened form of his name.
2. Reading *arrum* with AHw.
3. The narrative present is used in this passage, and has been interpreted as future tense by some translators.
4. Pun: *ahu* I, 'brother' and *ahu* II, 'side'.
5. Note the very abrupt change of theme.
6. Following Renger 1972, 190.
7. Perhaps a pun: 'destiny of the land', *šimti māti* and 'to die a natural death', *ina šimti mâtu*.
8. The word used is *mutu*, which also means a husband. It should be distinguished from the word translated 'warrior' as a divine epithet, *qarrādum*, which also means 'hero'.
9. See CAD, s.v. *sakkû*.
10. Probably read 'buttocks', *pūqu*, although 'net', *pūgu* has been suggested. The verb may also be taken as 'are open' rather than as imperative.
11. 'Upright': probably a *double entendre* with 'penis', both *išaru*.
12. The word also means a cow-pen.
13. The name of Gilgamesh's mother, Ninsun, here cannot be read Rimat-Ninsun, as has been suggested for SBV.
14. This colophon gives the opening line of this tablet's version, corresponding to line 27 of SBV.

Yale Tablet

15. Literally, 'the fire god, Gibil'.
16. Play on words 'go up', *elû* and 'the gods', *ilū*.
17. Compare Ecclesiastes 1 : 14 'I have seen all the works that are done under the sun, and behold, all is wind and vexation of spirit.' See also note 39 to SBV *Gilgamesh*.
18. 'Foolhardiness': reading *ze'rēti* with AHw. Possibly puns with *ṣehrēti* 'youthfulness'.
19. A particular type of bow characteristic of Anshan near Persepolis ir not yet identified.

20. See Wilcke 1985b, 207.
21. These instructions, from the Elders of Uruk to Gilgamesh, are referred to in an apotropaic ritual for digging a pit or well. See SBV, note 33.
22. These are presumably the regular funerary rites, *kispum*, that could be carried out when a man was travelling. The two main features were: pouring a libation of cool water, and reciting the names of dead ancestors.
23. Two other OBV tablets, van Dijk 1976, nos. 43 and 46, appear to cover some of the same material as SBV Tablets IV and V, but are still too difficult or fragmentary for translation.

Ishchali Tablet

24. The tablet was found in the temple of Shamash during excavations in a town near Eshnunna. It is not well preserved, and is very difficult to understand. This translation is tentative and provisional. In the Sumerian tale *The Death of Huwawa*, Gilgamesh offers gifts, including his two sisters, to Huwawa, and asks to enter his family(?). Huwawa then presents Gilgamesh with his mantles of radiance(?), which Gilgamesh's friends then cut to pieces, leaving Huwawa defenceless. See Ellis 1981–2, 123 ff. In the Sumerian poem *Shulgi, Ninsun, and An*, Gilgamesh is represented as the generous victor who spared Huwawa's life. See Klein, J. 1981, 11, note 31.

Meissner Tablet

25. This text comes from Sippar.
26. Compare Ecclesiastes 9: 7–9 '. . . Eat thy bread with joy, and drink thy wine with a merry heart; . . . Let thy garments be always white, and let thy head lack no ointment. Live joyfully with the wife whom thou lovest . . .' See also SBV, note 39.
27. Restorations suggested are: '[of mankind]' and '[of a wife]'.

The Descent of Ishtar to the Underworld

The Akkadian story is first attested in Late Bronze Age texts, in in both Babylonia and Assyria, and later from the palace library at Nineveh. It is a short composition of some 140 lines, and seems to end with ritual instructions for the *taklimtu*, an annual ritual known from Assyrian texts, which took place in the month of Dumuzi (Tammuz = June/July) and featured the bathing, anointing, and lying-in-state in Nineveh of a statue of Dumuzi.

The Sumerian version, *The Descent of Inanna*, is attested earlier, and is much longer, consisting of some 410 lines. It is a fuller, more detailed account, and shows clearly that Dumuzi periodically died and rose, causing seasonal fertility, a fact which had been doubted until 1963, when a newly published fragment disclosed the crucial evidence. This version contains no ritual or incantation. However, like the Akkadian story, it seems to represent the goddess as a cult statue, and it has been suggested that the goddess's statue makes a ritual journey from Uruk, her home town, to Kutha, seat of Underworld deities.

There is an obvious similarity in basic theme to the Greek myth of Persephone, who was abducted by Hades. He periodically released her to her mother Demeter, thus causing fertility on earth to be seasonal, but of course there are many major differences between the Greek and the Akkadian myths.

Certain lines of text in *The Descent of Ishtar* are also found in *Nergal and Ereshkigal* and in *Gilgamesh*.

THE DESCENT OF ISHTAR
TO THE UNDERWORLD

To Kurnugi, land of [no return],[1]
Ishtar daughter of Sin was [determined] to go;[2]
The daughter of Sin was determined to go
To the dark house, dwelling of Erkalla's god,
To the house which those who enter cannot leave,
On the road where travelling is one-way only,
To the house where those who enter are deprived of
    light,
Where dust is their food, clay their bread.
They see no light, they dwell in darkness,
They are clothed like birds, with feathers.[3]
Over the door and the bolt, dust has settled.
Ishtar, when she arrived at the gate of Kurnugi,
Addressed her words to the keeper of the gate,
    'Here gatekeeper, open your gate for me,
    Open your gate for me to come in!
    If you do not open the gate for me to come in,
    I shall smash the door and shatter the bolt,
    I shall smash the doorpost and overturn the
        doors,[4]
    I shall raise up the dead and they shall eat the
        living:
    The dead shall outnumber the living!'[5]
The gatekeeper made his voice heard and spoke,
He said to great Ishtar,
    'Stop, lady, do not break it down!
    Let me go and report your words to queen
        Ereshkigal.'
The gatekeeper went in and spoke to [Ereshkigal],
    'Here she is, your sister Ishtar [. . .]
    Who holds the great *keppû*-toy,[6]
    Stirs up the Apsu in Ea's presence [. . .]?'
When Ereshkigal heard this,
Her face grew livid as cut tamarisk,

Her lips grew dark as the rim of a *kunīnu*-vessel.[7]
  'What brings her to me? What has incited her
    against me?
  Surely not because I drink water with the
    Anunnaki,
  I eat clay for bread, I drink muddy water for
    beer?
  I have to weep for young men forced to abandon
    sweethearts.[8]
  I have to weep for girls wrenched from their
    lovers' laps.
  For the infant child I have to weep, expelled
    before its time.[8]
  Go, gatekeeper, open your gate to her.
  Treat her according to the ancient rites.'
The gatekeeper went. He opened the gate to her.
  'Enter, my lady: may Kutha give you joy,[9]
  May the palace of Kurnugi be glad to see you.'
He let her in through the first door, but stripped off
    (and) took away the great crown on her head.
  'Gatekeeper, why have you taken away the great
    crown on my head?'
  'Go in, my lady. Such are the rites of the
    Mistress of Earth.'
He let her in through the second door, but stripped
    off (and) took away the rings in her ears.
  'Gatekeeper, why have you taken away the rings
    in my ears?'
  'Go in, my lady. Such are the rites of the
    Mistress of Earth.'
He let her in through the third door, but stripped
    off (and) took away the beads around her neck.
  'Gatekeeper, why have you taken away the beads
    around my neck?'
  'Go in, my lady. Such are the rites of the
    Mistress of Earth.'
He let her in through the fourth door, but stripped
    off (and) took away the toggle-pins at her
    breast.[10]

'Gatekeeper, why have you taken away the
    toggle-pins at my breast?'
'Go in, my lady. Such are the rites of the
    Mistress of Earth.'
He let her in through the fifth door, but stripped off
    (and) took away the girdle of birth-stones
    around her waist.
'Gatekeeper, why have you taken away the girdle
    of birthstones around my waist?'
'Go in, my lady. Such are the rites of the
    Mistress of Earth.'
He let her in through the sixth door, but stripped
    off (and) took away the bangles on her wrists
    and ankles.
'Gatekeeper, why have you taken away the
    bangles from my wrists and ankles?'
'Go in, my lady. Such are the rites of the
    Mistress of Earth.'
He let her in through the seventh door, but stripped
    off (and) took away the proud garment of her
    body.
'Gatekeeper, why have you taken away the proud
    garment of my body?'
'Go in, my lady. Such are the rites of the
    Mistress of Earth.'
As soon as Ishtar went down to Kurnugi,[11]
Ereshkigal looked at her and trembled before her.
Ishtar did not deliberate (?), but leant over (?) her.
Ereshkigal made her voice heard and spoke,
Addressed her words to Namtar her vizier,
    'Go, Namtar [   ] of my [   ]
    Send out against her sixty diseases
        [   ] Ishtar:
    Disease of the eyes to her [eyes],
    Disease of the arms to her [arms],
    Disease of the feet to her [feet],
    Disease of the heart to her [heart],
    Disease of the head [to her head],
    To every part of her and to [   ].'

After Ishtar the mistress of (?) [had gone
    down to Kurnugi],
No bull mounted a cow, [no donkey impregnated a
    jenny],
No young man impregnated a girl in [the street (?)],
The young man slept in his private room,
The girl slept in the company of her friends.
Then Papsukkal, vizier of the great gods, hung his
    head, his face [became gloomy];
He wore mourning clothes, his hair was unkempt.
Dejected (?), he went and wept before Sin his
    father,
His tears flowed freely before king Ea.
    'Ishtar has gone down to the Earth and has not
      come up again.
    As soon as Ishtar went down to Kurnugi
    No bull mounted a cow, no donkey impregnated a
      jenny,
    No young man impregnated a girl in the street,
    The young man slept in his private room,
    The girl slept in the company of her friends.'
Ea, in the wisdom of his heart, created a person.[12]
He created Good-looks the playboy.[13]
    'Come, Good-looks, set your face towards the
      gate of Kurnugi.
    The seven gates of Kurnugi shall be opened
      before you.
    Ereshkigal shall look at you and be glad to see
      you.
    When she is relaxed, her mood will lighten.
    Get her to swear the oath by the great gods.
    Raise your head, pay attention to the waterskin,[14]
    Saying, "Hey, my lady, let them give me the
      waterskin, that I may drink water from it."'

      (*And so it happened. But*)

When Ereshkigal heard this,
She struck her thigh and bit her finger.
    'You have made a request of me that should no·
      have been made!

Come, Good-looks, I shall curse you with a great
   curse.[15]
I shall decree for you a fate that shall never be
   forgotten.
Bread (gleaned (?)) from the city's ploughs shall
   be your food,[16]
The city drains shall be your only drinking place,
The shade of a city wall your only standing place,
Threshold steps your only sitting place,
The drunkard and the thirsty shall slap your
   cheek.'
Ereshkigal made her voice heard and spoke;
She addressed her words to Namtar her vizier,
   'Go, Namtar, knock (?) at Egalgina,
Decorate the threshold steps with coral,[17]
   Bring the Anunnaki out and seat (them) on
      golden thrones,[18]
   Sprinkle Ishtar with the waters of life and conduct
      her into my presence.'
Namtar went, knocked at Egalgina,
Decorated the threshold steps with coral,
Brought out the Anunnaki, seated (them) on golden
   thrones,
Sprinkled Ishtar with the waters of life and brought
   her to her (sister).
He let her out through the first door, and gave back
   to her the proud garment of her body.[19]
He let her out through the second door, and gave
   back to her the bangles for her wrists and ankles.
He let her out through the third door, and gave
   back to her the girdle of birth stones around
   her waist.
He let her out through the fourth door, and gave
   back to her the toggle pins at her breast.
He let her out through the fifth door, and gave back
   to her the beads around her neck.
He let her out through the sixth door, and gave
   back to her the rings for her ears.
He let her out through the seventh door, and gave
   back to her the great crown for her head.

'Swear that (?) she has paid you her ransom, and
  give her back (in exchange) for him,[20]
For Dumuzi, the lover of her youth.
Wash (him) with pure water, anoint him with
  sweet oil,
Clothe him in a red robe, let the lapis lazuli pipe
  play (?).[21]
Let party-girls raise a loud lament (?)'[22]
Then Belili tore off (?) her jewellery,
Her lap was filled with eyestones.
Belili heard the lament for her brother, she struck
  the jewellery [from her body],
The eyestones with which the front of the wild cow
  was filled.[23]
'You shall not rob me (forever) of my only
  brother!
On the day when Dumuzi comes back up, (and)
  the lapis lazuli pipe and the carnelian ring come
  up with him,[24]
(When) male and female mourners come up with
  him,
The dead shall come up and smell the smoke
  offering.'

(*3 lines missing*)

NOTES TO *THE DESCENT OF ISHTAR*

Text: see Borger 1979, Ebeling 1949.

1. This passage occurs almost verbatim in *Nergal and Ereshkigal* (Sultantepe version) and in SBV *Gilgamesh*, VII. iv.
2. Ishtar is named as daughter of Sin rather than daughter of Anu, as she is
   in *Gilgamesh*. This may imply that the story is not closely associated
   with the literary traditions of Uruk.
3. Underworld creatures are often represented with feathers in
   Mesopotamian iconography.
4. The tablet from Assur adds an extra line: 'I shall break the hinges(?) and
   tear out the knob(?)'.
5. The same threat is made by Ereshkigal in *Nergal and Ereshkigal* if the

sky gods do not send Nergal back down to the Underworld, and by Ishtar in *Gilgamesh*, VI (see note 62).

6. *keppū*-toy: perhaps a whipping top; see note 80 on *Gilgamesh*, VII. iv.

7. Namtar's reactions in *Nergal and Ereshkigal*, when he saw Nergal at the gate, are expressed in identical similes. The *kunīnu* was a particular kind of vessel often made of reeds, of which the rim was coated with bitumen, thus black-lipped.

8. Alternatively these lines may be interpreted as rhetorical questions.

9. Buccellati 1982 suggested that the Sumerian *Descent of Inanna* is based on the ritual journey made by a statue of the goddess from Uruk to Kutha, and George 1985a remarked that the goddess is described as if she were a statue in this version. The reference to Kutha here may be a relic of the journey theme in the Sumerian version; or since Kutha had Nergal as patron god, the city name may be used as a name for the Underworld as Nergal's dwelling.

10. The identification of *tudittu* as 'toggle-pin' rather than 'pectoral' was made by Klein, H. 1983.

11. Note that Ishtar does not cross a river in order to reach the Underworld, nor does Nergal in *Nergal and Ereshkigal*.

12. Pun on *zikru*, 'word, name' and *zikaru/zikru*, 'man, male', as also in *Gilgamesh*, II.

13. Literally, 'His appearance is bright'. He may have been a boy castrated as an act of devotion. Such a practice is described by Lucian, *The Syrian Goddess* (see Strong and Garstang 1913). The name may be an intentional play on a name of the moon-god, who like the boy could travel to and from the Underworld without being harmed. In the Sumerian version of the story, two impotent creatures are sent down to the Underworld and they take a plant of life and water of life with them.

14. Kilmer 1971 suggests this is a cryptic reference to Ishtar's corpse. *halziqqu* is a very rare word for a waterskin, and a pun may be intended on the two words *alû*, 'ghost' and *ziqqu*, 'gust'; I suggest this to support her idea. (SMD)

15. The same line is used in *Gilgamesh*, VII. i.

16. Similar formulation of the curse, and two identical lines, are found in Enkidu's curse of Shamhat in *Gilgamesh*, VII. i. The Sumerian version does not include any cursing. 'City's ploughs': the variant, 'city's bakers', may be due to mis-hearing by oral tradition, since 'bakers' and 'plough' are both Akkadian words beginning *epi*.

17. 'Coral' or 'cowries'; the meaning of the noun is not quite certain.

18. Possibly a reference to a ritual against seizure by ghosts. See Introduction to *Nergal and Ereshkigal*. Akkadian *kussû* is both a chair and a throne. In the Sumerian story the Anunnaki seize the goddess, demand a substitute for her, and send her out of the Underworld with demons who are to bring her back if their demand is not met.

19. Either Namtar or the doorkeeper is the subject.

20. Equivalent instructions are given to the demons in the Sumerian story. A variant Akkadian text gives the information that Ereshkigal ' speaking to Namtar.

21. Corpses were wrapped in red cloth for burial; traces have occasionally been recovered by excavations.
22. 'Party girls': attached to the staff of Ishtar's temples.
23. Probably beads of banded agate and similar stones, which were often inscribed with the name of the donor; see Lambert 1969b.
24. In the Sumerian story Dumuzi's sister Geshtin-anna pleads for his periodic release. Also in the Sumerian story, Inanna took the 'rod and ring', emblems of kingship, down to the Underworld; this may be a reference to those emblems.

Nergal and Ereshkigal

Two very different versions of this story are extant. The earlier one was found at Tell el-Amarna in Egypt, dating from the fifteenth or fourteenth centuries BC, and is told in a highly abbreviated manner in about ninety lines. Nergal visits the Underworld accompanied by demons, seizes the throne of Ereshkigal, queen of the Underworld, by force, and remains thereafter as king.

The version known from Sultantepe of the seventh century BC and from Uruk in the Late Babylonian period is much longer, consisting of perhaps 350 lines. In this story Nergal makes two visits to the Underworld, and takes down with him not demons but a special chair or throne. The meaning of the chair may be explained by reference to a particular piece of furniture called a 'ghost's chair' in lexical texts; its purpose is explained in a ritual text as preventing seizure by ghosts:

If a man is chosen for death, and a ghost has seized him, you must purify everything, . . . place a bread ration before Shamash, Ea, and Marduk, threefold; scatter dates, flour, set up three *adagurru*-vessels, set up three censers with aromatics, scatter all kinds of cereals. You must put down a chair to the left of the offerings for the ghost of his kin, . . .

Thus, Nergal takes the chair down in an attempt to ensure that he can escape from the Underworld and elude death.

Both myths share the same basic theme: that the gods hold a banquet and, since Ereshkigal as queen of the Underworld cannot come up to join them, she sends her vizier to fetch a portion for her. Nergal behaves disrespectfully to the vizier, and for the insult to Ereshkigal he must be punished by her. He ends up as her husband.

It might appear that this myth records the transition of rule in the Underworld from a solitary female deity to a pair. However, Nergal is called 'the Ellil of the Netherworld' in a composition from the late third or early second millennium, so it may be preferable to ascribe to the myth a different purpose, such as harmonizing two separate traditions. No Sumerian version of the story is known.

For the character and names of Nergal, see the Glossary, and the Introduction to *Erra and Ishum*.

Nergal's ability to travel between heaven and the Underworld may be related to a major event in Phoenician religion. The name of Melqart, chief god of Tyre, is a Phoenician translation of the Sumerian name Nergal, and they are thus very closely assimilated. There is now evidence that Melqart was a dying and rising god, although the precise timing of events during the ritual of his death and resurrection has still to be established. Possible Phoenician influence upon *Nergal and Ereshkigal* is found in the use of the 'plural of majesty', in referring to Nergal as 'gods'.

NERGAL AND ERESHKIGAL

SBV i   (*About 6 lines missing?*)[1]

[Anu made his voice heard and spoke, he addressed
    his words to Kakka],
  ['Kakka, I shall send you to Kurnugi].
  You must speak thus to Ereshkigal [   ],
  Saying, "It is impossible for you to come up].
  [In your year you cannot come up to see us]
  [And it is impossible for us to go down].
  [In our month(s) we cannot go down to see you].
  [Let your messenger come]
  [And take from the table, let him accept a present
    for you].
  [I shall give something to him to present to
    you]." '
[Kakka went down the long stairway of heaven].
When he reached [the gate of Ereshkigal (he said)],
  ['Gatekeeper, open] the gate to me!'
  ['Kakka, come] in, and may the gate bless you.'
He let the god Kakka in through the first gate,
He let the god Kakka in through the second gate,
He let the god Kakka in through the third gate,
He let the god Kakka in through the fourth gate,
He let the god Kakka in through the fifth gate,
He let the god Kakka in through the sixth gate,
He let the god Kakka in through the seventh gate.
He entered into her spacious courtyard,
He knelt down and kissed the ground in front of
  her.
He straightened up, stood and addressed her,
  'Anu your father sent me
  To say, "It is impossible for you to go up;
  In your year you cannot go up to see us,
  And it is impossible for us to go down;
  In our month we cannot go down to see you.

Let your messenger come
And take from the table, let him accept a present
    for you.
I shall give something to him to present to you.''' '
Ereshkigal made her voice heard and spoke, she
    addressed her words to Kakka,
'O messenger of Anu our father, you who have
    come to us,
May peace be with Anu, Ellil, and Ea, the great
    gods.
May peace be with Nammu and Nash, the pure
    god(desse)s.[2]
May peace be with the husband of the Lady of
    Heaven.[3]
May peace be with Ninurta, [champion] in the
    land.'
Kakka made his voice heard and spoke; he addressed
    his words to Ereshkigal,
'Peace is indeed with Anu, Ellil, and Ea, the great
    gods.
Peace is indeed with Nammu and Nash the pure.
Peace is indeed with the husband of the Lady of
    Heaven.
Peace is indeed with Ninurta, champion in the
    land.'
Kakka made his voice heard and spoke, he addressed
    his words to Ereshkigal,[4]
'[   ] may be well with you.'
Ereshkigal made her voice heard and spoke, she
    addressed her words to her vizier Namtar,
'O Namtar my vizier, I shall send you to the
    heaven of our father Anu.
Namtar, go up the long stairway of heaven.
Take from the table and accept a present (for me).
Whatever Anu gives to you, you must present to
    me.'

(*about 16 lines missing*)

ii   (*about 10 lines missing*)

(*Ea addresses Nergal*)

[   ]
'[When he arrived [   ]
[   ] path [   ]
The gods are kneeling together before him.
The great gods, the lords of destiny.
For it is he who controls the rites, controls the
    rites of [   ]
The gods who dwell within Erkalla.
Why do you not kneel down before him?
I keep winking at you,
But you pretend not to realize,
And . . .

>   (*6 lines missing*)

>   (*Nergal addresses Ea*)

[   ] I will rise to my feet[5]
[   ] you said.
[   ] will double it.'
When Ea heard this he said to himself,
'. . .   . .'
(Then) Ea made his voice heard and spoke, he
    addressed his words to Nergal.
'My son, you shall go on the journey you want
    (to make), . . . grasp (?) a sword in your hand.
Go down to the forest of *mēsu*-trees.
Cut down *mēsu*-trees, *tiāru*-trees, and juniper!
Break off *kanaktu*-trees and *simberru*-trees.'[6]
When [Nergal] heard this, he took an axe up in his
    hand,
Drew the sword from his belt,
Went down to the forest of *mēsu*-trees,
Cut down *mēsu*-trees, *tiaru*-trees, and juniper,
Broke off *kanaktu*-trees and *simberru*-trees,
[   ] and Ningishzida.[7]
He painted it with [as a substitute for silver],[8]
Painted it with yellow paste and red paste as a
    substitute for gold,
Painted it with blue glaze as a substitute for lapis
    lazuli.
The work was finished, the chair complete.

Then he (Ea) called out and laid down instructions
    for him,
  'My son, (about) the journey which you want to
    make: from the moment you arrive,
[Follow whatever instructions [I give you].
From the moment they bring a chair to you,
Do not go to it, do not sit upon it.
(When) the baker brings you bread, do not go to
    it, do not eat the bread.
(When) the butcher brings you meat, do not go
    to it, do not eat the meat.
(When) the brewer brings you beer, do not go to
    it, do not drink the beer.
(When they) bring you a foot bath, do not go to
    it, do not wash your feet.
(When) she (Ereshkigal) has been to the bath
And dressed herself in a fine dress,[9]
Allowing you to glimpse her body . . .
You must not [do that which] men and women
    [do].'
Nergal [   ]

(*about 12 lines missing*)

[Nergal set his face towards Kurnugi,
To the dark house, dwelling of Erkalla's god,
To the house which those who enter cannot leave,]
iii On the road where travelling is one way only,
To the house where those who enter are deprived of
    light,
Where dust is their food, clay their bread.
They are clothed, like birds, with feathers.
They see no light, they dwell in darkness.
[   ]
[they moan](?) like doves.
[   ]
[The gatekeeper opened his mouth and addressed his
    words to Nergal,
  'I must take back a report about the [god(?)
    standing] at the door.'

The gatekeeper entered and addressed his words to
    Ereshkigal,
  'My lady, a [   ] has come to see us.
  [   ] who will identify him.'

    (*a few lines missing*)

Ereshkigal made her voice heard and spoke to
    Namtar,

    (*3 lines missing, comprising Ereshkigal's
    speech*)

    (*Namtar replies:*)

  'Let me identify him [   ]
  Let me . . . him at the outer gate.
  Let me bring back to my lord [a description of
    him].'
Namtar went and looked at Erra in the shadow of
    the door.
Namtar's face went as livid as cut tamarisk.
His lips grew dark as the rim of a *kunīnu*-vessel.[10]
Namtar went and addressed his lady,
  'My lady, when you sent me to your father,
  When I entered the courtyard of Anu
  All the gods were kneeling, humbled [before
    him(?)],
  All the gods of the land were kneeling [humbled
    before him.]
  "The gods" rose to their feet in my presence.[11]
  Now "they" have gone down to Kurnugi.'
Ereshkigal made her voice heard and spoke, she
    addressed her words to Namtar,
  'My dear Namtar, you should not seek
    Ellil-power,
  Nor should you desire to do heroic deeds.
  (What,) come up and sit on the throne of the
    royal dais?
  You, perform the judgements of the broad Earth?
  Should I go up to the heaven of Anu my
    father?[12]

Should I eat the bread of the Anunnaki?
Should I drink the water of the Anunnaki?
Go and bring the god [into my presence!]'
Namtar went and let in "the gods", Erra.
He let Nergal in through the first, the gate of
    Nedu.[13]
He let Nergal in through the second, the gate of
    Kishar.
He let Nergal in through the third, the gate of
    Endashurimma.
He let Nergal in through the fourth, the gate of
    Enuralla.
He let Nergal in through the fifth, the gate of
    Endukuga.
He let Nergal in through the sixth, the gate of
    Endushuba.
He let Nergal in through the seventh, the gate of
    Ennugigi.
He came into the broad courtyard,
And he knelt down, kissed the ground in front of
    her.
He straightened up, stood and addressed her,
    'Anu, your father sent me [to see you],
    Saying, "Sit down on [that] throne,
    Judge the cases [of the great gods],
    The great gods who live within Erkalla!"'
As soon as they brought him a throne
(He said to himself) 'Don't go to it!' and did not sit
    on it.[14]
(When) the baker brought him bread, 'Don't go to
    it!' and did not eat the bread.
(When) the butcher brought him meat, 'Don't go to
    it!' and did not eat his meat.
(When) the brewer brought him beer, 'Don't go to
    it!' and did not drink his beer.[15]
(When) they brought him a footbath, 'Don't go to
    it!' and did not wash his feet.[16]
(When) she went to the bath
And dressed herself in a fine dress
And allowed him to catch a glimpse of her body,

He [resisted] his heart's [desire to do what] men and
women [do].

(*about 10 lines missing*)

iv   (*3 lines fragmentary*)

Nergal [   ]
She went to the bath
And dressed herself in a fine dress
And allowed him to catch a glimpse of her body.
He [gave in to] his heart's [desire to do what men
        and women do].
The two embraced each other[17]
And went passionately to bed.
They lay there, queen Ereshkigal and Erra, for a
        first day and a second day.
They lay there, queen Ereshkigal and Erra, for a
        third day and a fourth day.[18]
They lay there, queen Ereshkigal and Erra, for a
        fifth day and a sixth day.
When the seventh day arrived,
Nergal, without [   ]
Took away after him [   ]
    'Let me go, and my sister [   ]
    Do not make tremble [   ]
    Let me go now, and I will return to Kurnugi
        [(later)].'
Her mouth turned dark (?) (with rage) [   ]
Nergal went [   ][19]
[   ] addressed his speech to the gatekeeper,
    'Ereshkigal your lady sent me,
    Saying, "I am sending you to the heaven of Anu
        our father",
    So let me be allowed out! The message [   ].'
Nergal came up the long stairway of heaven.
When he arrived at the gate of Anu, Ellil, and Ea,
Anu, Ellil, and Ea saw him and (said),
    'The son of Ishtar has come back to us,[20]
    She (Ereshkigal) will search for him and [   ].
    Ea his father must sprinkle him with spring
        water, and bareheaded,

Blinking and cringing let him sit in the assembly
   of all gods.'[21]
Ereshkigal [   ]
To the bath [   ]
[   ]
Her body [   ]
[   ]
She called out [   ]
   'The chair [   ]
   Sprinkle the room with the water [of   ]
   Sprinkle the room with the water [of   ]
   Sprinkle the room with the water [of   ]
   The [   ] of the two daughters of Lamashtu (?)
      and Enmesharra,
   Sprinkle with the waters of [   ].
   The messenger of Anu our father who came to
      see us
   Shall eat our bread and drink our water.'
Namtar made his voice heard and spoke,
Addressed his words to Ereshkigal his lady,
   'The messenger of Anu our father who came to
      see us—
   Before daylight he disappeared!'
Ereshkigal cried out aloud, grievously,
Fell from the throne to the ground,
Then straightened up from the ground.
Her tears flowed down her cheeks.
   'Erra, the lover of my delight—
   I did not have enough delight with him before he
      left!
   Erra, the lover of my delight—
   I did not have enough delight with him before he
      left.'
Namtar made his voice heard and spoke, addressed
      his words to Ereshkigal,
   'Send me to Anu your father, and let me arrest
      that god!
   [Let me take him to you,] that he may kiss you
      again!'
v Ereshkigal made her voice heard and spoke,

Addressed her words to Namtar her vizier,
   'Go, Namtar, [you must speak to Anu, Ellil, and
      Ea!]
   Set your face towards the gate of Anu, Ellil, and
      Ea,
   To say, ever since I was a child and a daughter,
   I have not known the playing of other girls,
   I have not known the romping of children.
   That god whom you sent to me and who has
      impregnated me—let him sleep with me again!
   Send that god to us, and let him spend the night
      with me as my lover!
   I am unclean, and I am not pure enough to
      perform the judging of the great gods,
   The great gods who dwell within Erkalla.
   If you do not send that god to me
   According to the rites of Erkalla and the great
      Earth
   I shall raise up the dead, and they will eat the
      living.
   I shall make the dead outnumber the living!'[22]
Namtar came up the long stairway of heaven.
When he arrived at the gate of Anu, Ellil, and Ea,
Anu, Ellil, and Ea saw him, and (said),'
   'What have you come for, Namtar?'
   'Your daughter sent me,
   To say, "Ever since I was a child and a daughter,
   I have not known the playing of other girls,
   I have not known the romping of children.
   That god whom you sent to me and who has
      impregnated me—let him sleep with me again!
   Send that god to us, and let him spend the night
      with me as my lover!
   I am unclean, and I am not pure enough to
      perform the judging of the great gods,
   The great gods who dwell within Erkalla.
   If you do not send that god to me,
   I shall raise up the dead, and they will eat the
      living.
   I shall make the dead outnumber the living!"'

Ea made his voice heard and spoke, addressed his
    words to Namtar,
  'Enter, Namtar, the court of Anu,
  [Search out your wrongdoer and bring him!].'[23]
When he entered the court of Anu,
All the gods were kneeling humbled [before him],
[All] the gods of the land were kneeling [humbled
    before him].
He went straight up to one, but did not recognize
    that god,
Went straight up to a second and a third, but did
    not recognize that god either.
Namtar went (away), and addressed his words to his
    lady,
  'My lady, about your sending me up to the
    heaven of Anu your father:
  My lady, there was only one god who sat
    bareheaded, blinking and cringing at the
    assembly of all the gods.'
  'Go, seize that god and bring him to me!
  (I expect) Ea his father sprinkled him with spring
    water,
  And he is sitting in the assembly of all the gods
    bareheaded, blinking and cringing.'
Namtar came up the long stairway of heaven.
When he reached the gate of Anu, Ellil, and Ea,
Anu, Ellil, and Ea saw him and (said),
  'What have you come for, Namtar?' 'Your
    daughter sent me,
  To say, "Seize that god and bring him to me."'
  'Then enter, Namtar, the courtyard of Anu, and
  Search out your wrongdoer and take him.'
He went straight up to one god, but did not
    recognize him,
Went straight up to a second and third, but did not
    recognize him either.
[Then X] made his voice heard and spoke,
    [addressed his words] to Ea,
  'Let Namtar, the messenger who has come to us,
  Drink our water, wash, and anoint himself.'

(break of about 15 lines)

vi   'He is not to strip off [   ]
          Erra, [   ]
          I shall [   ].'
          Namtar [made his voice heard and addressed his
                  words to Erra],
          'Erra, [   ]
          All the rites of the great Underworld [   ]
          When you go from [   ]
          You shall carry the chair [   ]
          You shall carry [   ]
          You shall carry [   ]
          You shall carry [   ]
          You shall carry [   ]
          You shall carry [   ]24
          [   ]
          [Do not grapple with him (?) lest] he bind (?)
                  your chest.'
          [Erra to]ok to heart [the speech of Namtar].
          He [   ] oiled his strap and slung his bow.
          Nergal went down the long stairway of heaven.
          When he arrived at the gate of Ereshkigal (he
                  said (?)),
            'Gatekeeper, open [the gate for me (?)]!'
          He struck down Nedu, the doorman [of the first]
                  gate, and did not let him gr[apple with
                  him (?)].25
          He struck down the second [doorman] (and did not
                  let him grapple with him).
          He struck down the third [doorman] (and did not let
                  him grapple with him).
          He struck down the fourth [doorman] (and did not
                  let him grapple with him).
          He struck down the fifth [doorman] (and did not let
                  him grapple with him).
          He struck down the sixth [doorman] (and did not let
                  him grapple with him).
          He struck down the seventh [doorman] (and did not
                  let him grapple with him).

He entered her wide courtyard,
And went up to her and laughed.
He seized her by her hairdo,
And [pull]ed (?) her from [the throne].
He seized her by her tresses
[   ].
The two embraced each other
And went passionately to bed.
They lay there, queen Ereshkigal and Erra, for a
    first day and a second day.
They lay there, queen Ereshkigal and Erra, for a
    third day.[26]
They lay there, queen Ereshkigal and Erra, for a
    fourth day.
They lay there, queen Ereshkigal and Erra, for a
    fifth day.
They lay there, queen Ereshkigal and Erra, for a
    sixth day.
When the seventh day arrived,
Anu made his voice heard and spoke,
Addressed his words to Kakka, his vizier,
   'Kakka, I shall send you to Kurnugi,
   To the home of Ereshkigal who dwells within
    Erkalla,
   To say, "That god, whom I sent to you,
   Forever [   ]
   Those above [   ]
   Those below [   ]

      (*break, about 12 lines missing to end*)

NOTES TO *NERGAL AND ERESHKIGAL*
(SULTANTEPE AND URUK VERSION)

Text: Gurney 1960, Hunger 1976.

1. The opening of the myth as suggested by Gurney 1960 was wrongly
   assigned to this composition, and is now joined to a different tablet.
2. Nash is an abbreviated and assimilated form of the name Nanshe.
   Nammu and Nanshe are the mother and daughter of Ea.

3. Possibly a reference to Dumuzi.
4. This line appears to be an unnecessary addition.
5. Or, 'Should I rise to my feet?'
6. *mēsu*-wood: a dark wood used in making divine statues, probably a form of rosewood (Dalbergia). *tiāru*: described as 'white pine' in explanatory texts. *kanaktu*: an aromatic timber, not identified. *simberru*: an aromatic fruit tree; maybe Umbrella pine/pine-nuts, Arabic ṣnōbar; the Uruk text established this reading, replacing Gurney's restoration of the Sultantepe text, which was damaged at that point, as 'staff'.
7. Uruk version has: '[   ] he made a throne for far-sighted Ea.'
8. The Sultantepe version has 'lapis lazuli' here, perhaps as a scribal confusion because it is a school exercise tablet; so the Uruk version is preferred here.
9. 'Fine robe': restoring the broken signs to give *lamahuššu*. (SMD)
10. *kunīnu*-vessel: see note 7 to *Descent of Ishtar*.
11. 'The gods' is used to refer to Nergal. This is a Phoenician and Punic usage, also found in the Old Testament when Yahweh is called Elohim 'gods', and in Amarna letters from Phoenician cities where Pharaoh is addressed as 'my gods' (RlA, s.v. Elohim).
12. These three questions should probably be taken as sarcastic and rhetorical, emphasizing that each deity has a separate and appropriate sphere.
13. The Uruk version names the gates as: Nedu, Enkishar, Endashurimma, Nerulla, Nerubanda, Endukuga, and Ennugigi, which are all Sumerian names or epithets. The cuneiform text uses ditto signs for the main areas of repetition here.
14. Uruk version has: 'He did not go to it' instead of 'Don't go to it'.
15. Uruk version has 'cupbearer' instead of 'brewer'.
16. Uruk version has: 'The foot-washer brought him water'.
17. Reading *aha-meš*, 'together' rather than logographically 'brothers'.
18. Dittos are again used.
19. Later in this column the story implies that he departed without her realizing.
20. 'son of Ishtar' implies that he is a lover with the capacity for fertility.
21. Either Nergal exhibits apparent congenital deformities through Ea's magic, or (as translated) the disguise is momentary.
22. This is identical to Ishtar's threat in *The Descent of Ishtar*.
23. Line restored from a presumed repeat eighteen lines later.
24. Several entirely different restorations are possible.
25. Read *lúatû ša* KÁ *[ina l-en]* KÁ *i-nar-šu-ma ana ti-[iṣ-bu-ti?] ul i-din* (SMD).
26. The text has dittos again.

NERGAL AND ERESHKIGAL
(AMARNA VERSION)

When the gods organized a banquet,[1]
They sent a messenger
To their sister Ereshkigal.
  'We cannot come down to you,
  And you cannot come up to us.
  So send someone to fetch a share of the food for
    you!'
Ereshkigal sent Namtar her vizier,
  'Go up, Namtar, to high heaven!'
He went into [where] the gods were [sitting],
And they [bowed (?)] and greeted Namtar,
The messenger of their eldest sister.
They bowed respectfully (?) when they saw him
    and . . .
The high gods [   ]
[   ] food for the goddess his mistress.
[   ] wept and was overcome.
[   ] the journey (?)

       (about 6 lines missing)

Ea [   ]
Went [to Namtar and] sent (him) back.
  'Go and [tell] my words to [our] sister.
  She will say, "Where (?) is the one who did not
    rise to his feet in the presence of my
    messenger?
  Bring him to me for his death (?), that I may kill
    him!"'[2]

      (And so it happened)

Namtar came (back) and spoke to the gods,
The gods summoned him and discussed the death
    with him.

'Look for the god who did not rise to his feet in
   your presence,
And take him before your mistress!'
Namtar counted them. The last god was crouching
   down.
'That god who did not rise to his feet in your
   presence—he is not here!'
Then Namtar went and gave his report, (saying):
'[My mistress, I went and counted] them.
The last god [was crouching down].
[The god who did not rise to his feet in my
   presence] was not there.'
[Ereshkigal made her voice heard],
[And addressed Namtar] her messenger,
'[   ] month.'
[   ] Ea, honoured lord.
'Identify the one', [   ] to the hand of [Ea].[3]
'Take (him) to Ereshkigal!' He was wee[ping]
Before his father Ea: 'He will see me!
He will not let me stay alive!' 'Don't be
   afraid [   ]
I shall give to you seven and seven [demons]
To go with you: ...,   ...,   ..., Flashes-of-
   Lightning,
Bailiff, Croucher, Expulsion, Wind,
Fits, Staggers, Stroke, Lord-of-the-Roof,
Feverhot, Scab [   ]
With you [   ] door
Ereshkigal will call out: "Doorkeeper, [   ]
   your door."

     (You must say)

"Loosen the thong, that I may enter into the
   presence of your mistress,
Ereshkigal. I have been sent!" The doorkeeper
   went
And said to Namtar: 'One god is standing at the
   entrance of the door,
Come, inspect him and let him enter.' Namtar
   came out

And saw him and gladly: '[Wait (?)] here!' He said
To his mistress: 'My lady, here is the god who in
    previous
    Months had vanished (?), and who did not rise to
        his feet in my presence!'[4]
    'Bring him in. As soon as he comes, I shall kill
        him!'
Namtar came out and [   ], 'Come in, my
    lord,
    To your sister's house and . . .   . . .'
Nergal [said], 'You should be glad to see me.
[   ] Nergal [   ]

        (2 *lines missing*)

. . . at the third, Flashes-of-Lightning at the fourth,[5]
Bailiff at the fifth, Croucher at the sixth, Expulsion
At the seventh, Wind at the eighth, Fits
At the ninth, Staggers at the tenth, Stroke
At the eleventh, Lord-of-the-Roof at the twelfth,
Feverhot at the thirteenth, Scab at the fourteenth
Door, he managed to seal her in (?). In the
    forecourt he cut off[6]
Namtar. He gave his troops orders: 'Let the doors
    Be opened! Now I shall race past (?) you!'
Inside the house, he seized Ereshkigal
By her hair, pulled her from the throne
To the ground, intending to cut off her head.
    'Don't kill me, my brother! Let me tell you
        something.'
Nergal listened to her and relaxed his grip, he wept
    and was overcome (when she said),
    'You can be my husband, and I can be your wife.
        I will let you seize[7]
    Kingship over the wide Earth! I will put the
        tablet
    Of wisdom in your hand! You can be master,
        I can be mistress.' Nergal listened to this speech
        of hers,
And seized her and kissed her. He wiped away h'
    tears.

'What have you asked of me? After so many
months,
It shall certainly be so!'[8]

NOTES TO *NERGAL AND ERESHKIGAL*
(AMARNA VERSION)

Text: Knudtzon 1915.

1. Some confusion is caused in this text by the arrangement of lines. Probably a tablet with very short lines was badly copied on to one with longer lines so that ends of lines do not always correspond to ends of sentences as would be normal.
2. Pun: *mutu*, 'husband' and *mūtu*, 'death'.
3. 'Identify': reading as imperative of *wussûm*.
4. Rituals and customs for honouring and placating the dead were carried out on a monthly schedule linked to the phases of the moon.
5. Ishtar/Inanna has similar shamanistic control of demons in the Sumerian story, *The Descent of Inanna*. In the cult of Ishtar at Nineveh, the goddess controlled demons who formed her entourage (Haas 1979).
6. Tentatively reading *huṭṭumaša*, 'to seal her in'. (SMD)
7. Exactly the same words are used by Ishtar in *Gilgamesh*, VI. i.
8. Some scholars think this ending is too cryptic and abrupt to be intentional, and that the story would have continued.

Adapa

Adapa was the first of the antediluvian seven sages who were sent by Ea the wise god of Eridu, to bring the arts of civilization to mankind. Eridu was traditionally the earliest Mesopotamian city; in the Sumerian king list it is the very first city to receive kingship from the gods in heaven. It lies at the head of the Arabian Gulf, originally beside the Euphrates river, not far from Ur of the Chaldees. Adapa was also known as Uan, which is the name given as Oannes by Berossus to the first sage; the name Uan also forms a pun on the Sumero-Akkadian word for a craftsman.

As the first sage, Adapa-Oannes introduced the correct rites of religious observance to mankind, and was the priest of Ea in his temple in Eridu. The story explains how the first sage, like the subsequent six, angered Ea, so Adapa lost the chance to obtain immortality from the sky gods. From *Erra and Ishum* II we know that all the sages were banished from earth because they angered the gods, and went back to the Apsu where Ea lived, and it is possible that the story, whose end is not yet extant, ended with Adapa's banishment. The Apsu was the home of fresh water and the name of Ea's dwelling, and the sages are described elsewhere in Mesopotamian literature as 'pure *purādu*-fish', possibly carp, a fish still kept as a holy duty in the precincts of Near Eastern mosques and monasteries. It is likely that Adapa as a fisherman was represented as a fish or fish–man composite in ancient iconography, although definite identifications are hard to make, and no specific scenes from the myth of Adapa have been recognized on cylinder seals. Adapa, acting both as a sage and as a priest, exemplifies the fact that, in early Akkadian of the third millennium BC and then much later in the Nabatean language around the time of Christ, the word *apkallum*, 'sage', is used to mean a kind of priest as a term of profession.

Scholars are still unclear about the precise meaning of the story. Did Ea deliberately trick Adapa out of immortality, or did he sincerely intend to help him, despite Adapa's crime against him, and fail, despite Ea's divine wisdom? Did Adapa defy the unwritten laws of hospitality by refusing food and drink in heaven, and thus oblige Anu to punish him? The story is outlined too sketchily in Akkadian to be clear, but its audience in ancient times would have understood the implications of what they heard, and a crucial *double entendre* may attribute man's folly to a simple misunderstanding.

The fragmentary tablets from which the story is known come from Tell el-Amarna in Egypt, of the fifteenth or fourteenth centuries BC, and from Assur, the traditional capital of the Assyrians on the Tigris, of the late second millennium BC. It is impossible on present evidence to give an accurate estimate of the length of the composition. If the Assur tablet contained the whole composition, and, if, like Etana, it contained about sixty lines per side, then that version would be about 120 lines in length.

ADAPA

(several lines missing)

Thoughtfulness [   ]
His word commands like the word of [Anu]
He (Ea) made broad understanding perfect in him
    (Adapa), to disclose the design of the land.
To him he gave wisdom, but did not give eternal life.
At that time, in those years, he was a sage, son of
    Eridu.[1]
Ea created him as a protecting spirit (?) among
    mankind.
A sage—nobody rejects his word—
Clever, extra-wise, he was one of the Anunnaki,[2]
Holy, pure of hands, the *pašīšu*-priest who always
    tends the rites.
He does the baking with the bakers,[3]
Does the baking with the bakers of Eridu,
He does the food and water of Eridu every day,
Sets up the offerings table with his pure hands,
Without him no offerings table is cleared away.
He takes the boat out and does the fishing for Eridu.
At that time Adapa, the son of Eridu,
When he had got the [leader (?)] Ea out of bed,
Used to 'feed' the bolt of Eridu every day.[4]
At the holy quay *Kar-usakar* he embarked in a
    sailing boat
And without a rudder his boat would drift,
Without a steering-pole he would take his boat out
[   ] into the broad sea.

(gap of uncertain length)

[   ]
South Wind [   ][5]
Send him (?) to live in the fishes' home.[6]
  'South Wind, though you send your brothers
    against me, however many there are,

I shall still break your wing!'
No sooner had he uttered these words
Than South Wind's wing was broken;
For seven days South Wind did not blow towards
the land.
Anu called out to his vizier Ilabrat,
'Why hasn't South Wind blown towards the land
for seven days?'
His vizier Ilabrat answered him,
'My lord, Adapa the son of Ea has broken South
Wind's wing.'[7]
When Anu heard this word,
He cried '(Heaven) help (him)!', rose up from his
throne.
'[Send for him to] be brought here!'
Ea, aware of heaven's ways, touched him[8]
And [   ] made him wear his hair unkempt,
[Clothed him in] mourning garb,
Gave him instructions,
'Adapa, you are to go before king Anu.
You will go up to heaven,
And when you go up to heaven,
When you approach the Gate of Anu,
Dumuzi and Gizzida will be standing in the Gate
of Anu,
Will see you, will keep asking you questions,
"Young man, on whose behalf do you look like
this?
On whose behalf do you wear mourning garb?"

   (*You must answer*)

"Two gods have vanished from our country,
And that is why I am behaving like this."

   (*They will ask*)

"Who are the two gods that have vanished from
the country?"

   (*You must answer*)

"They are Dumuzi and Gizzida."

They will look at each other and laugh a lot,
Will speak a word in your favour to Anu,
Will present you to Anu in a good mood.
When you stand before Anu
They will hold out for you bread of death, so you
    must not eat.[9]
They will hold out for you water of death, so you
    must not drink.
They will hold out a garment for you: so put it
    on.
They will hold out oil for you: so anoint
    yourself.[10]
You must not neglect the instructions I have
    given you:
Keep to the words that I have told you.'
The envoy of Anu arrived.
    'Send to me Adapa,
    Who broke South Wind's wing.'
He made him take the way of heaven
And he (Adapa) went up to heaven.
When he came up to heaven,
When he approached the Gate of Anu,
Dumuzi and Gizzida were standing in the Gate of
    Anu.
They saw Adapa and cried '(Heaven) help (him)!
    Young man, on whose behalf do you look like
      this?
    Adapa, on whose behalf do you wear mourning
      garb?'
'Two gods have vanished from the country,
And that is why I am wearing mourning garb.'
'Who are the two gods who have vanished from
    the country?'
'Dumuzi and Gizzida.'
They looked at each other, and laughed a lot.
When Adapa drew near to the presence of King
    Anu,
Anu saw him and shouted,
    'Come here, Adapa! Why did you break South
      Wind's wing?'

Adapa answered Anu,

> 'My lord, I was catching fish in the middle of the
> sea
> For the house of my lord (Ea).
> But he inflated (?) the sea into a storm (?)[11]
> And South Wind blew and sank me!
> I was forced to take up residence in the fishes'
> home.
> In my fury I cursed South Wind.'

Dumuzi and Gizzida responded from beside him,
Spoke a word in his favour to Anu.
His heart was appeased, he grew quiet.

> 'Why did Ea disclose to wretched mankind
> The ways of heaven and earth,
> Give them a heavy heart?
> It was he who did it!
> What can we do for him?
> Fetch him the bread of (eternal) life and let him
> eat!'[12]

They fetched him the bread of (eternal) life, but he
would not eat.
They fetched him the water of (eternal) life, but he
would not drink.
They fetched him a garment, and he put it on
himself.
They fetched him oil, and he anointed himself.
Anu watched him and laughed at him.

> 'Come, Adapa, why didn't you eat? Why didn't
> you drink?
> Didn't you want to be immortal? Alas for
> downtrodden people!'
> '(But) Ea my lord told me: "You mustn't eat!
> You mustn't drink!"'
> Take him and send him back to his earth.'

> (*gap of unknown length to end of story*)

> (*A piece of text known as Fragment D may give an
> alternative ending, and is followed by an
> incantation against disease, invoking Adapa*)

NOTES TO *ADAPA*

Text: Knudtzon 1915, Picchioni 1981.

1. In very early texts and in the cognate word in pre-Islamic Arabia, the word for sage, *apkallu*, means some kind of priest.
2. This epithet, *atra-hasis*, 'extra-wise', is also applied to the survivor of the Flood.
3. Dittos are used in the cuneiform for the repeated phrases in the following lines.
4. The bolt in Eridu may have been a ritual object corresponding to the cosmic bolt of the sea mentioned in *Atrahasis*, which Ea's *lahmu*-heroes guarded, and which could let through more fish to feed people in times of agricultural crop failure. Thus the bolt symbolized the harvest of fish from the sea, and was of special concern to Adapa as temple fisherman. (SMD)
5. The South Wind is clearly feminine in the story; her brothers in the following lines are presumably the other winds.
6. Or, 'home of his master'. The cuneiform signs are ambiguous.
7. One version of the story may have had 'son of Eridu' here rather than 'son of Ea'.
8. This verb is often used with the meaning 'to touch someone with evil intentions'.
9. An unusual verb seems to be chosen here for alliteration with the words for 'food' and 'eat', *akalu*, *kalu*, and *akālu*. An unusual plural form of the word 'heaven' produces a pun, 'bread of heaven / bread of death', *šamūti/ša mūti*.
10. Ea appears to be advising Adapa to accept the rites of a dead man, but they can also be seen as the first tokens of hospitality. Thus Ea may trick Adapa with a *double entendre* into accepting from Anu the fate of mortality.
11. The normal translation of this line is: 'The sea was like a mirror', which disregards several considerable difficulties. This translation derives both noun and verb very tentatively from *esēlu*.
12. Presumably understand three more lines here, corresponding to Ea's earlier instructions, dealing with the water of life, with garments, and with oil.

Etana

The story centres on a king of Kish who is attested in the Sumerian king list as a quasi-historical character. Presumably the legend had its origin in Kish, although the patron deities of Kish, Zababa, and Ishtar, play no part, for the sun-god Shamash alone is involved. The length and ending of the story are still disputed; if it was a three-tablet composition in its 'Standard' form, it should consist of about 450 lines in all.

Tablets of the Old Babylonian version come from Susa in Elam and from Tell Harmal; a Middle Assyrian version comes from Assur, and the 'Standard' version from Nineveh, to which may be added unprovenanced tablets in museum collections. But the story is certainly much older, for Lu-Nanna, the demi-sage of Shulgi, king of Ur (2150–2103 BC), is credited as the author, and the ascent of Etana on an eagle's back is shown on cylinder seals of the Akkadian period (2390–2249 BC). The late version omits some episodes which are quite crucial to the understanding of the story, although in other ways the versions seem close, with mainly rephrasing of individual lines or passages.

The bare motif, of a man's ascent to heaven on an eagle's back, is also found in the Greek myth of Ganymede; it was incorporated into the Alexander Romance, and is also found in Iranian stories and Islamic legends. The motif of a tree inhabited by a snake and a bird also occurs in the Sumerian text *Gilgamesh and the halub tree,* as described in the notes to *Gilgamesh*, XII.

Etana is the only Mesopotamian tale to have been identified unequivocally on ancient cylinder seals.[1]

---

[1] See Collon 1982, nos. 151 and 152.

ETANA

TABLET I

SBV [The great gods, the Igigi] designed a city,
[The Igigi] laid its foundation.
[The Anunnaki] designed the city of Kish,
[The Anunnaki] laid its foundation,
The Igigi made its brickwork firm
[   ].
'Let [   ] be their shepherd [   ]
Let Etana be their builder (?) [   ] the staff
of [   ].'
The great Anunnaki who decree destinies
Sat and conferred their counsel on the land.
They were creating the four quarters (of the world)
and establishing the form (of it).
The Igigi [   ] decreed names (?) for
them all.[1]
They had not established a king over all the teeming
people.[2]
At that time the headband and crown had not been
put together,[3]
And the lapis lazuli sceptre had not been
brandished (?),[4]
At the same time (?) the throne-dais had not been
made.[5]
The Sebitti barred the gates against armies (?),
[The   ] barred them against (other) settled
peoples.
The Igigi would patrol the city [   ].[6]
Ishtar [was looking for] a shepherd
And searching high and low for a king.
Inninna [was looking for] a shepherd
And searching high and low for a king.
Ellil was looking for a throne-dais for Etana.
'The young man for whom Ishtar [is looking so
dilige]ntly

And searches endlessly [   ].
A king is hereby affirmed for the land, and in
    Kish [it is established (?)]'
He brought kingship [   ]
[   ]
The gods of the lands [   ]⁷

    (*about 120 lines missing*)

TABLET II

He named him [   ]-man [   ]⁸
He built a fort (?) [   ]
The throne-dais of Adad his god [   ]⁹
In the shade of that throne-dais a poplar
    sprouted [   ]
On its crown an eagle crouched, [and a serpent lay
    at its base].
Every day they would keep watch [for their
    prey (?)].
The eagle made its voice heard and said to the
    serpent,
  'Come, let us be friends,
  Let us be comrades, you and I.'
The serpent made its voice heard and spoke to the
    eagle,
  '[You are not fit for] friendship [in the sight of
    Shamash!]
  You are wicked and you have grieved his heart.
  You have done unforgivable deeds, an
    abomination to the gods.¹⁰
  (But) come, let us stand up and [make a
    pledge (?)]
  Let us swear an oath on [the net of
    Shamash (?)]'¹¹
In the presence of Shamash the warrior they swore
    an oath,
  'Whoever oversteps the limit set by Shamash,
  Shamash shall deliver into the hands of the
    Smiter for harm.¹²

Whoever oversteps the limit set by Shamash,
May the mountain keep its pass far away from
    him,
May the prowling weapon make straight for him,
May the snares (on which) the oath to Shamash
    (is sworn) overturn him and ensnare him!'[13]
When they had sworn the oath on [the net of
    Shamash (?)],
They stood up (?) and went up the mountain.[14]
Each day they kept watch [for their prey (?).]
The eagle would catch a wild bull or wild ass,
And the serpent would eat, (then) turn away so that
    its young could eat.
The serpent would catch mountain goats or
    gazelles,[15]
And the eagle would eat, (then) turn away so that
    its young could eat.
The eagle would catch wild boar and wild sheep,
And the serpent would eat, (then) turn away so that
    its young could eat.
The serpent would catch cattle from the plains and
    wild beasts from the countryside,
And the eagle would eat, (then) turn away so that
    its young could eat.
The young of the serpent [had an abundance] of
    food.
The eagle's young grew large and flourished.
When the eagle's young had grown large and
    flourished,
The eagle plotted evil in its heart,
And in its heart it plotted evil,
And made up its mind to eat its friend's young
    ones.
The eagle made its voice heard and spoke to its
    young,
    'I am going to eat the serpent's young ones,
    The serpent [is sure to be an]gry
    So I shall go up and abide in the sky.
    I shall come down from the tree top only to eat
        the fruit!'

A small fledgling, especially wise, addressed its
    words to the eagle, its father,
  'Father, don't eat! The net of Shamash will
    ensnare you.
  The snares (on which) the oath of Shamash (is
    sworn) will overturn you and ensnare you.
  (Remember:) Whoever oversteps the limit set by
    Shamash,
  Shamash shall deliver into the hands of the
    Smiter for harm.'
It would not listen to them, and would not listen to
    the word of its sons.
It went down and ate the serpent's young.
In the evening at the close of day,
The serpent came and was carrying its load,
Laid the meat down at the entrance to its nest,
Stared, for its nest was not there.
Morning came (?), but [the eagle] did not [appear],
For with its talons it had [clawed at] the ground,
And its dust cloud [covered] the heavens on high.
The serpent lay down and wept,
Its tears flowed before Shamash.
  'I trusted in you, Shamash the warrior,
  And I was helpful (?) to the eagle who lives on
    the branches.[16]
  Now the serpent's nest [is grief-stricken].[17]
  My own nest is not there, while its nest is safe.
  My young ones are scattered and its young ones
    are safe.
  It came down and ate my young ones!
  You know the wrong which it has done me,
    Shamash!
  Truly, O Shamash, your net is as wide as earth,
  Your snare is as broad as the sky!
  The eagle should not escape from your net,
  As criminal as Anzu, who wronged his
    comrade.'[18]
[When he heard] the serpent's plea,
Shamash made his voice heard and spoke to the
    serpent,

'Go along the path, cross the mountain
Where a wild bull [   ] has been bound for
    you.[19]
Open up its innards, slit open its stomach,
Make a place to sit inside its stomach.
All kinds of birds will come down from the sky
    and eat the flesh.
The eagle too [will come down] with them.
[Since] it will not be aware of danger to itself,
It will search out the tenderest morsels, will comb
    the area (?),
Penetrate to the lining of the innards.
When it enters the innards, you must seize it by
    the wing,
Cut its wings, feather and pinion,
Pluck it and throw it into a bottomless pit,
Let it die there of hunger and thirst!'
At the command of the warrior Shamash,
The serpent went, it crossed the mountain.
The serpent came upon the wild bull,
And opened up its innards and slit open its stomach,
And made a place to sit inside its stomach.
All kinds of birds came down from the sky and
    began to eat the flesh.
But the eagle was aware of the danger to itself
And would not eat the flesh with the other birds.
The eagle made its voice heard and spoke to its son,
    'Come, and let us go down and let us eat the
    flesh of this wild bull!'
But the young fledgling was exceptionally wise, and
    said to the eagle its father,
    'Don't go down, father; perhaps the serpent is
    lying in wait inside this wild bull!'
The eagle reasoned thus to itself:
    'If the birds felt any fear,
    How would they be eating the flesh so
    peacefully?'
It did not pay heed to them, did not listen to the
    words of its sons,
Came down and stood upon the wild bull.

The eagle inspected the flesh,
But kept scanning ahead of it and behind it.
It inspected the flesh again,
But kept scanning ahead of it and behind it.
It kept going further in (?) until it penetrated to the
     lining of the innards.
As it went right in, the serpent seized it by the
     wing.
   'You robbed (?) my nest, you robbed my nest!'[20]
The eagle made its voice heard and began to speak
     to the serpent,
   'Spare me, and I shall give you, as one betrothed,
     a *nudunnû*-payment.'[21]
The serpent made its voice heard and spoke to the
     eagle,
   'If I were to free you, how would I answer
     Shamash the Most High?
   The punishment due to you would revert to me,
   The punishment that I now inflict on you!'
It cut its wings, pinion and feather,
Plucked it and threw it into a pit,
To die of hunger and thirst.
[The eagle   ]
Every day it prayed repeatedly to Shamash,
   'Am I to die in the pit?
   Who realizes that it is your punishment I bear?
   Save my life for me, the eagle,
   So that I may broadcast your fame for eternity!'
Shamash made his voice heard and spoke to the
     eagle,
   'You are wicked, and you have grieved my heart.
   You did an unforgivable deed, an abomination to
     the gods.
   You are dying, and I shall not go near you!
   But a man, whom I am sending to you, is
     coming—let him help you.'
Every day, Etana prayed repeatedly to Shamash,
   'O Shamash, you have enjoyed the best cuts of
     my sheep,
   Earth has drunk the blood of my lambs,

I have honoured the gods and respected the spirits
 of the dead,
The dream-interpreters have made full use of my
 incense.
The gods have made full use of my lambs at the
 slaughter.
O Lord, let the word go forth from your mouth
And give me the plant of birth,
Show me the plant of birth!
Remove my shame and provide me with a son!'[22]
Shamash made his voice heard and spoke to Etana,
 'Go along the road, cross the mountain,
 Find a pit and look carefully at what is inside it.
 An eagle is abandoned down there.
 It will show you the plant of birth.'
At the command of Shamash the warrior,
Etana went, crossed the mountain,
Found the pit and looked at what was inside it.
An eagle was abandoned down there.
The eagle raised itself up at once.

TABLET III

LV The eagle made its voice heard and spoke to
    Shamash,[23]
   'O Lord, [   ]
   The offspring (?) of a bird [   ]
   I am [   ]
   Whatever he says, [   ]
   Whatever I say, [   ].'
  At the command of Shamash, [   ]
  The offspring (?) of the bird [   ].
  The eagle made its voice heard and spoke to Etana,
   'Why have you come to me? Tell me!'
  Etana made his voice heard and spoke to the eagle,
   'O my friend, give me the plant of birth,
   Show me the plant of birth!
   Remove my shame and provide me with a son!
   Leave [   ]

When you get out (?) [   ].'
Then the eagle said [to Etana (?)],
    'All alone I shall [search the mountains (?)].[24]
    Let me bring [the plant of birth (?)] to you.'

MAV   When Etana heard this,[25]
He covered the front of the pit with juniper,
Made for it and threw down [   ]
And kept [   ]
Thus he kept (?) the eagle alive in the pit.
He began to teach it to fly again.
For one [month], then a second [month]
He kept (?) the eagle alive in the pit
And began to teach it to fly again.
For a third [month], then a fourth mo[nth]
He kept (?) the eagle alive in the pit
And began to teach it to fly again.

OBV   [Etana] helped it for seven months.
In the eighth month he helped it out of its pit.[26]
The eagle, now well fed, was as strong as a fierce
    lion.
The eagle made its voice heard and spoke to Etana,
    'My friend, we really are friends, you and I!
      Tell me what you wish from me, that I may give
        it to you.'
Etana made his voice heard and spoke to the eagle,
    'Change my destiny (?) and disclose what is
        concealed!'

(gap of about 6 lines?)

SBV   Etana (?) went and [helped the eagle out (?)].[27]
The eagle hunted around [in the mountains (?)]
But [the plant of birth] was not [to be found there].
    'Come, my friend, let me carry you up [to the
        sky],
      [Let us meet] with Ishtar, the mistress [of birth].
      Beside Ishtar the mistress [of birth let us   ].
      Put your arms over my sides,
      Put your hands over the quills of my wings.'
He put his arms over its sides,
Put his hands over the quills of its wings.

[The eagle] took him upwards for a mile.
  'My friend, look at the country! How does it
    seem?'
  'The affairs of the country buzz (?) [like
    flies (?)]²⁸
And the wide sea is no bigger than a sheepfold!'
[The eagle took him] up a second mile,
  'My friend, look at the country! How does it
    seem?'
  'The country has turned into a garden [   ],
  And the wide sea is no bigger than a bucket!'
It took him up a third mile.
  'My friend, look at the country! How does it
    seem?'
  'I am looking for the country, but I can't see it!
  And my eyes cannot even pick out the wide sea!
  My friend, I cannot go any further towards
    heaven.
  Retrace the way, and let me go back to my city!'
The eagle shrugged him off for one mile,
Then dropped down and retrieved him on its wings.
The eagle shrugged him off for a second mile,
Then dropped down and retrieved him on its wings.
The eagle shrugged him off for a third mile,
Then dropped down and retrieved him on its wings.
A metre from the ground, the eagle shrugged him
    off,
Then dropped down and retrieved him on its wings.

  (*gap of uncertain length*)

  (*They go back to Kish. Etana has a series of
  three (?) dreams which encourage him to
  make a second attempt to reach heaven.*)

Etana said to the eagle,
  '[My friend, I saw a first (?) dream.]
  The city of Kish was sobbing [   ]
  Within it [the people were in mourning (?)]
  I sang [a song of lamentation (?)].
  "O Kish, giver of life!

Etana [cannot give you an heir (?)]
O Kish, giver of life,
[   ]
Etana [cannot give you an heir (?)]

(gap of uncertain length)

His wife said to Etana,[29]
   '[The god] showed me a dream.
   Like Etana my husband [I have had a dream (?)],
   Like you [the god has shown me a dream (?)].
   Etana was king [of Kish for x years (?)]
   And his ghost [   ]

(gap of uncertain length)

Etana opened his mouth and spoke to the eagle,
   'My friend, that god showed me [another
      dream (?)].
   We were going through the entrance of the gate
      of Anu, Ellil, and Ea.
   We bowed down together, you and I.
   We were going through the entrance of the gate
      of Sin, Shamash, Adad, and Ishtar,
   We bowed down together, you and I.
   I saw a house with a window that was not sealed.
   I pushed it open and went inside.
   Sitting in there was a girl
   Adorned with a crown, fair of face.
   A throne was set in place, and [   ]
   Beneath the throne crouched snarling lions.
   I came up and the lions sprang at me.
   I woke up terrified.'
The eagle said to Etana,
   'My friend, [the significance of the dreams] is
      quite clear!
   Come, let me carry you up to the heaven of Anu.
   Put your chest over my breast,
   Put your hands over the quills of my wings.
   Put your arms over my sides.'
He put his chest over its breast,
Put his hands over its feathers,

Put his arms over its sides.
The eagle tied its load on securely,
Took him up a mile
And spoke to him, to Etana,
   'See, my friend, how the country seems!
   Inspect the sea, look carefully for its features!
   The country is only the edge (?) of (?) a
      mountain!
   And whatever has become of the sea?'[30]
The eagle took him up a second mile
And spoke to Etana,
   'See, my friend, how the country seems!
   Whatever [has become of (?)] the country?'
The eagle took him up a third mile
And spoke to Etana,
   'See, my friend, how the country seems!
   The sea has turned into a gardener's ditch!'
When they came up to the heaven of Anu,
They went through the gate of Anu, Ellil, and Ea.
The eagle and Etana bowed down together.
They went through the gate of Sin, Shamash, Adad,
     and Ishtar.[31]
The eagle and Etana bowed down together.
[   ]
He pushed it open [and went inside].

(*The rest of the text is missing*)

(*According to the Sumerian king list, Etana
was succeeded by his son Balih.*)

NOTES TO *ETANA*

Text: Kinnier Wilson 1985.
The different versions were almost certainly divided into tablets at different
points in the text. SBV is followed here.

1. OBV has 'festival' for 'names(?)'.
2. 'Teeming', *apâti*, used to be translated 'beclouded' owing to an incorrect
   etymology.

3. Early crowns consisted of two parts: a rigid conical or high oval cap, and a band encircling its edge.

4. Taking the verb as *ṣabāru* II, not *ṣapāru*. Alternatively, 'The sceptre had not been inlaid with lapis lazuli'.

5. This line is taken from OBV, since it connects with a subsequent line, eight lines later.

6. OBV adds: 'Sceptre and crown, headband and staffs, Were set before Anum in heaven. There was no advice for its people, (Until) kingship came down from heaven.'

7. In the following gap, Kinnier Wilson inserted a fragment that may better be placed in Tablet III. It is too fragmentary for translation here.

8. Perhaps 'They' instead of 'He'.

9. 'Throne-dais' may be used here to mean a whole shrine.

10. 'You have done . . . an abomination': literally, 'You ate *asakku*-food'. When pacts were made, ritual food was eaten which would 'turn against' the one who broke the pact.

11. Oaths were sworn while touching an appurtenance or symbol of a deity, which then could act as a weapon enforcing retribution upon a perjurer. The net thus may be referred to as a 'prowling weapon' six lines later.

12. Or, 'hunter' rather than 'smiter'.

13. MAV adds: 'May Shamash lift his head for the slaughterer, May Shamash deliver the evil one into the hands of the smiter, May he station an evil *gallu*-demon over him.'

14. OBV inserts a perfunctory line: 'All conceived, all gave birth', which MAV elaborates to: 'In the crown of the tree the Eagle gave birth, And at the base of the poplar the serpent gave birth, In the shade of that poplar The Eagle and the Serpent became friends, They swore an oath together, they were partners, They confided their worries to each other.'

15. OBV has: 'The serpent would catch a leopard (or) a tiger.'

16. Reading: *ana erî tumanî anāku ašrum*. (SMD)

17. Restored from OBV.

18. As it stands in SBV, this line alludes to Anzu's betrayal of Ellil while acting as his trusted doorkeeper. However, MAV has the similar-sounding word *anzillu*, 'abomination', at the same point, so the allusion to Anzu may derive from a corrupt text. Cf. also *Erra and Ishum*, note 39.

19. Or, 'Where [Shakkan] has bound a wild bull for you', or: 'Where [I, Shamash,] have bound a wild bull for you.'

20. Very uncertain. von Soden reads as: 'you entered and changed my nest'; Kinnier Wilson: 'You entered upon my nestlings.' Edzard 1987, 137, suggests a serpentine tongue-twister.

21. The word implies payment to a bride before marriage which ensured her livelihood after her husband's death.

22. Reading *piltu* (from *pištu*) rather than *biltu*, 'load, burden', which is the traditional translation, but inappropriate. (SMD)

23. Kinnier Wilson's IV c (p. 112) is taken here as a better-preserved variant of III A (p. 104) in his edition. His fragment III/B on p. 106 may not belong to this myth. I am indebted to Dr Jeremy Hughes for the

observation that Kinnier Wilson and others had assigned obverse and reverse to his Text M (plates 24–5) incorrectly (collated).

24. Restorations are based on line endings preserved in III A, p. 104 of Kinnier Wilson's edition.

25. The translation differs from that of Kinnier Wilson here, rejecting the restoration of a ladder with rungs, and taking the phrase *ṣabābu + kappu* in its attested sense of 'to teach to fly'. (SMD)

26. Taking the verb as *ṣâdu*.

27. Kinnier Wilson would place this episode in a hypothetical fourth tablet (see his IV/A on p. 108). The present reconstruction supposes that line 8 of OBV in Kinnier Wilson p. 40 is a version of line 13 of SBV on p. 114, but this is far from certain.

28. Reading *ihambuba* instead of *ihammuš*.

29. This fragment, given by Kinnier Wilson, p. 125 as LV, V, may come as the second in the preceding sequence of three dreams. Both in *Etana* and in *Gilgamesh* the reconstructions given here allow for a sequence of threes for confirmation. The dream may have indicated that Etana would have a son to carry out his funerary rites.

30. For the phrase *ana mimmê tuāru* see AHw, s.v. *mimmû* B2. (SMD)

31. The text has 'ditto' at the repetitions.

Anzu

The *Epic of Anzu* is principally known in two versions. The Old Babylonian version of the early second millennium exists as a small portion of the tale, giving the hero as Ningirsu, a warrior-god who was patron of the city Girsu in central Mesopotamia. That city is chiefly known in the late third millennium from the inscriptions of Gudea, a Sumerian governor who rebuilt Eninnu, Ningirsu's temple, and composed long inscriptions in honour of the event, and from many fine objects found by the French in the excavation of strata which date around that time: the lion-headed eagle Anzu is often depicted on them. However, no Sumerian account of the story is known, and Anzu in the Sumerian *Epic of Lugalbanda* has a quite different character and role: he is a benevolent bird whose offspring are fed during his absence by the hero of the epic. As far as its fragmentary condition allows us to judge, the Old Babylonian version of *Anzu* was written in an abbreviated form in which repetitious passages are not written verbatim. Ningirsu is given the title 'the God' or perhaps 'Il' in this version. The god Shara also plays a prominent role. He was the patron god of Umma, a city in central Mesopotamia which likewise flourished in the late third millennium and was not important thereafter.

The Standard Babylonian version, dating to the first millennium BC, may have consisted of about 720 lines on three four-column tablets. Some were found on the Late Assyrian sites of Nineveh, Tarbiṣu and Sultantepe, and probably belong to the seventh century BC. Another tablet comes from a museum collection in the USA and is of unknown provenance. It is Late Babylonian, but seems to have followed the Nineveh version closely. In this version the hero is Ninurta whose great cult centre at that time was Kalah, modern Nimrud, one of the Assyrian kings' capital cities in the ninth and eighth centuries BC. The walls of Ninurta's temple there are faced with monumental stone sculptures illustrating a cosmic battle, probably a version of the Anzu epic. The story gives Ninurta the title 'Bel', 'The Lord', equivalent to West Semitic Ba'al. Repeated episodes are written out in full. The colophon to the Tarbiṣu version implies that the written story was known to the Hurrians, who were powerful in the mid- to late second millennium and at times controlled Assyria from their cities north-west of Assyria.

The story centres around possession of the Tablet of Destinies. The narrative structure is very similar to that of the *Epic of Creation*, both in the struggle to regain possession by the good gods, and in the pronouncement of names and hypostases for the victorious hero-god.

The opening lines of the epic introduce the theme in the first person, representing the singer or poet, and are very closely comparable to the opening lines of *Erra and Ishum*. Nergal and Ninurta are quite close in some aspects of their characters, and in *Erra and Ishum* the defeat of Anzu with a net and the conquest of *asakku*-demons are attributed to Nergal/Erra. The fight of Ninurta to defeat the *asakku*-demons is known from the mainly Sumerian epic story of cosmic warfare called *Lugal-e*, and a companion story *An-gim*. These were very popular tales during both the second and the early first millennia. Sumerian Ninurta is armed with his trusty weapon Sharur; in *Anzu* Sharur plays a significant role as Ninurta's courier in the field of conflict. In *Lugal-e* his mother, the great goddess Nin-mah, speaks in support of him and is given the name Ninhursag, just as in *Anzu*, the mother of Ninurta as Belet-ili or Mami speaks in support of her son and is given the new title 'Mistress of All Gods'.

Other epic deeds of Ninurta are known only from passing references: he slew the bull-man in the sea; he slew the six-headed wild ram on the mountain; he slew the seven-headed serpent.

The Anzu epic and its ramifications in other tales illustrate how a common stock of narrative themes was used in different stories, and adapted in various places for diverse gods.

ANZU

SBV i I sing of the superb son of the king of populated
    lands,
  Beloved of Mami, the powerful god, Ellil's son;
  I praise superb Ninurta, beloved of Mami,
  The powerful god, Ellil's son,
  Ekur's child, leader of the Anunnaki, focus of
    Eninnu,
  Who waters cattle-pens, irrigated gardens, ponds (?),
    in country and town.
  Flood-wave of battles, who darkens the sash,
    warrior.[1]
  The fiercest *gallū*-demons, though tireless, fear his
    attack.
  Listen to the praise of the powerful one's strength,
  Who subdued, who bound the Mountain of Stones
    in his fury,[2]
  Who conquered soaring Anzu with his weapon,
  Who slew the bull-man inside the Sea.[3]
  Strong warrior who slays with his weapon,
  Powerful one who is quick to form a battle array.
  Until now, no dais had been created for the Igigi;
  The Igigi would assemble for their Ellil-power.
  Rivers were formed—the Tigris, the Euphrates—
  But springs (?) had not yet sent their water to the
    land.
  Seas [   ]
  Clouds were still far away on the horizon [( )].
  All the Igigi gathered
  To Ellil their father, warrior of the gods,
  They, his sons, brought a report.
   'Pay attention to reliable words!
   On Hehe, a wooded mountain of [   ]
   In the lap of (?) the Anunnaki [   ]

[   ] has given birth to Anzu.
[His] beak is a saw [   ]
[   ]
ii   Which [   ]
      Eleven coats of mail (?) [   ]
      The mountains [   ]
      [   ]
      At his shout [   ]
      The south wind [   ]
      The powerful [   ] wind [   ]
      The mass [   ]
      Whirlwinds [   ]
      They met and [   ]
      The four winds [   ]'
Father of the gods, Duranki's god, looked at him,
But kept his thoughts to himself.
He studied Anzu closely [   ]
He considered with (?) [   ]
      'Who gave birth to [   ]?
      Why is this [   ]?'
Ea answered his heart-searching,
The far-sighted one addressed his words to Ellil,
      'Surely water of the spate [begot Anzu],
      Holy water of the gods of Apsu.
      Broad Earth conceived him,
      And he was born from mountain rocks.
      You have looked at Anzu himself [   ].
      Let him serve you and never [cease]!
      In the hall let him bar the way to the innermost
         chamber, forever.'

         (*gap of 2 or 3 lines*)

iii   [   ] the words spoken to him.
      He (Ellil) took a cult centre [   ]
      And administered the orders of all the gods.
      He made an extra (?) fate, and Anzu
         administered (?) it.
      Ellil appointed him to the entrance of the chamber
         which he had perfected.
      He would bathe in holy water in his presence.

His eyes would gaze at the trappings of Ellil-power:
His lordly crown, his robe of divinity,
The Tablet of Destinies in his hands. Anzu gazed,
And gazed at Duranki's god, father of the gods,
And fixed his purpose, to usurp the Ellil-power.
Anzu often gazed at Duranki's god, father of the
    gods,
And fixed his purpose, to usurp the Ellil-power.
  'I shall take the gods' Tablet of Destinies for
      myself
  And control the orders for all the gods,
  And shall possess the throne and be master of
      rites!
  I shall direct every one of the Igigi!'
He plotted opposition in his heart
And at the chamber's entrance from which he often
    gazed, he waited for the start of day.
While Ellil was bathing in the holy water,
Stripped and with his crown laid down on the throne,
He gained the Tablet of Destinies for himself,
Took away the Ellil-power. Rites were abandoned,
Anzu flew off and went into hiding.
Radiance faded (?), silence reigned.
Father Ellil, their counsellor, was dumbstruck,
For he had stripped the chamber of its radiance.
The gods of the land searched high and low for a
    solution.
Anu made his voice heard and spoke,
Addressed the gods his sons,
  'Whichever [god] slays Anzu
  Will make our name great in all populated lands!'
They called the canal-controller, Anu's son,
The decision-maker spoke to him;[4]
They called Adad the canal-controller, Anu's son,
The decision-maker spoke to him,
  'Powerful Adad, ferocious Adad, your attack
      cannot be deflected;
  Strike Anzu with lightning, your weapon!
  Your name shall be great in the great gods'
      assembly,

You shall have no rival among the gods your
   brothers.
Then surely shall shrines be created!⁵
Establish your cult centres all over the four
   quarters!
Your cult centres shall enter Ekur!⁶
Show prowess to the gods, and your name shall
   be Powerful!'
Adad answered the speech,
Addressed his words to Anu his father,
   'Father, who could rush off to the inaccessible
     mountain?
   Which of the gods your sons will be Anzu's
     conqueror?
   For he has gained the Tablet of Destinies for
     himself,
   Has taken away the Ellil-power: rites are
     abandoned!
   Anzu flew off and went into hiding!
   His utterance has replaced that of Duranki's god!
   He has only to command, and whoever he curses
     turns to clay!
   At his utterance the gods (must now) tremble!'
He turned away, saying he would not make the
   expedition.
They called Gerra, Anunitu's son.
The decision-maker spoke to him,
   'Powerful Gerra, ferocious Gerra, your attack
     cannot be deflected;
   Burn (?) Anzu with fire (?), your weapon!
   Your name shall be great in the great gods'
     assembly,
   You shall have no rival among the gods your
     brothers.
   Then surely shall shrines be created!
   Establish your cult centres all over the four
     quarters!
   Your cult centres shall enter Ekur!
   Show prowess to the gods and your name shall be
     Powerful!'

Gerra answered the speech,
Addressed his words to Anu his father,
  'Father, who could rush off to the inaccessible
    mountain?
  Which of the gods your sons will be Anzu's
    conqueror?
  For he has gained the Tablet of Destinies for
    himself,
  Has taken away the Ellil-power: rites are
    abandoned!
  Anzu flew off and went into hiding!
  His utterance has replaced that of Duranki's god;
  He has only to command, and whoever he curses
    turns to clay!
  At his utterance the gods (must now) tremble!'[7]
He turned away, saying he would not make the
  expedition.
They called Shara, Ishtar's son.
He (Anu) proposed a solution, spoke to him,
  'Powerful Shara, ferocious Shara, your attack
    cannot be deflected;
  [Strike] Anzu with [. . .], your weapon!
  Your name shall be great in the great gods'
    assembly.
  You shall have no rival among the gods your
    brothers.
  Then surely shall shrines be created!
  Establish your cult centres all over the four
    quarters!
  Your cult centres shall enter Ekur!
  Show prowess to the gods, and your name shall
    be Powerful!'
Shara answered the speech,
Addressed his words to Anu his father,
  'Father, who could rush off to the inaccessible
    mountain?
  Which of the gods your sons will be Anzu's
    conqueror?
  For he has gained the Tablet of Destinies for
    himself,

Has taken away the Ellil-power: rites are
    abandoned!
Anzu flew off and went into hiding!
His utterance has replaced that of Duranki's god.
He has only to command, and whoever he curses
    turns to clay!
At his utterance the gods (must now) tremble!'
He turned away, saying he would not make the
    expedition.
The gods fell silent and despaired of advice.
The Igigi grew despondent where they sat, troubled.
The Lord of intelligence, wise one who dwells in the
    Apsu,[8]
Formed an idea in the depths of his being;[9]
Ea formed intelligence in his heart.
He told Anu what he was thinking in his inmost
    being.
    'Let me give orders and search among the gods,
    And pick from the assembly Anzu's conqueror.
    I myself shall search among the gods
    And pick from the assembly Anzu's conqueror.'
The Igigi listened to this speech of his;
The Igigi were freed (from anxiety) and kissed his
    feet.[10]
The far-sighted one made his voice heard and spoke,
Addressed his words to Anu and Dagan,
    'Have them call for me Belet-ili, sister of the gods,
    Wise counsellor of the gods her brothers.
    Have them announce her supremacy in the
        assembly,[11]
    Have the gods honour her in their assembly;
    I shall then tell her the idea which is in my
        heart.'
They called Belet-ili, sister of the gods, to him,
Wise counsellor of the gods her brothers.
They announced her supremacy in the assembly,[11]
The gods honoured her in their assembly.
(Then) Ea told the idea in the depths of his inmost
    being.
    'Previously [we used to call you] Mami

(But) now [your name shall be] Mistress of All
   Gods.[12]
Offer the powerful one, your superb beloved,
Broad of chest, who forms the battle array!
Give Ninurta, your superb beloved,
Broad of chest, who forms the battle array.
[Then shall his name be] Lord in the great gods'
   assembly.[13]
Let him show prowess to [the gods, that his name
   may be Powerful].
[Let his name be made great] in all populated
   lands,
[His] cult centre [   ]
Lord [.]'

   (*2 lines very fragmentary*)

[Mami listened to this speech of his (?)]
[And Belet-ili the supreme uttered 'Yes' (?)].
[The gods of the land (?) were glad at her
   utterance];
[The Igigi were freed (from anxiety) and kissed her
   feet.]
[She called her son into the gods' assembly,]
iv   And instructed her favourite, saying to him,
      'In the presence of Anu and Dagan],
      [They announced] the course of [their rites in the
         assembly].
      [I gave birth to all] the Igigi,
      I created every [single one of the Anunnaki],
      And I created the [gods'] assembly. [I, Mami,]
      [Assigned (?)] the Ellil-power [to my brother],
      [Designated] the kingship of heaven for Anu.
      Anzu has disrupted the kingship that I
         designated!
      He has obtained for himself the Tablet of
         Destinies [   ]
      He has robbed Ellil; he rejected your father,
      Stole the rites and turned them to his own use.
   (*Catchline*)
      Make (?) a path, fix the hour,

TABLET II

Make (?) a path, fix the hour,[14]
Let light dawn for the gods whom I created.
Muster your devastating battle force,
Make your evil winds flash as they march over
    him.
Capture soaring Anzu
And inundate the earth, which I created—wreck
    his dwelling.
Let terror thunder above him,
Let fear (of?) your battle force shake in (?) him,
Make the devastating whirlwind rise up against
    him.
Set your arrow in the bow, coat it with poison.
Your form must keep changing, like a
    gallu-demon.
Send out a fog, so that he cannot recognize your
    features!
May your rays proceed above him,
Make a high, attacking leap; have glare
More powerful than Shamash generates.
May broad daylight turn to darkness for him.
Seize him by the throat: conquer Anzu,
And let the winds bring his feathers as good
    news[15]
To Ekur, to your father Ellil's house.
Rush and inundate the mountain pastures[16]
And slit the throat of wicked Anzu.
Then shall kingship enter Ekur again,
Then shall rites return for the father who begot
    you!
Then surely shall shrines be created!
Establish your cult centres all over the four
    quarters!
Your cult centres shall enter Ekur!
Show prowess to the gods and your name shall be
    Powerful!'
The warrior listened to his mother's words.

He hunched (?) in trepidation, and went into hiding.
The Lord marshalled the Seven of Battle,
The warrior marshalled the seven evil winds,
Who dance in the dust, the seven whirlwinds.
He mustered a battle array, made war with a
    terrifying formation;
Even the gales were silent at his side, (poised) for
    conflict.
On the mountainside Anzu and Ninurta met.
Anzu looked at him and shook with rage at him,
Bared his teeth like an *ūmu*-demon; his mantle of
    radiance covered the mountain,
He roared like a lion in sudden rage,
In utter fury shouted to the warrior,
  'I have taken away every single rite
  And I am in charge of all the gods' orders!
  Who are you, to come to do battle against me?
  Give your reasons!'
Insolently his speech rushed out at him.
The warrior Ninurta answered Anzu,
  'I am the [avenger (?)] of Duranki's god,
  Who established Duranki, the . . . of the broad
  Earth of (?) Ea king of destinies.[17]
  I have come to . . . to battle against you, to
  trample on you!'
Anzu listened to his speech,
Then hurled his shout furiously amid the
    mountains.
Darkness fell over (?) the mountain, their faces were
    overcast.[18]
Shamash, the light of the gods, was overcast by
    darkness.
Adad roared like a lion (?), his din joined that of
    Anzu.
A clash between battle arrays was imminent, the
    flood-weapon massed (?).
The armour-plated breast (?) was bathed in blood.[19]
Clouds of death rained down, an arrow flashed
    lightning,
Whizzed, the battle force roared between them.

The powerful, superb one, Mami's son,
Trusted of Anu and Dagan, beloved of the far-
  sighted one,
Set the shaft to the bow, drew it taut,
Aimed (?) the shaft at him from the bow's curve.
But it did not go near Anzu: the shaft turned back.
Anzu shouted at it,
  'You, shaft that came: return to your reed
    thicket!
  Bow-frame: back to your copse!
  Bow-string: back to the ram's gut! Feathers,
    return to the birds!'
He was holding the gods' Tablet of Destinies in his
  hand,
And they influenced (?) the string of the bow; the
  arrows did not come near his body.
Deadly silence came over the battle, and conflict
  ceased.
Weapons stopped and did not capture Anzu amid
  the mountains.
He (Ninurta) shouted out and instructed Sharur:
  'Repeat to far-sighted Ea the actions you have
    seen!
  The Lord's message is: Ninurta was encircling
    Anzu
  And Ninurta the warrior was wrapped in
    devastation's dust.
  But when he set the shaft to the bow, drew it taut
  And aimed the shaft at him from the bow's curve,
  It did not go near Anzu: the shaft turned back
  As Anzu shouted at it:
  "You, shaft that came: return to your reed
    thicket!
  Bow-frame: back to your copse!
  Bow-string: back to the ram's gut! Feathers,
    return to the birds!"
  He was holding the gods' Tablet of Destinies in
    his hand,
  And they influenced (?) the string of the bow; the
    arrows did not come near his body.

Deadly silence came over the battle, and conflict
  ceased.
Weapons stopped and did not capture Anzu amid
  the mountains.'
Sharur bowed, took the message,
Carried the battle dispatch to far-sighted Ea.
Everything the Lord had told him, he repeated to
  Ea.
  'The Lord's message is: Ninurta was encircling
    Anzu
  And Ninurta was wrapped in devastation's dust.
  But when he set the shaft to the bow, drew it
    taut
  And aimed the shaft at him from the bow's curve,
  It did not go near Anzu: the shaft turned back
  As Anzu shouted at it:
  ''You, shaft that came: return to your reed
    thicket!
  Bow-frame, back to your copse!
  Bow-string, back to the ram's gut! Feathers,
    return to the birds!''
  He was holding the gods' Tablet of Destinies in
    his hand,
  And they influenced (?) the string of the bow; the
    arrows did not come near his body.
  Deadly silence came over the battle, and conflict
    ceased.
  Weapons stopped and did not capture Anzu amid
    the mountains.'
The far-sighted one listened to his son's words,
Called out and instructed Sharur,
  'Repeat to your lord what I say,
  And everything I tell you, repeat to him:
  Don't let the battle slacken, press home your
    victory!
  Tire him out so that he sheds his pinions in the
    clash of tempests.
  Take a throw-stick (?) to follow your arrows[20]
  And cut off his pinions, detach both right and
    left.

When he sees his wings and emits (?) his
    utterance,
Shouts "Wing to wing", don't panic:[21]
Draw taut from the curve of your bow, let shafts
    fly like lightning,
Let the wing feathers dance like butterflies (?).[22]
Seize him by the throat (?), conquer Anzu
And let the winds bring his feathers as good news
To Ekur, to your father Ellil's house.
Rush and inundate the mountain pastures
And slit the throat of wicked Anzu.
Then shall kingship enter Ekur again,
Then shall rites return for the father who begot
    you!
Then surely shall shrines be created!
Establish your cult centres all over the four
    quarters!
Your cult centres shall enter Ekur!
Show prowess to the gods, and your name shall
    be Powerful!'
Sharur bowed, took the message,
Carried the battle dispatch to his lord.
Everything Ea had told him, he repeated to him.
    'Don't let the battle slacken, press home your
        victory!
    Tire him out so that he sheds his pinions in the
        clash of tempests!
    Take a throw-stick (?) to follow your arrows
    And cut off his pinions, detach both right and
        left.
    When he sees his wings and emits (?) his
        utterance,
    Shouts "Wing to wing", don't panic:
    Draw taut from the curve of your bow, let shafts
        fly [like lightning],
    Let the wing feathers dance like butterflies.
    Seize him by the throat (?), conquer Anzu
    And let the winds bring his feathers as good news
    To Ekur, to your father Ellil's house.
    Rush and inundate the mountain pastures

And slit the throat of wicked Anzu.
Then shall your kingship enter Ekur again,
Then shall rites return for the father who begot
  you!
Then surely shall shrines be created!
Establish your cult centres all over the four
  quarters!
Your cult centres shall enter Ekur!
Show prowess to the gods, and your name shall
  be Powerful!'
The Lord listened to the words of far-sighted Ea.
He hunched (?) in trepidation, and went into hiding.
The Lord marshalled the Seven of Battle,
The warrior marshalled the seven evil winds,
Who dance in the dust, the seven whirlwinds.
He mustered a battle array, made war with a
  terrifying formation;
Even the gales were silent at his side, (poised) for
  conflict.

TABLET III
(*3 lines fragmentary*)

Devastation . . . [   ]
A heatwave blazed, confusion (?) [   ]
A tempest [   ] to the four winds,
Weapons slew (?) the protection of frost,
Both were bathed in the sweat of battle.
Anzu grew weary and in the clash of tempests shed
  his pinions.
He (Ninurta) took a throw-stick (?) to follow his
  arrows
And cut off his pinions, detached both right and
  left.
He (Anzu) saw his wings, and emitted his
  utterance;
But as he shouted 'Wing to wing', a shaft came
  up (?) at him,

A dart passed through his very heart.
He (Ninurta) made an arrow pass through pinion
    and wing,
A dart passed through heart and lungs.
He slew the mountains, inundated their proud
    pastures;
Ninurta slew the mountains, inundated their proud
    pastures,
Inundated the broad earth in his fury,
Inundated the midst of the mountains, slew wicked
    Anzu.
And warrior Ninurta regained the gods' Tablet of
    Destinies for his own hand.
As a sign of his good news,
The wind brought Anzu's feathers.
Dagan saw his sign and rejoiced,
Called all the gods and joyfully he spoke,
    'The strong one has indeed slain (?) Anzu on his
        mountain,
    Has regained for his own hands the . . .s of Anum
        and Dagan.
    Come! Let him come to us,
    Let him rejoice, play, make merry.
    Let him stand with the gods his brothers and hear
        (their) secrets,
    . . . the secrets of the gods.
    Let [Ellil (?)], the . . . of the gods his brothers
        bestow on him the rites.'
[Ellil (?)] made his voice heard and spoke,
Addressed his words to Dagan,
    '[   ] water . . .
    [When] he . . .   . . . he took.
    When he slew wicked Anzu in the midst of the
        mountains,
    Warrior Ninurta regained the gods' Tablet of
        Destinies for his own hands.
    Send for him and let him come to you.
    Let him place the Tablet of Destinies in your lap.'
Ellil made his voice heard and spoke,
Addressed his words to Nusku his vizier,
    'Nusku, go outside,

Bring Birdu into my presence.'
Nusku went outside,
Brought Birdu into Ellil's presence.
Ellil made his voice heard and spoke,
Addressed his words to Birdu,
   'Birdu, I shall send you, I shall . . .'

      (gap of a few lines)

Ninurta made his voice heard and spoke,
Addressed his words to Birdu,
   'Birdu, why have you come here
   So aggressively?'
Birdu made his voice heard and spoke,
Addressed his words to Ninurta his lord,
   'My lord, Ellil your father
   Sent me to you . . . to say,
   "The gods have heard
   That you slew wicked Anzu amid the mountains.
   They rejoiced, were glad and [   ]
   Made me come to your presence and [   ]
   Go to him, that he may [   ]"

     *(11 lines fragmentary, about 34 lines
     missing, then 3 lines fragmentary)*

Let him (Ellil) in his powerfulness gaze upon
   wicked Anzu (in Ekur).
Warrior, in your powerfulness, when you slew
   the mountain,
You captured Anzu, slew him in his powerfulness,
Slew soaring Anzu in his powerfulness.
Because you were so brave and slew the
   mountain,
You made all foes kneel at the feet of Ellil your
   father.
Ninurta, because you were so brave and slew the
   mountain,
You made all foes kneel at the feet of Ellil your
   father.
You have won complete dominion, every single
   rite.

Who was ever created like you? The mountain's
    rites
Are proclaimed (?), the shrines of the gods of
    fates granted to you.
They call upon Nissaba for your purification
    ceremony;
They call your name in the furrow NINGIRSU.
They designate for you the entire shepherding of
    peoples,
Give your great (?) name as DUKU (?) for
    kingship.
In Elam they give your name as HURABTIL,
They speak of you as SHUSHINAK in Susa.
Your name in Anu's . . . they give as LORD OF
    THE SECRET
[   ] among the gods your brothers.
[   ] your father.
[   ] who marches in front.
They give [your name as PABILSAG] in Egalmah,
Call [your name . . .] in Ur,
Give your name as NIN-AZU in Ekurmah.
[   ] Duranki was your birthplace.
[In . . .] they speak of you as ISHTARAN,
[In . . .] ZABABA.
[   ] they call his name.
Your bravery much greater than all the other
    gods,
[   ] your divinity is surpassing:
Wholehearted (?) I praise you!
They give [your name] in . . . as LUGALBANDA.
In E-igi-kalama (?) they give [your name] as
    LUGAL-MARADA.
[Your name in] E-sikil they give as WARRIOR
    TISHPAK,
[They call you (?)] . . . OF . . . in E-nimma-anku.
Your name in Kullab they call WARRIOR OF URUK,
[   ] son of Belet-ili your mother,
[   ] LORD OF THE BOUNDARY-ARROW,
[   ] PANIGARA,
[In E-akkil (?)] they call

[Your name] PAPSUKKAL who marches in front.
[   ] surpassing are your names among the
  gods by far!
[   ] you are thoughtful, capable, awesome,
Your [counsellor (?)] the far-sighted one, your
  father Anu.
[   ] battle and combat,
He granted to you . . . [   ],
Called you [   ] of their [   ]s.

(*7 lines fragmentary, about 5 lines missing,
1 line fragmentary. After a ruled line, 5
fragmentary lines and a few missing lines
appear to give a concluding passage.*)

(*Colophon*)
[   ] land of Hanigalbat
[   ] speedily excerpted
[   ] read (?), inspected (?), reviewed (?).

ANZU (OLD BABYLONIAN VERSION)

Tablet I not extant

TABLET II

He stole the Ellil-power; rites were abandoned,
Father Ellil their counsellor was dumbstruck.
Radiance faded (?), silence reigned,
Every one of the Igigi was thrown into confusion,
For he had stripped the chamber of its radiance.
The gods of the land assembled for a solution;
Anum made his voice heard,
Addressed the gods his sons,
  'Whichever god slays Anzum,
  I shall make his name greatest of all!'
They called the canal-controller, Anum's son; the
    decision-maker spoke to him,
  'O canal-controller, your battle force must never
    turn aside! Strike Anzum with lightning, your
    weapon!
  [Your name shall be great] among the great gods.
  You shall have no rival among the gods your
    brothers!
  Show prowess to the gods, and your name shall
    be Powerful!'
He addressed his words to Anum,
  'Father, who could rush off to the inaccessible
    mountain?
  Which of your sons will be Anzum's conqueror?
  For he has robbed Duranki's god of the rites.
  [He flew off (?)] into hiding and waited (?).
  [His utterance has] replaced that of Duranki's
    god.
  [Whoever he curses] turns to clay!

At his utterance the gods must now tremble!'
He turned away, saying he would not make the
    expedition.
They called Gerra, Anunitum's son;
The decision-maker spoke to him.

      (*understand virtual repeat of the previous
      speech*)

They called Shara, Ishtar's son;
The decision-maker spoke to him.

      (*understand virtual repeat of the previous
      speech*)

They were silenced; the gods despaired of advice.
The Igigi assembled, despondent, troubled.
The Lord of intelligence, wise one who dwells in the
    Apsu,
Spoke to his father (Anum) from his heart,
  'Let me give the command and pick from the
    assembly Anzum's conqueror.'
The Igigi listened to him saying this;
They were freed (from anxiety) and kissed his feet.
[He called (?)] the Great Goddess Mistress of . . .
    and announced her supremacy in the assembly,
  'Offer the powerful one, your superb beloved,
  Broad of chest, who forms the Seven of Battle:
  Ningirsu the powerful one, your superb beloved,
  Broad of chest, who forms the Seven of Battle.'
The Great Goddess, the supreme, listened to his
    saying this, and uttered, 'Yes'.[23]
The gods of the land were glad at her utterance; they
    were freed (from anxiety) and kissed her feet.
She called into the gods' assembly
Her son; she instructed her favourite, saying to
    him,
  'In the presence of Anum and Dagan . . .
They announced the course of their rites in the
    assembly.
  I gave birth to all the Igigi,
  Created the gods' assembly, I, Mammi,

Designated the Ellil-power for my brother, even
    kingship of heaven for Anum.
[Anzum has disrupted] the kingship that I
    designated.
He has rob[bed Ellil], rejected your father.
[Make (?)] a path, fix the hour,
Let light dawn for the gods whom I created.
Muster your devastating battle force,
Let your seven evil winds concentrate (?) on . . .
Conquer soaring Anzum,
And give peace to the earth, which I created—
    wreck (?) his dwelling.
Let terror move over him,
Let fear of (?) your battle force shake [in (?)
    him].

      (2 *lines missing*)

Make the devastating whirlwind rise up against
    him,
Set your arrow in the bow to carry poison.
May your shouted curse cast panic over him,
May he grope through the darkness, let his vision
    weaken and fail.
May he not flee from you, may his pinions fall in
    the clash.
Your face must keep changing, like a *gallu*-
    demon! Send out a fog, so that he cannot
    recognize your features.
May the moon's crescent not glow overhead, let
    broad daylight be as darkness for him.
Seize him by the throat; conquer Anzum
And let the winds bring the feathers as good news
To Ekur, to your father Ellil.
Let the winds bring the feathers as good news.'
The warrior listened to his mother's speech.
Keen for the fight, he felt powerful enough: he
    went back to the mountain (?).
She who harnesses the seven demons of wind (?),
Who dance in the dust, the seven whirlwinds,

[The Great Goddess] who harnesses the seven
    demons of wind (?)
Mustered his devastating battle force.
[   ] the gods (?) concentrate (?) on . . .
On the side of Anzum's mountain, the God met
    (him).
Anzu looked at him and shook with rage at him.
He charged (?), baring his teeth like an *ūmu-*
    demon; his mantle of radiance surrounded the
    mountain.

TABLET III

[Anzum looked at him] and shook with rage at him.
[He charged (?), baring his teeth like an *ūmu-*
    demon; his mantle of radiance surrounded the
    mountain.]
[He roared] like a lion in sudden rage.
[In utter fury] he shouted to the Warrior,
    ['I have taken away] every single rite!
    [Who are you,] to come to do [battle] against me?
    [Give] your reasons!'
His utterance [came out aggressively at him.] The
    warrior Ningirsu answered Anzum,
    '[I am the avenger (?) of] Duranki's god, who
    established Duranki, who decreed destinies.
    I have come [to . . . do battle against you,] to
    trample on you!
    [   ] whirlwinds, armour.'
[Anzum listened to] his speech,
Then roared his shout furiously amid the
    mountains.
[The armour-plated breast] was bathed in blood,
The battle force [whizzed and] roared [between
    them].
[The powerful, superb one,] Mammi's [son], trusted
    of Anum and Dagan, beloved of the far-sighted
    one,
Set the shaft to the bow, aimed it at him; but it did
    not go near Anzum: the shaft turned back.

Anzum shouted at it, 'You, shaft, that came: return
to your reed-thicket!

(*gap of about 46 lines*)

'[Cut off his pinions, detach both] right [and left].
[When he sees and emits] his utterance,
[Shout: "Wing to wing" (?)], don't panic!

(*2 lines fragmentary*)

Inundate [the mountain pastures], cause
confusion,
[   ] his throat.
[Then shall kingship enter] Ekur again. Then
shall rites return for the father who begot you!
[Then surely shall] shrines be created!
Establish your cult centres all [over the four
quarters!]'
[The God listened] to his father's message.
Keen for the fight, he felt powerful enough, and
went back to [the mountain (?)]
[The God prepared the Seven] of battle;
he [   ] the four winds.
[   ] the Earth quaked, tremors filled it.
His [   ] grew overcast, the sky darkened (?).
He tired him out, so that Anzum [shed] his pinions
in the clash of the tempest.

(*break*)

NOTES TO *ANZU*

Text: Hruška 1975, Hallo and Moran 1979, Saggs 1986.

1. 'Who darkens the sash': perhaps in the sense of sexual arousal.
2. This is an allusion to the Sumerian myth *Lugal-e* (van Dijk 1983).
3. Nothing is known of this heroic exploit from extant literature.
4. The epithet *šākin ṭēmi* translated 'decision-maker' here, is also the title
   of a high Babylonian administrative official.
5. For this use of *libšû-ma*, 'surely', compare AHw, 113a sub *bašû* G 1 f.
   (SMD)

6. A prestigious deity who was patron of a particular city could have stands or cellas within the main temples of other major gods in the latters' cities.

7. Or, the speech may end in the previous line.

8. 'Intelligence': literally, 'ear'.

9. 'Being': literally, 'stomach'.

10. The same couplet occurs in *Atrahasis*, I.

11. The text has 'his supremacy', probably by mistake.

12. The same couplet occurs in *Atrahasis*, I.

13. 'Lord': i.e. Bel. Contrast the equivalent title 'God', i.e. El or Ilu in OBV.

14. Reading the first word tentatively as *bi-šim*, since *bi-riq* cannot be a transitive form of the verb with 'path' as its object.

15. The old translation, 'carry his feathers to secret places', should almost certainly be abandoned.

16. Or, 'the insides of the mountains'.

17. Variant: 'Anu'.

18. Or, 'its surface'.

19. Body armour, made of overlapping bronze or copper scales sewn on to a leather garment, is attested in material remains from around 1400 BC.

20. The identification of this weapon *tilpānu* is still not certain.

21. Variant: 'My wing, my wing', *kappī kappī*, perhaps a corruption with *Gilgamesh*, VI in mind. See note 56 to *Gilgamesh*.

22. Variant shows that the text may be corrupt here; perhaps originally 'dance among the enemy'.

23. Literally: 'She made yes'. See note 7 to *Atrahasis*.

The Epic of Creation

The *Epic of Creation* is named an epic in a sense quite different to that of the *Epic of Gilgamesh*. Here is no struggle against fate, no mortal heroes, no sense of suspense over the outcome of events. The success of the hero-god Marduk (in the Babylonian version, Assur in the Assyrian version) is a foregone conclusion. None of the good gods is injured or killed; no tears are shed. Yet cosmic events are narrated: the earliest generations of gods are recounted leading up to the birth of the latest hero-god; the forces of evil and chaos are overcome, whereupon the present order of the universe can be established, with its religious centres, its divisions of time, its celestial bodies moving according to proper rules, and with mankind invented to serve the gods. The gods themselves behave in an orderly fashion: they assemble, discuss, agree, and elect their leaders in a gathering of males; after Tiamat's primeval parturition and the spawning of monsters, goddesses play no part in creating the civilized world, not even in creating mankind.

DATE OF COMPOSITION

The date of the epic cannot be fixed precisely. Tablets on which the work was written date mainly to the first millennium, and the epic continued well into the Seleucid period when it was used by Berossus in his *Babyloniaca*, and was still known in the fifth to sixth centuries AD, when the writer Damascius quoted from Berossus. But the tradition must be earlier. No date can be given to the hymnic-epic dialect in which it was written, for such dialectic features are not found in any groups of non-literary or more easily datable inscriptions. It is usually assumed that the version featuring Marduk is primary and the version featuring Assur is secondary, for no traces of Assyrian dialect are apparent. Although plenty of literary texts of the early second millennium have been found, none of them contains the *Epic of Creation*, but this, of course, is an argument from silence. A surprising lack of textual variation is to be found in the tablets, which came from a variety of sites and periods. This may be explained either as indicating that composition is relatively late, and that there is no oral background; or as showing that a text became 'canonized' if it was used for a particular ritual, as this epic was. When Sennacherib described scenes from the epic with which he decorated the doors of the Temple of the New Year Festival, he included details which are not found in the extant version, such as that the god Amurru was Assur's charioteer, and so we may deduce that there were indeed different versions in circulation.

If it is correct that the version with Marduk is the original one, the epic cannot have been composed before the reign of Sumu-la-el (1936–1901 BC), an Amorite ruler under whom Babylon, with Marduk as its patron god, first achieved eminence. Unfortunately, nothing is yet known of literary activity, style, or dialect during his rule. Hammurabi's reign (1848–1806 BC) has been suggested as a possibility, but there are no allusions to the epic in the poetic prologue and epilogue to his great Code of Laws, nor does that work contain features of the hymnic-epic dialect. The next possibility comes from the reign of an early Kassite king Agum-Kakrime in the sixteenth century, under whom the cult statue of Marduk was brought back from years in captivity and reinstated in Babylon. Such an occasion is likely to have inspired the composition of new hymns, and an inscription of that king described new doors for the temple as being decorated with composite monsters similar to those who join Tiamat's army in the epic. But they are not exactly the same, and some scholars have questioned the authenticity of the inscription; it may have been written several centuries later as a pious fraud, although a motive for such deception is hard to find. The reign of Nebuchadnezzar I (1125–1104 BC) has also been suggested, during which the cult statue of Marduk was returned once again from captivity, and Marduk is attested with the title 'King of the gods', but there is now good evidence to show that such a date for composition is too low. A lexical text known as *An-Anum* lists the major gods of the Babylonian pantheon together with their secondary names by assimilation and some of their epithets. A long section with the names of Marduk includes a subsection that corresponds very closely indeed to the names of Marduk which are found in Tablet VII of the epic. A slightly less close comparison can be made between Tablet VI and other names of Marduk in *An-Anum*. Evidence from a tablet with a list of gods found at the Hittite capital in Anatolia shows that *An-Anum* must have included the *Epic of Creation*'s list of Marduk's names long before the time of Nebuchadnezzar I, and probably excludes a dating to his reign.

Tablets VI and VII of the epic are not essential to the main work; they are obviously inappropriate to Assur, and so in dating the final two tablets to the Kassite period we still retain a number of options for dating the main epic, Tablets I–V, to some earlier period. A possible indication of Amorite origins comes from the West Semitic name of the weather-god, Addu, which is included among Marduk's names. The general theme of a god triumphing over the Sea to bring new order to the world is found in a myth from Ugarit and alluded to in the Old Testament, although much of the detail is very different from that of the epic. Sumerian temple hymns and poems refer to the heroic exploits of gods, but never to a triumph over the Sea; the Sea, whether as a god or goddess, is not important in the Sumerian pantheon. The evidence is very tenuous, but it remains possible that the basic story of the epic is Amorite, and that the last two tablets were added during the Kassite period, a time which is recognized increasingly as one of composition as well as compilation. If so, an Amorite god, rather than Marduk, may have been the 'original' hero.

RELATED THEMES IN *ANZU*

Considerable similarities are evident between the *Epic of Creation* and the *Epic of Anzu*, which was certainly popular from the Old Babylonian period onwards. Both tales involve possessing the Tablet of Destinies as a key element; the weapons used in the big fight are largely the same, and the structure of the crisis, in which three gods are sent in turn and the third alone triumphs, is alike in both. The proclamation of new names and titles for the victor is likewise remarkably similar. Direct dependence, however, is impossible to prove, and such similarities may better be interpreted as showing how a common stock of motifs existed, from which each composition drew freely. This way of looking at parallel items can also be applied to stock phrases, epithets, and similes, for a huge range of folk-tales must have existed in oral narrative, few of which were ever recorded in writing; *Anzu* and *Atrahasis* both contain references to tales of which we know nothing.

THE RITUAL CONNECTION

A ritual tablet is extant giving instructions for the performance of the New Year Festival in Babylon, and it says specifically that the *Epic of Creation* is to be recited (or possibly enacted) on the fourth day. The text has a long gap, and it is possible that more than one recital was envisaged. In any case, the epic is definitely used as part of a ritual, and it has a type of opening, like *Atrahasis*, consisting of a statement 'When . . .', which is quite distinct from the type 'I shall sing . . .', found in the standard version of *Gilgamesh* and in *Erra and Ishum*. The latter may introduce oral narrative in general, or may be a feature of the Late Bronze and Early Iron Ages rather than earlier periods; Old Babylonian *Gilgamesh* almost certainly did not have such an opening.

In *Gilgamesh* we are aware of an audience constantly demanding detail, whereas the *Creation* is vaguely phrased, designed to impress rather than to entertain. Compare and contrast how the bow, Marduk's weapon, and the various weapons of Gilgamesh, are described. In the *Creation* we are told: 'He created a bow and assigned it as his weapon'; later we are told that 'its form was extremely cunning'. This weapon was instrumental in slaying Tiamat, ending chaos and allowing orderly creation to proceed. But we do not hear the audience asking, 'How was it made? What materials were used? How much did it cost?' By contrast, we are told of Gilgamesh's weapons how, down at the forge, 'craftsmen sat down and gave it thought . . . they cast large axes, they cast axes weighing three talents each, they cast great daggers with blades weighing two talents each, and rivets at the sides of thirty minas each'.

The reason for this difference may be found in the nature of the New Year festival. This took place in the capital city in the month of Nisan (April), and the king had his mandate to rule renewed by the gods; to the ceremony came governors, plenipotentiaries, courtiers, top officials, and army officers to renew their oaths of loyalty to the king and royal family, just as the gods swore an oath to Marduk (or Assur), when he had been elected king. All of these subjects would have listened to the epic, and its recital would have impressed upon them how an orderly universe and its kingship should be organized: an ideal state of affairs used for propaganda purposes. When the king's subjects kiss his feet, they are doing no less than the great gods of heaven and earth did for Marduk. There is no question of rivalry; loyal support is absolute.

THE EPIC OF CREATION

When skies above were not yet named[1]
Nor earth below pronounced by name,
Apsu, the first one, their begetter
And maker Tiamat, who bore them all,[2]
Had mixed their waters together,
But had not formed pastures, nor discovered
    reed-beds;
When yet no gods were manifest,
Nor names pronounced, nor destinies decreed,
Then gods were born within them.
Lahmu (and) Lahamu emerged, their names
    pronounced.[3]
As soon as they matured, were fully formed,
Anshar (and) Kishar were born, surpassing them.
They passed the days at length, they added to the
    years.
Anu their first-born son rivalled his forefathers:
Anshar made his son Anu like himself,[4]
And Anu begot Nudimmud in his likeness.
He, Nudimmud, was superior to his forefathers:
Profound of understanding, he was wise, was very
    strong at arms.
Mightier by far than Anshar his father's begetter,
He had no rival among the gods his peers.
The gods of that generation would meet together
And disturb Tiamat, and their clamour reverberated.
They stirred up Tiamat's belly,
They were annoying her by playing inside
    Anduruna.
Apsu could not quell their noise
And Tiamat became mute before them;
However grievous their behaviour to her,
However bad their ways, she would indulge them.

Finally Apsu, begetter of the great gods,
Called out and addressed his vizier Mummu,
  'O Mummu, vizier who pleases me!
  Come, let us go to Tiamat!'
They went and sat in front of Tiamat,
And discussed affairs concerning the gods their
    sons.
Apsu made his voice heard
And spoke to Tiamat in a loud voice,
  'Their ways have become very grievous to me,
  By day I cannot rest, by night I cannot sleep.
  I shall abolish their ways and disperse them!
  Let peace prevail, so that we can sleep.'
When Tiamat heard this,
She was furious and shouted at her lover;
She shouted dreadfully and was beside herself with
    rage,
But then suppressed the evil in her belly.
  'How could we allow what we ourselves created to
    perish?
  Even though their ways are so grievous, we
    should bear it patiently.'
(Vizier) Mummu replied and counselled Apsu;
The vizier did not agree with the counsel of his
    earth mother.
  'O father, put an end to (their) troublesome ways,
  So that she may be allowed to rest by day and
    sleep at night.'
Apsu was pleased with him, his face lit up
At the evil he was planning for the gods his sons.
(Vizier) Mummu hugged him,
Sat on his lap and kissed him rapturously.
But everything they plotted between them
Was relayed to the gods their sons.
The gods listened and wandered about restlessly;
They fell silent, they sat mute.
Superior in understanding, wise and capable,
Ea who knows everything found out their plot,
Made for himself a design of everything, and laid it
    out correctly,

Made it cleverly, his pure spell was superb.
He recited it and it stilled the waters.
He poured sleep upon him so that he was sleeping
    soundly,
Put Apsu to sleep, drenched with sleep.
Vizier Mummu the counsellor (was in) a sleepless
    daze.
He (Ea) unfastened his belt, took off his crown,
Took away his mantle of radiance and put it on
    himself.
He held Apsu down and slew him;
Tied up Mummu and laid him across him.
He set up his dwelling on top of Apsu,
And grasped Mummu, held him by a nose-rope.
When he had overcome and slain his enemies,
Ea set up his triumphal cry over his foes.
Then he rested very quietly inside his private
    quarters
And named them Apsu and assigned chapels,
Founded his own residence there,
And Ea and Damkina his lover dwelt in splendour.
In the chamber of destinies, the hall of designs,
Bel, cleverest of the clever, sage of the gods, was
    begotten.
And inside Apsu, Marduk was created;
Inside pure Apsu, Marduk was born.
Ea his father created him,
Damkina his mother bore him.
He suckled the teats of goddesses;
The nurse who reared him filled him with
    awesomeness.
Proud was his form, piercing his stare,
Mature his emergence, he was powerful from the
    start.
Anu his father's begetter beheld him,[5]
And rejoiced, beamed; his heart was filled with joy.
He made him so perfect that his godhead was
    doubled.
Elevated far above them, he was superior in every
    way.

His limbs were ingeniously made beyond
     comprehension,
Impossible to understand, too difficult to perceive.
Four were his eyes, four were his ears;
When his lips moved, fire blazed forth.
The four ears were enormous
And likewise the eyes; they perceived everything.
Highest among the gods, his form was outstanding.
His limbs were very long, his height (?)
     outstanding.

   (*Anu cried out*)

 'Mariutu, Mariutu,[6]
 Son, majesty, majesty of the gods!'[7]
Clothed in the radiant mantle of ten gods, worn
     high above his head
Five fearsome rays were clustered above him.
Anu created the four winds and gave them birth,
Put them in his (Marduk's) hand, 'My son, let them
     play!'
He fashioned dust and made the whirlwind carry it;
He made the flood-wave and stirred up Tiamat.
Tiamat was stirred up, and heaved restlessly day
     and night.
The gods, unable to rest, had to suffer . . .
They plotted evil in their hearts, and
They addressed Tiamat their mother, saying,
 'Because they slew Apsu your lover and
 You did not go to his side but sat mute,
 He has created the four, fearful winds
 To stir up your belly on purpose, and we simply
  cannot sleep!
 Was your lover Apsu not in your heart?
 And (vizier) Mummu who was captured? No
  wonder you sit alone!
 Are you not a mother? You heave restlessly
 But what about us, who cannot rest? Don't you
  love us?
 Our grip(?) [is slack], (and) our eyes are sunken.

Remove the yoke of us restless ones, and let us
     sleep!
Set up a [battle cry] and avenge them!
Con[quer the enemy] and reduce them to
     nought!'
Tiamat listened, and the speech pleased her.
     'Let us act now, (?) as you were advising!
     The gods inside him (Apsu) will be disturbed,
     Because they adopted evil for the gods who begot
          them.'
They crowded round and rallied beside Tiamat.
They were fierce, scheming restlessly night and day.
They were working up to war, growling and raging.
They convened a council and created conflict.
Mother Hubur, who fashions all things,[8]
Contributed an unfaceable weapon: she bore giant
     snakes,
Sharp of tooth and unsparing of fang (?).
She filled their bodies with venom instead of blood.
She cloaked ferocious dragons with fearsome rays
And made them bear mantles of radiance, made
          them godlike,

          (*chanting this imprecation*)

     'Whoever looks upon them shall collapse in utter
          terror!
     Their bodies shall rear up continually and never
          turn away!'
She stationed a horned serpent, a *mušhuššu*-dragon,
     and a *lahmu*-hero,[9]
An *ugallu*-demon, a rabid dog, and a scorpion-man,
Aggressive *ūmu*-demons, a fish-man, and a
     bull-man
Bearing merciless weapons, fearless in battle.
Her orders were so powerful, they could not be
     disobeyed.
In addition she created eleven more likewise.
Over the gods her offspring who had convened a
     council for her

She promoted Qingu and made him greatest among
    them,
Conferred upon him leadership of the army,
    command of the assembly,
Raising the weapon to signal engagement,
    mustering combat-troops,
Overall command of the whole battle force.
And she set him upon a throne.
    'I have cast the spell for you and made you
        greatest in the gods' assembly!
    I have put into your power rule over all the gods!
    You shall be the greatest, for you are my only
        lover!
    Your commands shall always prevail over all the
        Anukki!'
Then she gave him the Tablet of Destinies and made
    him clasp it to his breast.
    'Your utterance shall never be altered! Your word
        shall be law!'
When Qingu was promoted and had received the
    Anu-power
And had decreed destinies for the gods his sons, (he
    said),
    'What issues forth from your mouths shall
        quench Fire!
    Your accumulated venom (?) shall paralyse the
        powerful!'
(*Catchline*)
Tiamat assembled his creatures
(*Colophon*)
First tablet, 'When skies above'. [Written] like [its]
    original [and inspected].
Tablet of Nabû-balaṭsu-iqbi son of Na'id-Marduk.
Hand of Nabû-balaṭsu-iqbi son of
        Na'id-Marduk [   ].

TABLET II

Tiamat assembled his creatures
And collected battle-units against the gods his
    offspring.
Tiamat did even more evil for posterity than Apsu.
It was reported (?) to Ea that she had prepared for
    war.
Ea listened to that report,
And was dumbfounded and sat in silence.
When he had pondered and his fury subsided,
He made his way to Anshar his father;
Came before Anshar, the father who begot him
And began to repeat to him everything that Tiamat
    had planned.
  'Father, Tiamat who bore us is rejecting us!
  She has convened an assembly and is raging out
    of control.
  The gods have turned to her, all of them,
  Even those whom you begot have gone over to
    her side,
  Have crowded round and rallied beside Tiamat.
  Fierce, scheming restlessly night and day,
  Working up to war, growling and raging,
  They have convened a council and created
    conflict.
  Mother Hubur, who fashions all things,
  Contributed an unfaceable weapon: she bore giant
    snakes,
  Sharp of tooth and unsparing of fang (?).
  She filled their bodies with venom instead of
    blood.
  She cloaked ferocious dragons with fearsome rays,
  And made them bear mantles of radiance, made
    them godlike,

        (*chanting this imprecation*)

  ''Whoever looks upon them shall collapse in utter
    terror!

Their bodies shall rear up continually and never
turn away!"
She stationed a horned serpent, a *mušḫuššu*-
dragon, and a *laḫmu*-hero,
An *ugallu*-demon, a rabid dog, and a
scorpion-man,
Aggressive *ūmu*-demons, a fish-man, and a
bull-man
Bearing merciless weapons, fearless in battle.
Her orders were so powerful, they could not be
disobeyed.
In addition she created eleven more likewise.
Over the gods her offspring who had convened a
council for her
She promoted Qingu, made him greatest among
them,
Conferred upon him leadership of the army,
command of the assembly,
Raising the weapon to signal engagement, to rise
up for combat,
Overall command of the whole battle force.
And she set him (*lit.* her) upon a throne.
"I have cast the spell for you and made you
greatest in the gods' assembly!
I have put into your power rule over all the
gods!
You shall be the greatest, for you are my only
lover!
Your commands shall always prevail over all the
Anukki!"
She gave him the Tablet of Destinies and made
him clasp it to his breast.
"Your utterance shall never be altered! Your
word shall be law!"
When Qingu was promoted and had received the
Anu-power,
And had decreed destinies for the gods her sons,
(he said),
"What issues forth from your mouths shall
quench Fire!

Your accumulated venom (?) shall paralyse the
   powerful!'' '
Anshar listened, and the report was very disturbing.
  'Woe!' he cried, he bit his lip,
His liver was inflamed, his belly would not rest.
His roar to Ea his son was quite weak.
  'My son, you who started the fight,
  You remain responsible for what you have done.
  You went and slew Apsu,
  And Tiamat, whom you enraged—where else
   is an opponent for her?'
Despairing of advice, the prince of good sense,
Creator of divine wisdom, Nudimmud,
With soothing speech, words of appeasement,
He answered Anshar his father nicely:
  'Father, you are the unfathomable fixer of fates!
  The power to create and to destroy is yours!
  O Anshar, you are the unfathomable fixer of fates!
  The power to create and destroy is yours!
  For the moment stay quiet at the words I shall tell you.
  Bear in mind what a good thing I did.
  Before I slew Apsu,
  Who else could he look to? Now (there are)
   these (monsters),
  Before I can rush up and extinguish him (Qingu)
  He will surely have destroyed me! Then what?'
Anshar listened, and the speech pleased him.
His heart prompted him to speak to Ea.
  'My son, your deeds were highly commendable,
  You can make a strike fierce, unbeatable.
  Ea, your deeds were highly commendable,
  You can make a strike fierce, unbeatable.
  But go towards Tiamat, sooth her uprising,
  May her fury abate at your spell.'
He listened to the words of his father Anshar.
He took the road, went straight on his way.
Ea went, he searched for Tiamat's strategy,
But then stayed silent and turned back.
He entered into the presence of the ruler Anshar,
In supplication he addressed him.
  'My father, Tiamat's actions were too much for me.

I searched for her course, but my spell was not
    equal to her.
Her strength is mighty, she is completely terrifying.
Her crowd is too powerful, nobody could defy her.
Her noise never lessens, it was too loud for me.
I feared her shout, and I turned back.
But father, you must not relax, you must send
    someone else to her.
However strong a woman's strength, it is not
    equal to a man's.
You must disband her regiments, confuse her advice,
Before she can impose her power on us.'

(*For the rest of this episode see Supplement 4, p. 342*)

Anshar was speechless, and stared at the ground;
He gnashed his teeth (?) and shook his head (in
    despair) at Ea.
Now, the Igigi assembled, all the Anukki.
They sat silently (for a while), tight-lipped.

      (Finally they spoke)

'Will no (other) god come forward? Is [fate]
    fixed?
Will no one go out to face Tiamat with [   ]?'
Then Ea from his secret dwelling called
[The perfect] one (?) of Anshar, father of the great
    gods,
Whose heart is perfect like a fellow-citizen or
    countryman (?),
The mighty heir who was to be his father's
    champion,
Who rushes (fearlessly) into battle: Marduk the
    Hero!
He told him his innermost design, saying,
    'O Marduk, take my advice, listen to your father!
You are the son who sets his heart at rest!
Approach Anshar, drawing near to him,
And make your voice heard, stand your ground:
    he will be calmed by the sight of you.'[11]
The Lord rejoiced at the word of his father,

And he approached and stood before Anshar.
Anshar looked at him, and his heart was filled with
    joy.
He kissed him on the lips, put away his
    trepidation.

   (*Then Marduk addressed him, saying*)

'Father, don't stay so silent, open your lips,
Let me go, and let me fulfil your heart's desire.
Anshar, don't stay so silent, open your lips,
Let me go, and let me fulfil your heart's desire.'

   (*Anshar replied*)

'What kind of man has ordered you out (to) his
    war?
My son, (don't you realize that) it is Tiamat, of
    womankind, who will advance against you with
    arms?'

   (*Marduk answered*)

'Father, my creator, rejoice and be glad!
You shall soon set your foot upon the neck of
    Tiamat!
Anshar, my creator, rejoice and be glad,
You shall soon set your foot upon the neck of
    Tiamat.'

   (*Anshar replied*)

'Then go, son, knowing all wisdom!
Quell Tiamat with your pure spell!
Set forth immediately (in) the storm chariot;
Let its [   ] be not driven out, but turn
    (them?) back!'
The Lord rejoiced at the word of his father;
His heart was glad and he addressed his father,
   'Lord of the gods, fate of the great gods,
   If indeed I am to be your champion,
   If I am to defeat Tiamat and save your lives,
   Convene the council, name a special fate,
   Sit joyfully together in Ubshu-ukkinakku:

My own utterance shall fix fate instead of you!
Whatever I create shall never be altered!
The decree of my lips shall never be revoked,
      never changed!'
(*Catchline*)
Anshar made his voice heard
(*Colophon*)
Second tablet, 'When skies above'. [Written]
      according to [   ]
[   ] a copy from Assur.
[   ]

                    TABLET III

Anshar made his voice heard
And addressed his speech to Kakka his vizier,
    'O Kakka, vizier who pleases me!
I shall send you to Lahmu and Lahamu.
You know how to probe, you are skilled in
      speaking.
Have the gods my fathers brought before me;
Let all the gods be brought to me.
Let there be conversation, let them sit at a
      banquet,
Let them eat grain, let them drink choice wine,
(And then) let them decree a destiny for Marduk
      their champion.
Set off, Kakka, go and stand before them, and
Everything that I am about to tell you, repeat to
      them,
"Anshar your son has sent me,
He has told me to report his heart's message,
To say, "Tiamat who bore us is rejecting us!
She has convened a council, and is raging out of
      control.
The gods have turned to her, all of them,
Even those whom you begot have gone over to
      her side,
Have crowded round and rallied beside Tiamat.

They are fierce, scheming restlessly night and
    day.
They are working up to war, growling and
    raging.
They convened a council and created conflict.
Mother Hubur, who fashions all things,
Contributed an unfaceable weapon: she bore giant
    snakes,
Sharp of tooth and unsparing of fang (?).
She filled their bodies with venom instead of
    blood.
She cloaked ferocious dragons with fearsome rays,
And made them bear mantles of radiance, made
    them godlike,

    (*chanting this imprecation*)

"Whoever looks upon them shall collapse in utter
    terror!
Their bodies shall rear up continually, and never
    turn away!"
She stationed a horned serpent, a *mušhuššu*-
    dragon, and a *lahmu*-hero,
An *ugallu*-demon, a rabid dog, and a
    scorpion-man,
Aggressive *ūmu*-demons, a fish-man, and a
    bull-man
Bearing merciless weapons, fearless in battle.
Her orders were so powerful, they could not be
    disobeyed.
In addition she created eleven more likewise.
Over the gods her offspring who had convened a
    council for her
She promoted Qingu, made him greatest among
    them,
Conferred upon him leadership of the army,
    command of the assembly,
Raising the weapon to signal engagement, to rise
    up for combat,
Overall command of the whole battle force.
And she set him upon a throne.

"I have cast the spell for you and made you
  greatest in the gods' assembly!
I have put into your power rule over all the gods!
You shall be the greatest, for you are my only
  lover!
Your commands shall always prevail over all the
  Anunnaki!"
She gave him the Tablet of Destinies, and made
  him clasp it to his breast.
"Your utterance shall never be altered! His
  (! Your) word shall be law!"
When Qingu was promoted and had received the
  Anu-power[12]
And had decreed destinies for the gods her sons,
  (he said),
"What issues forth from your mouths shall
  quench Fire!
Your accumulated venom (?) shall paralyse the
  powerful."
I sent Anu, but he was unable to face her.
Nudimmud panicked and turned back.
Then Marduk, sage of the gods, your son, came
  forward.
He wanted of his own free will to confront
  Tiamat.
He addressed his words to me,
"If indeed I am to be your champion,
To defeat Tiamat and save your lives,
Convene the council, name a special fate,
Sit joyfully together in Ubshu-ukkinakku:
And let me, my own utterance, fix fate instead of
  you.
Whatever I create shall never be altered!
Let a decree from my lips never be revoked, never
  changed!"
Hurry and decree your destiny for him quickly,
So that he may go and face your formidable
  enemy!" '
Kakka set off and went on his way,
And before Lahmu and Lahamu the gods his fathers

Prostrated himself and kissed the earth in front of
   them,
Then straightened up and stood and spoke to
   them,
   'Anshar your son has sent me.
   He has told me to report his personal message,
   To say, "Tiamat who bore us is rejecting us!
   She has convened a council, and is raging out of
      control.
   The gods have turned to her, all of them,
   Even those whom you begot have gone over to
      her side,
   Have crowded round and rallied beside Tiamat.
   Fierce, scheming restlessly night and day,
   Working up to war, growling and raging,
   They have convened a council and created
      conflict.
   Mother Hubur, who fashions all things,
   Contributed an unfaceable weapon: she bore giant
      snakes,
   Sharp of tooth and unsparing of fang (?).
   She filled their bodies with venom instead of
      blood.
   She cloaked ferocious dragons with fearsome rays,
   And made them bear mantles of radiance, made
      them godlike,

      (*chanting this imprecation*)

   "Whoever looks upon them shall collapse in utter
      terror!
   Their bodies shall rear up continually, and never
      turn away!"
   She stationed a horned serpent, a *mušuššu*-
      dragon, and a *lahmu*-hero,
   Ugallu-demons, rabid dogs, and a scorpion-man,
   Aggressive *ūmu*-demons, a fish-man, a bull-man
   Bearing merciless weapons, fearless in battle.
   Her orders were so powerful, they could not be
      disobeyed.
   In addition she created eleven more likewise.

Over the gods her offspring who had convened a
  council for her
She promoted Qingu, made him greatest among
  them,
Conferred upon him leadership of the army,
  command of the assembly,
Raising the weapon to signal engagement, to rise
  up for combat,
Overall command of the whole battle force.
And she set him upon a throne.
"I have cast the spell for you, and have made you
  greatest in the gods' assembly!
I have put into your power rule over all the gods!
You shall be the greatest, for you are my only
  lover!
Your commands shall always prevail over all the
  Anunnaki!"
She gave him the Tablet of Destinies, and made
  him clasp it to his breast.
"Your utterance shall never be altered! Your
  word shall be law!"
When Qingu was promoted and had received the
  Anu-power
And had decreed destinies for the gods her sons,
  (he said),
"What issues forth from your mouths shall
  quench Fire!
Your accumulated venom (?) shall paralyse the
  powerful!"
I sent Anu, but he was unable to face her.
Nudimmud panicked and turned back.
Then Marduk, sage of the gods, your son, came
  forward.
He wanted of his own free will to confront
  Tiamat.
He spoke his words to me:
"If indeed I am to be your champion,
To defeat Tiamat and to save your lives,
Convene the council, name a special fate,
Sit joyfully together in Ubshu-ukkinakku:

And let me, my own utterance, fix fate instead of
    you.
Whatever I create shall never be altered!
Let a decree from my lips never be revoked, never
    changed!''
Hurry and decree your destinies for him quickly,
So that he may go and face your formidable
    enemy."'
Lahmu and Lahamu listened and cried out aloud.
All the Igigi then groaned dreadfully,
    'How terrible! Until he (Anshar) decided to report
    to us,
    We did not even know what Tiamat was doing.'
They milled around and then came,
All the great gods who fix the fates,
Entered into Anshar's presence and were filled with
    joy.
Each kissed the other: in the assembly [   ]
There was conversation, they sat at the banquet,
Ate grain, drank choice wine,
Let sweet beer trickle through their drinking straws.
Their bodies swelled as they drank the liquor;
They became very carefree, they were merry,
And they decreed destiny for Marduk their
    champion.
(*Catchline*)
They founded a princely shrine for him

TABLET IV

They founded a princely shrine for him,
And he took up residence as ruler before his fathers,
    (*who proclaimed*)
    'You are honoured among the great gods.
    Your destiny is unequalled, your word (has the
    power of) Anu!
    O Marduk, you are honoured among the great
    gods.
    Your destiny is unequalled, your word (has the
    power of) Anu!

From this day onwards your command shall not
 be altered.
Yours is the power to exalt and abase.
May your utterance be law, your word never be
 falsified.
None of the gods shall transgress your limits.[13]
May endowment, required for the gods' shrines
Wherever they have temples, be established for
 your place.
O Marduk, you are our champion!
We hereby give you sovereignty over all of the
 whole universe.
Sit in the assembly and your word shall be
 pre-eminent!
May your weapons never miss (the mark), may
 they smash your enemies!
O lord, spare the life of him who trusts in
 you,[14]
But drain the life of the god who has espoused
 evil!'
They set up in their midst one constellation,[15]
And then they addressed Marduk their son,
 'May your decree, O lord, impress the gods!
 Command to destroy and to recreate, and let it be
  so!
 Speak and let the constellation vanish!
 Speak to it again and let the constellation
  reappear.'
He spoke, and at his word the constellation
 vanished.
He spoke to it again and the constellation was
 recreated.
When the gods his fathers saw how effective his
 utterance was,
They rejoiced, they proclaimed: 'Marduk is King!'
They invested him with sceptre, throne, and staff-
 of-office.
They gave him an unfaceable weapon to crush the
 foe.
 'Go, and cut off the life of Tiamat!

Let the winds bear her blood to us as good
news!'[16]
The gods his fathers thus decreed the destiny of the
lord
And set him on the path of peace and obedience.
He fashioned a bow, designated it as his weapon,
Feathered the arrow, set it in the string.
He lifted up a mace and carried it in his right hand,
Slung the bow and quiver at his side,
Put lightning in front of him,
His body was filled with an ever-blazing flame.
He made a net to encircle Tiamat within it,
Marshalled the four winds so that no part of her
could escape:
South Wind, North Wind, East Wind, West Wind,
The gift of his father Anu, he kept them close to
the net at his side.
He created the *imhullu*-wind (evil wind), the
tempest, the whirlwind,[17]
The Four Winds, the Seven Winds, the tornado, the
unfaceable facing wind.
He released the winds which he had created, seven
of them.
They advanced behind him to make turmoil inside
Tiamat.
The lord raised the flood-weapon, his great weapon,
And mounted the frightful, unfaceable
storm-chariot.
He had yoked to it a team of four and had
harnessed to its side
'Slayer', 'Pitiless', 'Racer', and 'Flyer';
Their lips were drawn back, their teeth carried
poison.
They know not exhaustion, they can only devastate.
He stationed on his right Fiercesome Fight and
Conflict,
On the left Battle to knock down every
contender (?).
Clothed in a cloak of awesome armour,[18]
His head was crowned with a terrible radiance.

The Lord set out and took the road,
And set his face towards Tiamat who raged out of
    control.
In his lips he gripped a spell,
In his hand he grasped a herb to counter poison.
Then they thronged about him, the gods thronged
    about him;
The gods his fathers thronged about him, the gods
    thronged about him.
The Lord drew near and looked into the middle of
    Tiamat:[19]
He was trying to find out the strategy of Qingu her
    lover.
As he looked, his mind became confused,[20]
His will crumbled and his actions were muddled.
As for the gods his helpers, who march(ed) at his
    side,[21]
When they saw the warrior, the leader, their looks
    were strained.
Tiamat cast her spell. She did not even turn her
    neck.
In her lips she was holding falsehood, lies,
    (wheedling),[22]
    '[How powerful is] your attacking force, O lord of
    the gods!
    The whole assembly of them has gathered to your
    place!'

        (*But he ignored her blandishments*)

The Lord lifted up the flood-weapon, his great
    weapon
And sent a message to Tiamat who feigned
    goodwill, saying:
    'Why are you so friendly on the surface
    When your depths conspire to muster a battle
    force?[23]
    Just because the sons were noisy (and)
    disrespectful to their fathers,
    Should you, who gave them birth, reject
    compassion?

You named Qingu as your lover,
You appointed him to rites of Anu-power,
  wrongfully his.
You sought out evil for Anshar, king of the gods,
So you have compounded your wickedness against
  the gods my fathers!
Let your host prepare! Let them gird themselves
  with your weapons!
Stand forth, and you and I shall do single
  combat!'
When Tiamat heard this,
She went wild, she lost her temper.
Tiamat screamed aloud in a passion,
Her lower parts shook together from the depths.
She recited the incantation and kept casting her
  spell.
Meanwhile the gods of battle were sharpening their
  weapons.
Face to face they came, Tiamat and Marduk, sage of
  the gods.
They engaged in combat, they closed for battle.
The Lord spread his net and made it encircle her,
To her face he dispatched the *imhullu*-wind, which
  had been behind:
Tiamat opened her mouth to swallow it,
And he forced in the *imhullu*-wind so that she could
  not close her lips.
Fierce winds distended her belly;
Her insides were constipated and she stretched her
  mouth wide.
He shot an arrow which pierced her belly,
Split her down the middle and slit her heart,
Vanquished her and extinguished her life.
He threw down her corpse and stood on top of her.
When he had slain Tiamat, the leader,
He broke up her regiments; her assembly was
  scattered.
Then the gods her helpers, who had marched at her
  side,
Began to tremble, panicked, and turned tail.

Although he allowed them to come out and spared
  their lives,
They were surrounded, they could not flee.
Then he tied them up and smashed their weapons.
They were thrown into the net and sat there
  ensnared.
They cowered back, filled with woe.
They had to bear his punishment, confined to
  prison.
And as for the dozens of creatures, covered in
  fearsome rays,
The gang of demons who all marched on her right,
He fixed them with nose-ropes and tied their arms.
He trampled their battle-filth (?) beneath him.
As for Qingu, who had once been the greatest
  among them,
He defeated him and counted him among the dead
  gods,[24]
Wrested from him the Tablet of Destinies,
  wrongfully his,[25]
Sealed it with (his own) seal and pressed it to his
  breast.
When he had defeated and killed his enemies
And had proclaimed the submissive (?) foe his slave,
And had set up the triumphal cry of Anshar ov   all
  the enemy,
And had achieved the desire of Nudimmud, Marduk
  the warrior
Strengthened his hold over the captive gods,
And to Tiamat, whom he had ensnared, he turned
  back.
The Lord trampled the lower part of Tiamat,
With his unsparing mace smashed her skull,
Severed the arteries of her blood,
And made the North Wind carry it off as good
  news.[26]
His fathers saw it and were jubilant: they rejoiced,
Arranged to greet him with presents, greetings
  gifts.[27]
The Lord rested, and inspected her corpse.

He divided the monstrous shape and created marvels
(from it).
He sliced her in half like a fish for drying:
Half of her he put up to roof the sky,
Drew a bolt across and made a guard hold it.
Her waters he arranged so that they could not
escape.
He crossed the heavens and sought out a shrine;
He levelled Apsu, dwelling of Nudimmud.
The Lord measured the dimensions of Apsu
And the large temple (Eshgalla), which he built in
its image, was Esharra:
In the great shrine Esharra, which he had created as
the sky,
He founded cult centres for Anu, Ellil, and Ea.
(*Catchline*)
He fashioned stands for the great gods
(*Colophon*)
146 lines. Fourth tablet 'When skies above'. Not
complete.
Written according to a tablet whose lines were
cancelled.
Nabu-belshu (son of) Na'id-Marduk, son of a smith,
wrote it for the life of himself
And the life of his house, and deposited (it) in
Ezida.

TABLET V

He fashioned stands for the great gods.
As for the stars, he set up constellations
corresponding to them.
He designated the year and marked out its divisions,
Apportioned three stars each to the twelve months.
When he had made plans of the days of the year,
He founded the stand of Neberu to mark out their
courses,
So that none of them could go wrong or stray.
He fixed the stand of Ellil and Ea together with it,

Opened up gates in both ribs,
Made strong bolts to left and right.
With her liver he located the heights;
He made the crescent moon appear, entrusted night
　　(to it)
And designated it the jewel of night to mark out the
　　days.
　'Go forth every month without fail in a corona,
　At the beginning of the month, to glow over the
　　land.
　You shine with horns to mark out six days;
　On the seventh day the crown is half.
　The fifteenth day shall always be the mid-point,
　　the half of each month.[28]
　When Shamash looks at you from the horizon,
　Gradually shed your visibility and begin to wane.
　Always bring the day of disappearance close to
　　the path of Shamash,[29]
　And on the thirtieth day, the [year] is always
　　equalized, for Shamash is (responsible for) the
　　year.
　A sign [shall appear (?)]: sweep along its path.
　Then always approach the [　　　　　　] and
　　judge the case.
　[　　　　　] the Bowstar to kill and rob.[30]

　　　　　(15 lines broken)

At the New Year's Festival
Year [　　　　　　　　　　　　　　　]
May [　　　　　　　　　　　　　　　]
The bolt of the exit [　　　　　　　　　]
From the days [　　　　　　　　　　　]
The watches of night and day [　　　　　]
The spittle of Tiamat [　　　　　　　　]'
Marduk [　　　　　　　　　　　　　　]
He put into groups and made clouds scud.
Raising winds, making rain,
Making fog billow, by collecting her poison,
He assigned for himself and let his own hand
　　control it.

He placed her head, heaped up [   ]
Opened up springs: water gushed out.
He opened the Euphrates and the Tigris from her
      eyes,[31]
Closed her nostrils, [   ].
He piled up clear-cut mountains from her udder,
Bored waterholes to drain off the catchwater.
He laid her tail across, tied it fast as the cosmic
      bond,
And [   ] the Apsu beneath his feet.
He set her thigh to make fast the sky,
With half of her he made a roof; he fixed the earth.
He [   ] the work, made the insides of Tiamat
      surge,
Spread his net, made it extend completely.
He ... [   ] heaven and earth
[   ] their knots, to coil [   ]
When he had designed its cult, created its rites,
He threw down the reins (and) made Ea take
      (them).
The Tablet of Destinies, which Qingu had
      appropriated, he fetched
And took it and presented it for a first reading (?) to
      Anu.[32]
[The gods (?) of] battle whom he had ensnared were
      disentangled (?);
He led (them) as captives into the presence of his
      fathers.
And as for the eleven creatures that Tiamat had
      created, he [   ],
Smashed their weapons, tied them at his feet,
Made images of them and had them set up at the
      door of Apsu.[33]
   'Let this be a sign that will never in future be
      forgotten!'
The gods looked, and their hearts were full of joy at
      him.
Lahmu and Lahamu and all his fathers
Embraced him, and Anshar the king proclaimed that
      there should be a reception for him.

Anu, Enlil, and Ea each presented him with gifts.
[   ] Damkina his mother exclaimed with joy
    at him;
She made him beam [inside (?)] his fine (?) house.
He (Marduk) appointed Usmu, who had brought his
    greetings present as good news,
To be vizier of the Apsu, to take care of shrines.
The Igigi assembled, and all of them did obeisance
    to him.
The Anunnaki, each and every one, kissed his feet.
The whole assembly collected together to prostrate
    themselves.
[   ] they stood, they bowed, 'Yes, King
    indeed!'
[   ] his fathers took their fill of his
    manliness,
[They took off his clothes] which were enveloped in
    the dust of combat.
[   ] the gods were attentive to him.
With cypress [   ] they sprinkled (?) his
    body.
He put on a princely garment,
A royal aura, a splendid crown.
He took up a mace and grasped it in his right hand.
[   ] his left hand.
[   ]
He set a [*mušhuššu*-dragon (?)] at his feet,
Placed upon [   ]
Slung the staff of peace and obedience at his side.
When the mantle of radiance [   ]
And his net was holding (?) fearful Apsu,
A bull [   ]
In the inner chamber of his throne [   ]
In his cellar [   ]
The gods, all that existed, [   ]
Lahmu and Lahamu [   ]
Made their voices heard and spoke to the Igigi,
    'Previously Marduk was (just) our beloved son
    But now he is your king. Take heed of his
        command.'

Next they spoke and proclaimed in unison,
   'LUGAL-DIMMER-ANKIA is his name. Trust in
      him![34]
   When they gave kingship to Marduk,
   They spoke an oration for him, for blessing and
      obedience.
   Henceforth you shall be the provider of shrines
      for us.
   Whatever you command, we shall perform
      ourselves.'
Marduk made his voice heard and spoke,
Addressed his words to the gods his fathers,
   'Over the Apsu, the sea-green dwelling,
   In front of (?) Esharra, which I created for you,
   (Where) I strengthened the ground beneath it for
      a shrine,
   I shall make a house to be a luxurious dwelling
      for myself
   And shall found his cult centre within it,
   And I shall establish my private quarters, and
      confirm my kingship.
   Whenever you come up from the Apsu for an
      assembly,
   Your night's resting place shall be in it, receiving
      you all.
   Whenever you come down from the sky for an
      assembly,
   Your night's resting place shall be in it, receiving
      you all.
   I hereby name it Babylon, home of the great
      gods.
   We shall make it the centre of religion.'
The gods his fathers listened to this command of
      his,
   '[   ] . . .
   Who has [   ] your [   ]
   More than you by yourself have created?
   Who has [   ] your [   ]
   More earth than you by yourself have created?
   Babylon, whose name you have just pronounced,

Found there our night's resting place forever!
[   ] let them bring our regular offerings
[   ]
Whatever our work that we [   ]
There [   ] his toil [   ].'
They rejoiced [   ]
The gods [   ] them
Who knows [   ] them light
He made his voice heard, his command [   ]
[   ] them [   ]
[   ]
They did obeisance to him and the gods spoke to
    him,
They addressed their lord Lugal-dimmer-ankia,
  'Previously the Lord was [our beloved] son.
  But now he is our king. We shall take heed of his
    command.
    [   ] gave long life [   ]
    [   ] the mantle of radiance, the mace,
    and staff.
    [   ] all the lore of sages.
    We [   ].'
(*Catchline*)
When Marduk heard the speech of the gods
(*Colophon*)
Fifth tablet, 'When skies above'
Palace of Assurbanipal, king of the world, king of
    Assyria.

TABLET VI

When Marduk heard the speech of the gods,
He made up his mind to perform miracles.
He spoke his utterance to Ea,
And communicated to him the plan that he was
    considering.
  'Let me put blood together, and make bones too.
  Let me set up primeval man: Man shall be his
    name.

Let me create a primeval man.
The work of the gods shall be imposed (on him),
   and so they shall be at leisure.
Let me change the ways of the gods miraculously,
So they are gathered as one yet divided in two.'
Ea answered him and spoke a word to him,
Told him his plan for the leisure of the gods.
   'Let one who is hostile to them be surrendered
      (up),
   Let him be destroyed, and let people be created
      (from him).
   Let the great gods assemble,
   Let the culprit be given up, and let them convict
      him.'
Marduk assembled the great gods,
Gave (them) instructions pleasantly, gave orders.
The gods paid attention to what he said.
The king addressed his words to the Anunnaki,
   'Your election of me shall be firm and foremost.
   I shall declare the laws, the edicts within my
      power.
   Whosoever started the war,
   And incited Tiamat, and gathered an army,
   Let the one who started the war be given up to
      me,
   And he shall bear the penalty for his crime, that
      you may dwell in peace.'
The Igigi, the great gods, answered him,
Their lord Lugal-dimmer-ankia, counsellor of
      gods,
   'It was Qingu who started the war,
   He who incited Tiamat and gathered an army!'
They bound him and held him in front of Ea,
Imposed the penalty on him and cut off his blood.
He created mankind from his blood,[35]
Imposed the toil of the gods (on man) and released
      the gods from it.
When Ea the wise had created mankind,
Had imposed the toil of the gods on them—
That deed is impossible to describe,

For Nudimmud performed it with the miracles of
    Marduk—
Then Marduk the king divided the gods,
The Anunnaki, all of them, above and below.
He assigned his decrees to Anu to guard,
Established three hundred as a guard in the sky;
Did the same again when he designed the
    conventions of earth,
And made the six hundred dwell in both heaven and
    earth.
When he had directed all the decrees,
Had divided lots for the Anunnaki, of heaven and of
    earth,[36]
The Anunnaki made their voices heard
And addressed Marduk their lord,
    'Now, O Lord, that you have set us free,
    What are our favours from you?
    We would like to make a shrine with its own
        name.
    We would like our night's resting place to be in
        your private quarters, and to rest there.
    Let us found a shrine, a sanctuary there.
    Whenever we arrive, let us rest within it.'
When Marduk heard this,
His face lit up greatly, like daylight.
    'Create Babylon, whose construction you
        requested!
    Let its mud bricks be moulded, and build high the
        shrine!'
The Anunnaki began shovelling.
For a whole year they made bricks for it.
When the second year arrived,
They had raised the top of Esagila in front of (?) the
    Apsu;
They had built a high ziggurrat for the Apsu.
They founded a dwelling for Anu, Ellil, and Ea
    likewise.
In ascendancy he settled himself in front of them,
And his 'horns' look down at the base of Esharra.[37]
When they had done the work on Esagila,

(And) the Anunnaki, all of them, had fashioned
    their individual shrines,
The three hundred Igigi of heaven and the
    Anunnaki of the Apsu all assembled.
The Lord invited the gods his fathers to attend a
    banquet
In the great sanctuary which he had created as his
    dwelling.
  'Indeed, Bab-ili (is) your home too![38]
  Sing for joy there, dwell in happiness!'
The great gods sat down there,
And set out the beer mugs; they attended the
    banquet.
When they had made merry within,
They themselves made a *taqribtu*-offering in
    splendid Esagila.
All the decrees (and) designs were fixed.
All the gods divided the stations of heaven and
    earth.
The fifty great gods were present, and
The gods fixed the seven destinies for the cult.
The Lord received the bow, and set his weapon
    down in front of them.
The gods his fathers looked at the net which he had
    made,
Looked at the bow, how miraculous her construction,
And his fathers praised the deeds that he had done.
Anu raised (the bow) and spoke in the assembly of
    gods,
He kissed the bow. 'May she go far!'[39]
He gave to the bow her names, saying,
  'May Long and Far be the first, and Victorious
    the second;
  Her third name shall be Bowstar, for she shall
    shine in the sky.'
He fixed her position among the gods her
    companions.
When Anu had decreed the destiny of the bow,
He set down her royal throne. 'You are highest of
    the gods!'

And Anu made her sit in the assembly of gods.
The great gods assembled
And made Marduk's destiny highest; they
    themselves did obeisance.
They swore an oath for themselves,
And swore on water and oil, touched their throats.[40]
Thus they granted that he should exercise the
    kingship of the gods
And confirmed for him mastery of the gods of
    heaven and earth.

Anshar gave him another name: ASARLUHI.
    'At the mention of his name we shall bow down!
    The gods are to pay heed to what he says:
    His command is to have priority above and below.
    The son who avenged us shall be the highest!
    His rule shall have priority; let him have no
        rival!
    Let him act as shepherd over the black-headed
        people, his creation.
    Let his way be proclaimed in future days, never
        forgotten.
    He shall establish great *nindabû*-offerings for his
        fathers.
    He shall take care of them, he shall look after
        their shrines.
    He shall let them smell the *qutrinnu*-offering,
        and make their chant joyful.
    Let him breathe on earth as freely as he always
        does in heaven.
    Let him designate the black-headed people to
        revere him,
    That mankind may be mindful of him, and name
        him as their god.
    Let their (interceding) goddess pay attention when
        he opens his mouth.
    Let *nindabû*-offerings be brought [to] their god
        (and) their goddess.
    Let them never be forgotten! Let them cleave to
        their god.

Let them keep their country pre-eminent, and
   always build shrines.
Though the black-headed people share out the
   gods,[41]
As for us, no matter by which name we call him,
   he shall be our god.
Come, let us call him by his fifty names!
His ways shall be proclaimed, and his deeds
   likewise!

MARDUK

Whose father Anu designated him at the moment
   of his birth,
To be in charge of pasturage and watering places,
   to enrich their stalls,
Who overwhelmed the riotous ones with his
   flood-weapon
And saved the gods his fathers from hardship.
Let THE SON, MAJESTY OF THE GODS be his name!
In his bright light may they walk forever more:
The people whom he created, the form of life that
   breathes.
He imposed the work of the gods (on them) so
   that they might rest.
Creation and abolition, forgiveness and
   punishment—
Such are at his disposal, so let them look to him.
MARUKKA—he is the god who created them.[42]
He pleases the Anunnaki and gives rest to the
   Igigi.
MARUTUKKU—he is the help of country, city, and
   his people.
Him shall the people revere forever.
MERSHAKUSHU—fierce yet considerate, furious yet
   merciful.[43]
Generous is his heart, controlled are his
   emotions.
LUGAL-DIMMER-ANKIA—his name which we gave
   him in our assembly.
We made his command higher than the gods his
   fathers'.

He is indeed BEL of the gods of heaven and earth,
  all of them,
The king at whose instruction the gods are awed
  above and below.
NARI-LUGAL-DIMMER-ANKIA is a name that we have
  given him as director of all the gods,
Who founded our dwellings in heaven and earth
  out of difficulties,
And who shared out the stations for the Igigi and
  Anunnaki.
At his names may the gods tremble and quake in
  (their) dwellings.

ASARLUHI (first) is his name which his father Anu
  gave him,
He shall be the light of the gods, strong leader,
Who like his name is the protecting spirit of god
  and country.
He spared our dwellings in the great battle despite
  difficulties.
Second, they called him Asarluhi as NAMTILA, the
  god who gives life,[44]
Who restored all the damaged gods as if they
  were his own creation.[45]
Bel, who revives dead gods with his pure
  incantation,
Who destroys those who oppose him but . . .s the
  enemy.
Asarluhi third as NAMRU, whose name was given
  (thus),
The pure god who purifies our path.'[46]

Anshar, Lahmu, and Lahamu called his three names;
They pronounced them to the gods their sons,
  'We have given him each of these three names.
  Now you, pronounce his names as we did!'
The gods rejoiced, and obeyed their command.
In Ubshu-ukkinakku they deliberated their counsel.
  'Let us elevate the name of the son, the warrior,
  Our champion who looks after us!'

They sat in their assembly and began to call out the
destinies,
Pronounced his name in all their rites.
(_Catchline_)
Asare, bestower of ploughland, who fixes (its)
boundaries

TABLET VII

'ASARE, bestower of ploughland, who fixes (its)
boundaries,[47]
Creator of grain and linseed, producer of
vegetation.
ASAR-ALIM, whose weighty counsel in the
Chamber of Council is most valued;
The gods, even those who know no fear, pay heed
to him.
ASAR-ALIM-NUNA, the honoured one, the light of
the father who begot him,
Who directs the orders of Anu, Ellil, Ea, and
D[amkina?].
He indeed is their provider, who allocates their
incomes,
Whose farmland makes a surplus for the country.

He is TUTU, (first) as creator of their renewal.
He shall purify their shrines, that they may stay
at rest.
He shall invent an incantation, that the gods may
be at peace.
Even if they should rise up in anger, he shall turn
them back.
He shall be pre-eminent in the assembly of the
gods his fathers;
None among the gods shall rival him.
He is Tutu, (second) as ZI-UKKINA, the inspiration
of his people,
Who fixed the pure skies for the gods,[48]
Who set their ways and marked out their
stations.

May he not be forgotten by teeming humanity,
     may they uphold his work.[49]
Thirdly, they named him Tutu as ZIKU, upholder
     of purification,
The god of sweet breath, lord of obedience and
     consent,
Producer of riches and abundance, who maintains
     a surplus,
Who turns whatever is scant into plenty.
Even in the worst hardship we can smell his
     sweet breath!
May they speak in worship and sing his praises!
Fourthly, let the people glorify Tutu as AGAKU,
Lord of the pure incantation, who revives the
     dying,
Who showed mercy even to the captured gods,
Who removed the yoke imposed upon the gods
     his enemies,
Who created mankind to set them free,
The merciful one who has the power to give life!
His words shall be firm; they shall never be
     forgotten
In the mouth of the black-headed people whom
     he created with his own hands.
Fifthly, let their mouths show forth Tutu as
     TUKU, whose spell (is) pure,
Who uprooted all the wicked with his pure
     incantation.

He is SHAZU, aware of the gods' intentions, who
     can see emotions,
Who does not allow evil-doers to escape him,
Establisher of the gods' assembly, gratifier of
     their wishes,
Who makes the arrogant kneel beneath his wide
     canopy.
Director of justice, who plucks out crooked
     speech,
In whose place lies can be distinguished from
     truth.

Secondly, let them worship Shazu as ZISI, silencer
of the aggressor,
Expeller of deathly silence from the bodies of the
gods his fathers.
Thirdly, he is Shazu as SUHRIM, uprooter of all
the foe by force of arms,
Dispelling their plots, scattering them to the
winds,
Extinguishing all the wicked, wherever they may
be.
May the gods always proclaim the triumph in the
assembly!
Fourthly, he is Shazu as SUHGURIM, responsible
for the obedience of the gods his fathers.
Uprooter of the foe, destroyer of their offspring,
Dispeller of their works, who left no trace of
them.
Let his name be proclaimed and spoken in the
land.
Fifthly, let future generations consider Shazu as
ZAHRIM,
Destroyer of all enemies, every one of them
arrogant,
Who brought all the refugee gods into shrines:
Let this be established as his name.
Sixthly, let them all praise Shazu as ZAHGURIM
too,
Who destroyed all the foe by himself in battle.

He is ENBILULU, the lord, their enricher;
Their deity is mighty, responsible for sacrificial
omens,
Who looks after pasturage and watering places,
establishes them for the land,
Who opens up wells (?) and apportions the waters
of abundance.[50]
Secondly, let them address Enbilulu as EPADUN,
lord of the countryside and . . .,
Canal-controller of heaven and earth, establisher
of the furrow,

Who maintains pure ploughland in the
   countryside,
Who directs ditches and canals and marks out the
   furrows.
Thirdly, let them praise Enbilulu as GUGAL
   ("canal-controller") of the gods' irrigated land.
Lord of abundance and the luxuriance of great
   grain-piles.
Responsible for riches, who gives surplus to
   homes,
Giver of cereals, producer of grain.
Fourthly (?), he is Enbilulu as HEGAL
   ("Abundance"), who heaps up a surplus for
   people,
Who brings rain of abundance over the broad
   earth, and makes vegetation grow profusely.

He is SIRSIR, who piled a mountain over Tiamat,
And took as booty the corpse of Tiamat, by his
   force of arms.
Governor of the land, their righteous shepherd,
Whose gifts are cultivation, garden plots and
   ploughland,
Who waded into the broad Sea-Tiamat in his
   fury:
Like a bridge he spanned her battlefield.
Secondly, they named Sirsir as MALAH
   ("Boatman")—may she, Tiamat,
Be his barque forever, and he her sailor.

He is GIL, who amasses mighty heaps and mounds
   of grain.
Producer of cereals and flocks, giver of the land's
   seed.
He is GILIMA, who established the cosmic bond of
   the gods, who created stability;
The ring that encompasses them, who prepares
   good things.
He is AGILIMA, the lofty, who tore out flood-waves,
   and controlled snows,

And built the earth above the water, established
    the heights.

He is ZULUM who designated fields for the gods,
    and divided up what he had created.
Bestower of incomes and food offerings, supplier
    of shrines.
He is MUMMU, fashioner of heaven and earth,
    director of . . .
The god who purifies heaven and earth, secondly
    as ZULUM-UMMU
Whom no other god equals for strength.

GISH-NUMUN-AB, creator of all people, maker of
    the world's quarters,
Destroyer of Tiamat's gods, maker of people in
    their entirety.
LUGAL-AB-DUBUR, the king who scattered Tiamat's
    brood and snatched her weapon,
Who made a firm base in the van and the rear.
PAGAL-GUENA, leader of all lords, whose might is
    supreme,
Who is greatest of the gods his brothers, prince of
    them all.
LUGAL-DURMAH, king, bond of gods, lord of the
    cosmic bond,
Who is greatest in the royal abode, highest of the
    gods by far.
ARANUNA, counsellor of Ea, creator of the gods
    [his (?)] fathers,
Whom no god equals in his princely way.
DUMU-DUKU, whose pure dwelling is marked out
    for him on the holy mound,
Dumu-duku, without whom rules cannot be
    decided, LUGAL-DUKU.
LUGAL-SHUANNA, king whose might is supreme
    among the gods.
Lord, might of Anu, who is pre-eminent as the
    namesake (?) of Anshar.
IRUGA, who took them all captive from inside
    Tiamat,

Who unites all wisdom, and is broad of
  understanding.

IRQINGU, who took Qingu captive as foe (?) in (?)
  battle,

Who administers decrees for everything, who
  confirms supremacy.

KINMA, director of all the gods, giver of counsel,

At whose name the gods themselves quake in fear
  as in a tempest.

As E-SIZKUR, he shall sit highest in the house of
  prayer,

And the gods shall bring their presents before
  him,

As long as he accepts revenues from them.

None may perform miracles without him.[51]

No (other) god shall designate the revenues of the
  black-headed people, his own creation,

Without him, nor decisions about their lifetimes.

GIBIL, who establishes the . . . of weapon(s),

Who performed miracles in the battle with
  Tiamat.

Profound in wisdom, skilled in understanding,

(So) profound, that none of the gods can
  comprehend.

ADDU shall be his name: let him cover all the
  sky,[52]

And may his fine noise rumble over the earth.

May he shed water (?) from the clouds,

And give sustenance to the people below.

ASHARU, who like his name is responsible for the
  gods of destinies:

He does indeed take charge over every single
  person.

NEBERU: he does indeed hold the crossings of
  heaven and earth.

Neither up nor down shall they cross over; they
  must wait on him.

Neberu is his star which is bright in the sky.

He controls the crossroads; they must look to
  him,

Saying: "He who kept crossing inside Tiamat
    without respite,
Shall have Neberu as his name, grasping her
    middle.
May he establish the paths of the heavenly stars,
And may he shepherd all the gods like sheep.
Let him defeat Tiamat, constrict her breath and
    shorten her life,
So that for future people, till time grows old,
She shall be far removed, not kept here, distant
    forever."
Because he had created the Place (heaven),
    and fashioned Dannina (earth),
ENKURKUR, father Ellil named him.
Ea heard that name, by which the Igigi all called
    him,
And was delighted, saying,
"He whose fathers have given him such a
    splendid name
Shall have the name Ea, just like me.
He shall have mastery over the arrangement of
    all my rites,
And shall direct every one of my decrees.'''

With fifty epithets the great gods
Called his fifty names, making his way supreme.
May they always be cherished, and may the older
    explain (to the younger).
Let the wise and learned consult together,
Let the father repeat them and teach them to the
    son.
Let the ear of shepherd and herdsman be open,
Let him not be negligent to Marduk, the Ellil of the
    gods.
May his country be made fertile, and himself be
    safe and sound.
His word is firm, his command cannot alter;
No god can change his utterance.
When he is angry, he does not turn his neck
    (aside);

In his rage and fury no god dare confront him.
His thoughts are deep, his emotions profound;
Criminals and wrongdoers pass before him.
He (the scribe?) wrote down the secret instruction
    which older men had recited in his presence,
And set it down for future men to read.
May the [people?]s of Marduk whom the Igigi gods
    created
Weave the [tale?] and call upon his name
In remembrance (?) of the song of Marduk
Who defeated Tiamat and took the kingship.

NOTES TO *EPIC OF CREATION*

Text: composite cuneiform text for students: Lambert and Parker 1966; outdated edition Labat 1935; new edition announced Lambert and Millard 1969 still awaited.

1. The epic is often referred to by the first two words of the first line as Enuma Elish.
2. The word 'maker' is *mummu*; the *bīt mummi* was the term for a workshop that produced statues of deities.
3. The Assyrian version has Ea and Damkina instead of Lahmu and Lahamu.
4. The Assyrian version has Marduk instead of Anshar. Assur was assimilated with Anshar from the eighth century at least, perhaps because of similarity in names.
5. Variant has Lahmu instead of Anu.
6. This appears to be a play on the logogram for Marduk's name AMAR.UTU; it has also been interpreted as a possible diminutive of the word 'son'.
7. *šamšī* is a title, literally 'my sun', meaning 'your/his majesty' which was taken by gods who headed their local pantheon and by great kings during the Late Bronze Age (c.1500–1000 BC).
8. Perhaps a pun: 'Hubur, river / *hubūru*, hubbub'.
9. Compare this list of Tiamat's monsters with those with which Agum-kakrime adorned the doors of Marduk's temple: 'I made a pair of great door leaves, pine door leaves, . . . I had them inlaid with a horned serpent, *lahmu*-hero, bull-man, *ugallu*-demon, rabid dog, fish-man, goat-fish in lapis lazuli, rock crystal, carnelian, and alabaster.' Either these creatures were there simply to ward off evil, or a different ver~ of the Epic was in circulation, illustrated by the doors.

10. Alliteration, *libbuš lippuš*.

11. It has been suggested that *emarukka*, translated here 'by the sight of you', is a name of Tiamat elsewhere unattested in Akkadian or Sumerian, corresponding to Omorka in Berossus' *Babyloniaca*; but Tiamat would be quite out of place in this sentence.

12. The variant *enūtu*, 'power of the *en*-priesthood', puns with *anūtu*, 'Anu-power'. The pun presumably applies also to other occurrences of this line.

13. Alliteration: *itukka la ittiq*.

14. Marduk's title 'Lord' (*Bēl*) = same as that used for Ninurta in SBV *Anzu*.

15. 'Constellation', *lumāšu*, was previously misread as 'garment', *lubāšu*; the cuneiform signs *ba* and *ma* are often very hard to distinguish.

16. Compare note 15 to *Anzu*. The phrase is identical here.

17. Apparently 'evil wind' is an explanatory gloss on *imhullu*, a Sumerian loan word, and seems quite unnecessary.

18. Alliteration on the letters HLP in the four words of this line. Cf. note 45 to SBV *Gilgamesh*.

19. Pun: 'middle/battle-force' (both Akkadian *qablu*).

20. Subject perhaps Qingu rather than Marduk.

21. Sennacherib's inscription, describing a scene from the Epic as depicted on the doors of his Temple of the New Year's Festival, makes it clear that the gods accompanied Assur into battle in the Assyrian version. 'A picture of Assur who goes inside Tiamat for battle; how he raises the bow in the chariot that he rides, the flood-weapon with which he is entrusted; Amurru who rides with him as rein-holder, ... the gods march in front of him and march behind him, those who ride in a vehicle, those who march on foot, and how those in front of Assur are arrayed, and how those behind Assur are arrayed; Tiamat and the creatures of her insides, against whom Assur, king of the gods, marches to battle; a picture of Sennacherib king of Assyria; the gods Sharur, Shargaz, Kakka, Nusku, Madanu, Tishpak, Ninurta-of-the-wall, Kubu, Haya, Sebitti—these are the gods who march in front of Assur. Mullissu, Sherua, Sin, Nikkal, Shamash, Aya, Kippat-mati, Anu, Antu, Adad, Shala, Ea, Damkina, Belet-ili, Ninurta—these are the gods who march behind Assur. The conquering weapons are positioned in Assur's chariot.'

22. 'Falsehood': see Borger 1980 for this interpretation.

23. A close parallel with this pair of lines is found in an inscription of Ashurbanipal (Streck 1916, p. 28, line 381).

24. The precise implication of 'dead gods' is uncertain.

25. Play on words and alliteration: *šimāti la simāti*.

26. The north wind was regarded as the most pleasant and favourable wind in ancient Mesopotamia as in Egypt.

27. 'Greetings gifts' may be an explanatory gloss of 'presents', and seems to be unnecessary.

28. The word for the fifteenth day of the month, *šabattu*, is cognate with the Sabbath.

29. i.e. the moon must disappear on the eastern horizon at sunrise.

30. A literary composition describing the Bowstar who is killed by Ea was published by Walker 1983. See also note 39 below.

31. The word *īnu* means both 'eyes' and 'springs'.

32. Anu or Ea; the logogram is ambiguous.

33. This may allude to the decoration of Ea's temple in Eridu, or may alternatively be modelled on the display of Ninurta's trophies in Sumerian mythology. See Cooper 1978, 141–54.

34. Lugal-dimmer-ankia: Sumerian for 'King of the gods of heaven and earth'.

35. The ambiguity of subject (Marduk or Ea) may be deliberate.

36. Division of land at inheritance among brothers was done by lot. See note 4 to *Atrahasis*.

37. Perhaps the pinnacles; or a reference to the crown with bulls' horns which all gods wore.

38. Written phonetically, which is unusual, perhaps emphasizing its (secondary?) etymology as 'Gate of God'.

39. By a different reading of the same signs, 'May she go far' can alternatively be translated, 'She shall be my daughter', and may possibly be a learned pun. The bow almost certainly refers to Ishtar, daughter of Anu, as the Bowstar *elamatum*. See Walker 1983, 147, note 14. He publishes there a fragment from the seventh tablet of an otherwise unattested myth *Gerra and Elamatum* which bears some close resemblances to this epic and to *Anzu*. The month in which the great festival of Ishtar of Arbil was held is described as: 'Month of the heliacal rising of the Bowstar'.

40. This gesture is attested as accompanying treaty oaths in the Old Babylonian period.

41. The expression 'black-headed people' is normally understood to be a poetic term for mankind in general. It may also imply contrast with fair-haired people living beyond the bounds of ancient Mesopotamia.

42. This name Marukka and the following one play upon the name Marduk.

43. Mershakushu was previously read as Agashadulu.

44. The temple of Ellil in Babylon as 'lord of the lands' was E-namtila.

45. Perhaps this refers to the repair and restoration of divine statues in the workshops of Esagila; but there may also be an allusion to a feat of Ninurta.

46. There is play on various forms and secondary etymologies of the name of Ellil: *ellu*, 'pure', and *mullilu*, the Sumerian *eme-sal* dialect form of Ellil's name.

47. It is not possible to give an accurate translation or explanation for many of the following Sumerian titles of Marduk. In some cases, e.g. Asare, Tutu, Enbilulu, and Addu, he is assimilated with venerable deities whose independent existence is attested. In other cases the titles appear to be epithets which describe various aspects of his power; they are occasionally paraphrased and elaborated in the Akkadian description which follows each title, but often the elaboration consists largely of an esoteric play on words and logograms that is impossible to convey in English even when it is understood, and which can hardly have been meaningful in spoken form. The most comprehensive discussion is by Bottéro 1977,

who uses an ancient, erudite commentary of extreme brevity to help explain the riddle-like complexities of the text.

48. The verb 'fixed', *ukinnu*, puns on the second element of the epithet, Ukkina.

49. The word 'teeming', *apâti*, used to be translated 'beclouded' owing to an incorrect etymology.

50. 'Wells', *berāti*, or 'irrigated land', *miṭrāti*. *be* and *miṭ* are both readings of a single sign.

51. This line seems to be intrusive according to the sense of the adjacent lines.

52. This is the only assimilation of Marduk with a major god of the Late Bronze–Iron Age pantheon as distinct from ancient Sumerian gods. An Old Babylonian text from Mari refers to Addu (the west-semitic form of the weather-god Adad) of Aleppo as the conqueror of Tiamat. This may show that a version of this creation story was current in west-semitic circles in the early second millennium, and may account for the specifically west-semitic form, phonetically written, of the god's name here. See J.-M. Durand 1993.

Theogony of Dunnu

This composition probably dates to at least the early second millennium, when Dunnu was a town of importance. Despite its incompleteness, the text is useful for showing that each city may have had its own local traditions about creation, which differed even in essentials from those of other cities. Unlike the *Epic of Creation*, in which the primeval forces were Sea-water and Fresh water, we have here Plough and Earth as the originators of creation and the parents of the Sea. In yet another text, an incantation against toothache, the prime mover of creation is Anu the sky-god, who creates the sky which creates the earth. Thus we cannot speak of 'the Mesopotamian view of creation' as a single, specific tradition, and this in turn shows the futility of claiming a direct connection between genesis as described in the Old Testament and any one Mesopotamian account of creation. Another ancient account of genesis is preserved in the *Theogony* of Hesiod, in which Sky and Earth begin the process of creation; it was probably composed in Bœotia in the eighth century BC, making use of much older, traditional material.

The recurrent themes of incest, patricide, and matricide which characterize the *Theogony of Dunnu* can be paralleled to some extent in Hittite myths about early generations of gods, and contrast strongly with the gentlemanly conduct shown by almost all the deities in the *Epic of Creation*. The monthly schedule of family violence seems to lead up to a change of habits at the New Year, which may indicate a connection between the recital of Creation and the New Year's Festival, but with more than half the composition lacking, no proper analysis can yet be made.

THEOGONY OF DUNNU

At the very beginning (?) [Plough married Earth]¹
And they [decided to establish (?)] a family (?) and
    dominion.
 'We shall break up the virgin soil of the land into
    clods.'²
In the clods of their virgin soil (?), they created
    Sea.³
The Furrows, of their own accord, begot the Cattle
    God.
Together they built Dunnu forever (?) as his
    refuge (?).
Plough made unrestricted dominion for himself in
    Dunnu.
Then Earth raised her face to the Cattle God his son
And said to him, 'Come and let me love you!'
The Cattle God married Earth his mother,
And killed Plough his father,
And laid him to rest in Dunnu, which he loved.
Then the Cattle God took over his father's
    dominion.
He married Sea, his older sister.
The Flocks God, son of the Cattle God, came
And killed the Cattle God, and in Dunnu
Laid him to rest in the tomb of his father.⁴
He married Sea his mother.
Then Sea slew Earth her mother.
On the sixteenth day of Kislimu, he took over
    dominion and rule.⁵
[   ] the son of the Flocks God married River
    his own sister,⁶
And killed (his) father the Flocks God and Sea his
    mother,⁷
And laid them to rest in the tomb undisturbed (?).
On the first day of Tebet, he seized dominion and
    rule for himself.

The Herdsman God son of the Flocks God married
    his sister Pasture-and-Poplar,
And made Earth's verdure abundant,
Supported sheepfold and pen
To feed (?) creatures of field and fen,
And [   ] for the gods' requirements.
He killed [   ] and River his mother
And made them dwell in the tomb.
On the [   ] day of Shabat, he took over
    dominion and rule for himself.
Haharnum son of the Herdsman God married his
    sister Belet-ṣeri
And killed the Herdsman God and Pasture-and-
    Poplar his mother,
And made them dwell in the tomb.
On the sixteenth day of Addar, he took over rule
    (and) dominion.
[Then Hayyashum] son of Haharnum
Married [   ] his own sister.
At the New Year he took over his father's
    dominion,
But did not kill him, and seized him alive.
He ordered his city to imprison his father . . . and

*(about 38 lines missing, then 20 fragmentary
lines which mention Nusku, Ninurta, and
Ellil)*

NOTES TO *THEOGONY OF DUNNU*

Text: Lambert and Walcot 1965, Jacobsen 1984.

1. Differences in readings for divine names between Lambert 1965 and Jacobsen 1984 are crucial in some cases, unimportant in others. I have mainly followed Jacobsen; alternative readings are given in the Glossary under Plough, Shakkan, Flocks, River, and Kush. By translating them mostly with the English for their main aspect, I have avoided purely technical choices over the supposed pronunciation of logograms.
2. Pun: 'virgin soil', *harbu* I; 'plough', *harbu* II.

3. Or, 'by striking with their(?) plough'.
4. The logogram É KI.SÌ.GA used for 'tomb', *qubūru*, could also be read as 'place of funerary offerings to dead ancestors', *bīt kispi*.
5. The sequence of months gives the last four months of the year, corresponding to December–March. The new year began in April.
6. Jacobsen thought there were two separate gods called 'Flocks'.
7. Pun on logograms 'father', AB.BA, and 'sea', A.AB.BA. If A.AB.BA is read *ayabbu* rather than *tâmtu*, the pun also operates in the Akkadian readings of the logograms.

Erra and Ishum

In the extant text known to us at present, *Erra and Ishum* may date no earlier than the eighth century BC, but it almost certainly incorporates older elements. It consists of five tablets comprising some 750 lines; the final tablet is shorter than the others. Tablets with the text come from both Assyria (Nineveh, Assur, Sultantepe) and Babylonia (Babylon, Ur, Tell Haddad). The main tablet, from Assur, takes the form of an amulet.

The introductory lines belong to the genre associated with oral narrative in Standard Babylonian compositions, in which the poet in the first person declares the main theme of his subject; similar introductions are found in the Standard versions of *Anzu* and of *Gilgamesh*.

A few quotations have been found in the inscriptions of Sargon II and his contemporary in Babylon, the notorious Merodach-Baladan II, of the late eighth century, but those kings may have been quoting from the work because it was popular then, and not necessarily because it was composed at that time. Although the various tablets show very little textual variation, much more variation is exhibited in extracts, which were written commonly on amulets, and they show that different versions did indeed exist, perhaps due to oral tradition. Certain evidence of older associations has been noted, particularly with reference to the Suteans, traditionally nomadic enemies who damaged Babylonian cities in the eleventh century BC, but they may have been incorporated deliberately to lend an air of antiquity and thus authority to the poem. Such a possibility is reinforced by an apparent element of pseudo-prophecy, which is expressed in Tablet IV, when Erra proclaims: 'But afterwards a man of Akkad shall rise up.' So a date in the ninth or eighth century BC seems likely. Erra and Ishum are quite similarly depicted in the *Crown Prince's Vision of the Nether World*, which was probably composed in the early seventh century BC.

Erra, also known as Nergal, one main subject of the poem, is a great god in the Mesopotamian pantheon whose aspects as a god of plague and lord of the Underworld made him particularly unpredictable and awesome. Partially assimilated with Gilgamesh on the one hand and with Heracles on the other, he was a fertility god, patron of copper smelting, controller of both wild and domesticated animals, and his weapon was floods and mountain torrents. As consort of the great fertility goddess Mami he had succeeded the Sumerian god Shulpae. As a heroic warrior of sudden and uncertain changes of mood, the poem presents him as an effective challenge to Marduk, now represented as the disgruntled and senile god of Babylon. The other main subject of the poem is Ishum, whose essential nature as god of fire and as leader in battle is tempered by his skill as a wise counsellor and cunning placator of Erra.

The poem does not describe a clear narrative of specific events, but rather consists of direct discourse in which the poet, Erra, Ishum, and Marduk all make speeches, mostly in a rhetorical and declamatory style. War threatens Babylonia because of Marduk's impotence and Erra's aggression, but total disaster is narrowly averted thanks to the soothing flattery of Erra by Ishum. There is no real enemy, no rivalry, no dangers faced and overcome, no failure. An element of ridicule and satire spices the characterization of both Erra and Marduk. Possibly the poem shows features of ritual drama: the poet speaks to the gods who are sometimes addressed in the second person, sometimes he speaks for them in the first person; at other times the narrative is in the third person. At times direct speech is given without preamble, as in the *Epic of Creation*; at times an epic type of formulaic introduction to direct speech is given in full. Thus the composition may offer information on the ancestry of true drama, which is thought to have arisen in Greece from a dithyrambic chorus that began a dialogue, in which a single actor played the god.

As for the purpose and form of the work, it is generally reckoned that it refers to the recent past history and tribulations of Babylonia which will now be put to right by the new 'man of Akkad', perhaps Nabonassar or Merodach-Baladan II, and the poem relates the events in a didactic manner. The ending of the work, and its use in extracts on amulets, makes it clear that certain passages served to ward off danger and illness. There is no clear evidence that the poem was used in the cult in specific circumstances, and there is no reason to connect its author with worship of Erra, whose main cult centre at Kutha plays no part in the poem.

The ending of the poem is unusual, for the scribe is named as Kabti-ilani-Marduk of the Dabibi clan, a family first attested around 765 BC and associated with high temple office in both Babylon and Uruk. A dream is the express source of his inspiration. In the final lines Erra in the first person exhorts the people to praise himself.

ERRA AND ISHUM

TABLET I

[I sing of the son of] the king of all populated lands,
  creator of the world,[1]
Of Hendursanga, Ellil's heir,
Holder of the lofty sceptre, herder of the black-
  headed people, shepherd of [populations],
Of Ishum, pious slaughterer whose hands are adept
  at carrying his furious weapons
And making his fierce axes flash! Erra, warrior of
  gods was stirring at home;[2]
His heart urged him to make war.
He spoke to his weapons, 'Rub yourselves with
  deadly poison!'
To the Sebitti, unrivalled warrior, 'Arm yourselves
  with your weapons!'
He said to you (Ishum), 'I shall go out into the
  open country—[3]
  You will be the torch, people can see your light.
  You are to march in front, and the gods [will
    follow you].
  You are the sword that slaughters [   ].'
'O Erra, rise up, and in overwhelming the land
How happy your mood, how joyous your heart!'[4]
Yet Erra himself felt as weak as a man short of
  sleep,
Saying to himself, 'Should I rise or sleep?'
He told his weapons, 'Stay propped in the cupboard!'
To the Sebitti, unrivalled warrior, 'Go back to your
  home.'
Until you (Ishum) rouse him, he will stay asleep in
  bed,
Enjoy himself with Mami his lover!
For he is Engidudu, lord who prowls by night,
  leader of princes,

Who leads on youths and girls in peace and makes
    (night) as bright as day.
Different is the divine nature of the Sebitti,
    unrivalled warrior;
Their birth was strange and full of terrible portents.
Anyone who sees them is smitten with terror, for
    their breath is lethal;
People are petrified and cannot approach them.[5]
Ishum is the door bolted before them.
When Anu, king of the gods, impregnated Earth,
She bore the Seven Gods for him and he named
    them Sebitti.
When they stood before him, he decreed their
    destiny.
He summoned the first and gave him orders,
    'Wherever you band together and march out, you
      shall have no rival.'[6]
He spoke to the second, 'Ignite like Gerra and blaze
    like a flame!'
He said to the third, 'You must put on the face of a
    lion, so that anyone seeing you will crumble in
    terror.'
He spoke to the fourth, 'Let the mountain flee
    before the one who bears your fierce
    weapons!'[7]
He ordered the fifth, 'Blow like the wind, and seek
    out the rim of the world!'
He commanded the sixth, 'Go through above and
    below, and do not spare anyone!'
The seventh he filled with dragon's venom, and 'Lay
    low living things!'
When Anu had decreed the destinies of all the
    Sebitti,
He gave them to Erra, warrior of the gods, 'Let
    them march at your side!
    Whenever the hubbub of settled people becomes
      unbearable to you,[8]
    And you want to wreak destruction,
    To kill off some black-headed people and lay low
      Shakkan's cattle,[9]

These shall act as your fierce weapons, and march
   at your side!'
They were indeed fierce, and their weapons rose up.
They said to Erra, 'Rise! Stand up!
   Why do you stay in town like a feeble old man?
   How can you stay at home like a lisping child?
   Are we to eat women's bread, like one who has
      never marched on to the battlefield?
   Are we to be fearful and nervous as if we had no
      experience of war?
   To go on to the battlefield is as good as a festival
      for young men!
   Anyone who stays in town, be he a prince, will
      not be satisfied with bread alone;
   He will be vilified in the mouths of his own
      people, and dishonoured.
   How can he raise his hand against one who goes
      to the battlefield?
   However great the strength of one who stays in
      town,
   How can he prevail over one who has been on the
      battlefield?
   City food, however fancy, cannot compare with
      what is cooked on the embers.
   Best beer, however sweet, cannot compare with
      water from a water-skin.
   A palace built on a platform cannot compare with
      the shelters of [a camp.]
   Go out to the battlefield, warrior Erra, make your
      weapons resound!
   Make your noise so loud that those above and
      below quake,
   So that the Igigi hear and glorify your name,
   So that the Anunnaki hear and fear your word,
   So that the gods hear and submit to your yoke,
   So that kings hear and kneel beneath you,
   So that countries hear and bring you their
      tribute,
   So that demons hear and avoid (?) you,
   So that the powerful hear and bite their lips,

So that mountain peaks hear and bow their heads
    in terror,
So that the rolling seas hear and are stirred up
    and destroy their produce,
So that tree trunks are lopped in a mighty grove,
So that the reeds of an impenetrable reed-bed are
    cut down,
So that people are frightened into controlling
    their noise,
So that cattle tremble and turn to clay,
So that the gods your fathers see and praise your
    valour!
Warrior Erra, why did you abandon the
    battlefield and stay in town?
Even Shakkan's cattle and wild beasts despise us.
Warrior Erra, we must tell you, and our words
    will surely be harsh for you,
As long as the whole land is too much for us,
Surely you will listen to our words!
Do a favour for the Anunnaki who love silence!
Sleep no longer pours over the Anunnaki, because
    of people's noise.[10]
Cattle are trampling down the pastureland, the
    life of the country.
The farmer weeps bitterly over his [yield].
The lion and the wolf lay low Shakkan's cattle.
The shepherd prays to you for his sheep, he
    cannot sleep by day nor by night.
And we, who know the mountain passes, we have
    quite forgotten the road!
Spiders' webs are spun over our campaign gear.
Our trusty bows have rebelled and become too
    tough for our strength.
The points of our sharp arrows are blunt.
Our daggers are corroded with verdigris for lack
    of butchery.'
Warrior Erra listened to them.
The speech which the Sebitti made was as pleasing
    to him as the best oil.
He made his voice heard and spoke to Ishum,

'How can you listen and stay silent?
Open up a path, and let me take the road!
Let me appoint the Sebitti, unrivalled
    warrior, [to   ]¹¹
Make them march at my side as my fierce
    weapons.
And as for you, go ahead of me, go behind me.'
When Ishum heard this,
He made his voice heard and spoke to the warrior
    Erra,¹²
    'Lord, Erra, why have you planned evil for the
        gods?
    You have plotted to overthrow countries and to
        destroy their people, but will you not turn
        back?'
Erra made his voice heard and spoke,
Addressed his words to Ishum who marches before
    him,
    'Ishum, be silent, and listen to my speech
    About settled people whom you say I should
        spare!
    Wise Ishum, who marches in front of the gods,
        whose advice is good,
    In heaven I am a wild bull, on earth I am a lion.
    In the country I am king, among the gods I am
        fierce.
    Among the Igigi I am the warrior, among the
        Anunnaki I am powerful.
    Among cattle I am the smiter, in the mountains I
        am a wild ram.¹³
    In the reed-thicket I am Gerra, in the grove I am
        the *magšaru*-axe.
    In the course of a campaign I am the standard.
    I blow like the wind, I rumble like Adad,
    I can see the rim of everything like Shamash.
    I go out on to the battlefield, and I am a wild
        sheep.
    I go into sheepfolds (?), and I make my dwelling
        there.¹⁴
    All the (other) gods are afraid of battle,

So that the black-headed people despise (them).
But I, because they no longer fear my name,
And since prince Marduk has neglected his word
    and does as he pleases,
    I shall make prince Marduk angry, and I shall
        summon him from his dwelling, and I shall
        overwhelm (his) people.'
Warrior Erra set his face towards Shuanna, city of
    the king of gods.
He entered Esagila, palace of heaven and earth, and
    stood in front of him (Marduk),
He made his voice heard and spoke (to) the king of
    gods,
    'Why does the finery, your lordship's adornment
        which is full of splendour like the stars of
        heaven, grow dirty?
    The crown of your lordship which made E-halanki
        shine like E-temen-anki—its surface is
        tarnished!'
The king of gods made his voice heard and spoke,
Addressed his words to Erra, warrior of gods,
    'Warrior Erra, concerning that deed which you
        have said you will do:
    A long time ago, when I was angry and rose up
        from my dwelling and arranged for the Flood,[15]
    I rose up from my dwelling, and the control of
        heaven and earth was undone.
    The very heavens I made to tremble, the positions
        of the stars of heaven changed, and I did not
        return them to their places.
    Even Erkalla quaked; the furrow's yield
        diminished, and forever after (?) it was hard to
        extract (a yield).
    Even the control of heaven and earth was undone,
        the springs diminished, the flood-water receded.
        I went back, and looked and looked; it was very
        grievous.
    The (remaining) offspring of living things was
        tiny, and I did not return them to their
        (former) state,

To the extent that I was like a farmer who can
  hold (all) his seed-corn in his hand.[16]
I made a house and settled into it.
As for the finery which had been pushed aside by
  the Flood, its surface dulled:
I directed Gerra to make my features radiant, and
  to cleanse my robes.[17]
When he had made the finery bright, and finished
  the work,
I put on my crown of lordship and went back to
  my place.
My features were splendid, and my gaze was
  awesome!
(As for) the people who were left from the Flood
  and saw the result of my action,
Should I raise my weapons and destroy the
  remnant?[18]
I made those (original) Craftsmen go down to the
  Apsu, and I said they were not to come back
  up.[19]
I changed the location of the *mēsu*-tree (and of)
  the *elmešu*-stone, and did not reveal it to
  anyone.[20]
Now, concerning that deed which you have said
  you will do, Warrior Erra,
Where is the *mēsu*-wood, the flesh of the gods,
  the proper insignia of the King of the World,[21]
The pure timber, tall youth, who is made into a
  lord,[22]
Whose roots reach down into the vast ocean
  through a hundred miles of water, to the base
  of Arallu,[23]
Whose topknot above rests on the heaven of
  Anu?
Where is the pure *zagindurû*-stone which
  [   ] threw away?[24]
Where is Nin-ildu the great carpenter-god of my
  Anu-power,
Who carries the pure axe of the sun, and knows
  ... timbers,

Who makes [the night (?)] as radiant as day and
    makes [people (?)] bow down beneath me?
Where is Gushkin-banda, creator of god and man,
    whose hands are pure?
Where is Ninagal, who carries the hammer and anvil
Who chews hard copper like hide and
    manufactures tools?
Where are the precious stones, produce of the
    vast ocean, fitting ornament for crowns?
Where are the Seven Sages of the Apsu, the holy
    carp, who are perfect in lofty wisdom like Ea
    their lord, who can make my body holy?'[25]
The warrior Erra listened to him as he stood (?)
    there.
He made his voice heard and spoke to prince
    Marduk,
    '[   ]
    [   ]
    The holy *elmešu*-stone [   ].'
When Marduk heard this,
He made his voice heard and spoke to warrior Erra,
    'I shall rise up from my dwelling, and the control
        of heaven and earth will be undone.
    The waters will rise and go over the land.
    Bright day will turn into darkness.
    A storm will rise up and cover the stars of
        heaven.
    An evil wind will blow, and the vision of people
        and living things will [be obscured (?)].
    Gallu-demons will come up and seize [   ]
    Those who are undressed will [   ] the one
        who opposes them.
    The Anunnaki will come up and trample on living
        things.
    Until I gird myself with weapons, who can make
        them go back?'
When Erra heard this,
He made his voice heard and spoke to prince
    Marduk,
    'Prince Marduk, until you re-enter that house and

Gerra cleanses your robes, and you return to
your place,
Until then shall I rule and keep firm control of
heaven and earth.
I shall go up into heaven, and give orders to the
Igigi;
I shall go down to the Apsu and direct the
Anunnaki.
I shall send ferocious *gallu*-demons to Kurnugi,
And I shall set my fierce weapons over them.
I shall tie the wings of the wicked wind like a
bird.
At that house which you shall enter, prince
Marduk,
I shall make Anu and Ellil lie down like bulls, to
right and left of your gate.'
Prince Marduk listened to him,
And the speech that Erra made was pleasing to him.
(*Catchline*)
He rose up from his inaccessible dwelling and set
his face towards the dwelling of the Anunnaki.

TABLET II

He rose up from his inaccessible dwelling
And set his face towards the dwelling of the
Anunnaki.
He entered . . . and sto[od before them,]
[Discarded] his radi[ance] and let his rays
fall [   ].[26]
[Because (?)] he had set his face towards another
place and no longer [   ] the earth,
[The winds (?)] rose up, and bright day was turned
into darkness.
[   ] of the land together [   ]
[   ] went up [   ]
[   ] and the bottom of [   ]
[   ] all of the rim of [   ]

(*gap of 7 lines*)

The crown [   ]
His heart [   ]
Of the governor [   ]
  'The mantle of radiance [   ]
  Let Ea in the Apsu [   ]
  Let Shamash see [   ] and let the
    people [   ]
  Let Sin look, and at his sign [   ] to the land.
  Concerning that work Ea [   ] is
    expert (?).'
The warrior Erra was filled with anger,[27]
  'Why, because of foam on the surface of water,
    did Marduk
  Give the [   ] of mankind, whom I myself
    created
  To bring promptly the *taklīmu*-offerings of the
    Anunnaki,
  At the wrong time?
  He plotted evil, to devastate the land, to destroy
    people [.]'
Ea-sharru considered, and then he said,
  'Now, (it was) prince Marduk who rose up, who
    told those craftsmen that they were not to
    come back up.
  Statues of them, which I made among the people,
    for [his great divinity]
  Which no god goes and approaches [(?)   ]'[28]
He gave to the Craftsmen a generous heart, and
  [   ]-ed their base.
He bestowed on them wisdom and made their
  handiwork beautiful.
They made that finery radiant, and more choice (?)
  than before.
The warrior Erra stood before him night and day
  without cease;
Whatever (?) was placed there to make the finery
  radiant for the king of kings, he would say:
  'You can't come near the work!
  [   ] I shall cut off his life, I shall stretch
  out his . . .

[   ] hasten to the work.
[   ] has no rival.
[   ] . . .
[   ] shall rival princes.' (?)
        ] his head
          [made his finery
            radiant]
[   ] . . .
[   ] at his door.
[   ] king Shamash was clothed.
[   ] set down his dwelling
[   ] light was established
[   ] assembled.
[   ] Marduk

    (8 lines fragmentary)

The king of gods made his voice heard and spoke,
  '[   ] and they will go up to heaven.
  [   ] return to your dwelling.
  [   ] . . .
  [   ] upon your cheek
  [   ] their people
  [   ] you did not turn back.'
[   ] spoke to the king of gods,
  '[   ] of the day

    (gap of about 17 lines)

[   ] father of the gods [   ]
Ellil [   ]
The gods, all of them in [   ]
Among Shakkan's cattle, all of them [   ]
Erra among all the gods [   ]
Among the stars of heaven the Fox Star [ ][29]
Was twinkling and its rays [   ] to him.
The stars of all the gods were dazzling [ ]
Because they were angry with each other and Prince
    Marduk [   ] put [   ].
  'The star of Erra is twinkling and carries rays,
    [   ] of Anunitu.

His mantle of radiance will be activated (?) and all
    people will perish.
As for (?) the dazzling stars of heaven that carry
    a sword (?),
As for (?) the titch (?) of creation, the ant, it does
    not . . . [   ].
Among Shakkan's cattle, their astral image is that
    of the Fox [   ]
Endowed with strength, a fierce (?) lion [   ]
Ellil is the father of populations (?) and he has
    made the final [decision (?)].'
Innina replied from the gods' assembly, gave advice
    [   ],
[Addressed] her words to Anu and Dagan [   ],
    'Pay attention, all of you, go into your private
        quarters;
    Cover your lips. Did you not smell the
        qut[*rinnu*-offering (?)]
    In the presence of Prince Marduk, nor give
        advice, nor bese[ech him (?)]?
    Until the time is fulfilled, the [hour] is passed,
    The word Marduk spoke is like a mountain where
        trees (?) [grow]; he does not change
        it (?) [   ]
    Erra [   ]

      (gap of 4 lines)

Ishtar went and they entered the private quarters.
She urged Erra, but he would not agree [   ][30]
Ishum [made his voice heard and spoke],
Addressed [his words to Innina   ],[31]
    'He has ill-treated (?) [   ]
    Erra is angry and will not be silent [   ].
    Let the mountains be at peace, [   ] to
        him.'
Ellil's lofty son, who does not take the road without
    the leader Ishum,
Entered Emeslam and made his dwelling there.
He deliberated (?) with himself concerning that
    work.[32]

But his heart [   ]; it gave him no reply.
He asked himself, 'How can you sit still? (?)[33]
  Open up a path, and let me take the road!
  The time has elapsed, the hour has passed.
  I promise that I shall destroy the rays of the Sun;
  I shall cover the face of the Moon in the middle
      of the night.
  I shall say to Adad, "Hold back [your]
      well-springs,
  Drive away the clouds and cut out snow and
      rain."
  To Marduk (?) and to Ea I shall bring a reminder:
  He who grows up in times of plenty shall be
      buried in times of deprivation.
  He who travels out on a path with water shall
      return along a way of dust-storms.
  I shall say to the king of gods, "Stay in Esagila!"
  They will do as you have told them, they will
      carry out your command in full.
  The black-headed people will revile you, and you
      will not accept their prayers.
  I shall finish off the land and count it as ruins.
  I shall devastate cities and make of them a
      wilderness.
  I shall destroy mountains and fell their cattle.
  I shall stir up oceans and destroy their produce.
  I shall dig out reed-thickets and graves and I shall
      burn them like Gerra.
  I shall fell people and [I shall leave no] life,
  I shall not keep a single one back [   ]!
  I shall not leave out any of the cattle of Shakkan
      nor any wild beasts [whatsoever].
  From city to city I shall seize the one who
      governs.
  A son will not ask after the health of his father,
      nor the father of his son.
  A mother will happily plot harm for her
      daughter.
  I shall let a [barbarian] enter a god's shrine where
      evil men should not go.

I shall let a rogue sit down in the dwelling of
     princes.
I shall let a wild beast of . . . enter [cult centres].
I shall stop anyone entering any city which he
     encounters.
I shall let wild beasts of the mountains go down
     (into cities).
I shall devastate public places, wherever people
     tread.
I shall let wild beasts of the countryside which are
     not . . . come into the public square.
I shall let a bad omen occur to devastate a city.
I shall let the demon "Supporter of Evil" enter
     the gods' [inaccessible] dwelling.
I shall devastate the royal palace and make it into
     a ruin [(   )].
I shall cut off the noise of mankind and deprive
     him of joy,
Like [   ] like fire where there was once
     peace.
[   ] I shall let evil enter.'
(*Catchline*)
[   ] he would pay attention to nobody.

TABLET III

[   ] he would pay attention to nobody,
The words of caution that they spoke [   ]
Lions [   ]
[   ]
To [   ]
    'I shall make them take [   ] and I shall
       shorten their lifetime,
    I shall sever the life of the just man who takes on
       paternal responsibility,
    I shall set up [at the head (?)] the wicked man
       who cuts off life.
    I shall change the minds of people, so that the
       father will not listen to the son;

The daughter will speak words of rejection to the
    mother.
I shall make their words wicked, and they will
    forget their god,
Will speak great insolence to their goddess.
I shall muster the bandit and cut off the highway.
They will even plunder each other's property in
    the city centre.
The lion and the wolf will fell Shakkan's cattle.
[   ] I shall cause to rage and he will cut
    off offspring.
I shall deprive the nurse of the baby's cry and
    toddler's prattle.
I shall make Alala leave the pasture.
Shepherd and herdsman will forget the shelter.
I shall cut off the garment from a man's body
And I shall make the young man walk naked in
    the city square.
I shall make the young man go down into the
    Earth unshrouded.
The young man—his supply of sacrificial sheep
    will be interrupted and endanger his own life.
The prince—his supply of lambs will become too
    scarce to obtain oracles from Shamash.[34]
The sick man will demand roast meat (perversely)
    to satisfy his craving.
He will not free for ... he will go.
[   ] I shall stop the steeds of princes.
[   ] I shall cut off.
[   ] I shall cause to seize.

      (gap of uncertain length)[35]

Rain [   ]
Evil winds [   ]

      (gap of uncertain length)[35]

'You have (?) set up the weapons of *kidinnu*-men
    as an abomination to Anu and Dagan.[36]
You have made their blood flow like water in the
    drains of public squares.

You have opened their veins and let the river
   carry off (their blood).
Ellil has cried "Woe!" and clutched at his heart.
[He has risen up from] his dwelling.
An irredeemable curse is set in his mouth,
He has sworn not to drink the river's waters,
He shuns their blood and will not enter into
   Ekur.'
Erra addressed his words to Ishum, who marches
   before him,
   'The Sebitti, unrivalled warrior [   ]
   All of them [   ]
   Who [   ]
   Who marches before [   ]
   Who [   ]
   Who like Gerra [   ]
   In front of the house [   ]
   Who like [   ]
   Who [   ]
   Whom Erra [   ]
   The face of a lion [   ]
   In my rage [   ]
   Open the path, let me take the road!
   Let me appoint the Sebitti, unrivalled
      warrior [   ].
   Make them march at my side as my fierce
      weapons.
   And as for you, go ahead of me, go behind me!'
Ishum listened to this speech of his;
He felt compassion and said to himself,
   'Woe to my people against whom Erra rages
      and [   ]
   Whom the warrior Nergal, as in the moment of
      battle, [   ] Asakku.[37]
   His arms, like those which (slew (?)) the ruined
      god, are not too weak to slay them,[38]
   His net, like that (which overwhelmed) wicked
      Anzu, is spread to overwhelm them.'[39]
Ishum made his voice heard and spoke,
Addressed his words to the warrior Erra,

'How could you plot evil for gods and men?
Even though you have plotted evil against the
   black-headed people, will you not turn back?'
Erra made his voice heard and spoke,
Addressed his words to Ishum who marches before
   him,
   'You know the decisions of the Igigi, the counsels
      of the Anunnaki.
   You give the command for the black-headed
      people, and gain their attention (?).
   How can you speak like one who is ignorant,
   Advise me as if you did not know of Marduk's
      words to me!
   The king of gods has risen up from his dwelling
   So how can all the lands stay firm?
   He has taken off his lordly crown:
   King and princes [   ] will forget their
      rites.
   He has undone his girdle:
   The belt of god and man is loosened and cannot
      be retied.
   Furious Gerra has made his finery bright as day,
      and has displayed his radiance.
   He holds a mace in his right hand, his great
      weapon;
   The glance of Prince Marduk is terrifying.
   Yet to me you speak [   ]
   Leader of the gods, wise Ishum, whose counsel is
      good,
   How can you now sit and [   ]
   Was Marduk's word not pleasing to you?'
Ishum made his voice heard and spoke to warrior
      Erra,
   'Warrior Erra, [   ]
   Trample on the people and [   ]
   Where the cattle [   ]
   The reed-thicket and grove which [   ]
   Now, as for what you say, warrior Erra, [(   )]
   One was put in charge, but you [   ]
   You killed seven and did not spare one.

Cattle [   ]
Erra, you clash your weapons together
And the mountains shake, the seas surge
At the flashing of your sword [   ] they
   look towards the mountain.
The palace [   ]'

   (*gap of uncertain length*)

Ishum made his voice heard and spoke to warrior
   Erra,
'Warrior Erra, you hold the nose-rope of
   heaven,[40]
You control the whole earth, and you rule the
   land.
You made the sea rough and encompass
   mountains,
You govern people and herd cattle.
Esharra is at your disposal; E-engurra in your
   hands.
You look after Shuanna and rule Esagila,
You control all the rites and the gods respect you.
The Igigi revere you, the Anunnaki fear you,
Ellil agrees with you. Does conflict happen
   without you,
Or warfare take place in your absence?
The armoury of war belongs to you
And yet you say to yourself, "They despise me!"
(*Catchline*)
O warrior Erra, did you not fear prince Marduk's
   name?

               TABLET IV

O warrior Erra, did you not fear prince Marduk's
   name?
You have untied the bond of Dimkurkurra, city of
   the king of gods, the bond of lands!
You have changed your divine nature and become
   like a human![41]

You have donned your weapons and entered in,
Into the heart of Babylon, and have spoken like a
  braggart (?), that you would seize the city.
The sons of Babylon, who have none to take
  charge of them, like reeds in a reed-thicket,
  have all gathered about you.
He who is ignorant of weapons is unsheathing his
  dagger,
He who is ignorant of bows is stringing his bow,
He who is ignorant of battle is making war,
He who is ignorant of wings is flying like a bird.
  The weakling covers the master of force;[42]
The fatty is overtaking the sprinter.
To the governor in charge of their shrines they
  utter great blasphemies.
Their hands have dammed up the city gate of
  Babylon, the artery of their wealth.
They have thrown firebrands into the shrines of
  Babylon like looters of the country.
You are the one who marches at the head, and
  you take the lead for them.
You press down arrows upon Imgur-Ellil until he
  says "Woe is me!"
You have founded a dwelling for Muhra, keeper
  of its city-gate, in the blood of young men and
  women.
You are the decoy for the inhabitants of Babylon,
  and they are the bird;
You ensnared them in your net and caught and
  destroyed them, warrior Erra.
You left the city and went off elsewhere;
You put on the face of a lion and entered the
  palace.
The army saw you and donned their weapons.
The governor, who had treated Babylon well,
  became enraged,
Directed his troops to loot like enemy looters,
Incited the leader of the army to crime,
"You are the man whom I shall send to that city!
You shall respect neither god nor man.

Put young and old alike to death.

You shall not leave any child, even if he still
sucks milk.

You shall pillage the accumulated wealth of
Babylon."

The royal troops were put into units and entered
the city.

The bow twanged, the dagger pricked.

You set up the weapons of *kidinnu*-men as an
abomination to Anu and Dagan.

You have made their blood flow like water in the
drains of public squares.

You have opened their veins and let the river
carry off (their blood).

The great lord Marduk saw and cried "Woe!" and
clutched at his heart.

An irredeemable curse is set in his mouth.

He has sworn not to drink the river's waters.

He shuns their blood and will not enter into
Esagila,

"Woe to Babylon, which I made as lofty as a
date-palm's crown, but the wind shrivelled it.

Woe to Babylon, which I filled with seeds like a
pine-cone, but whose abundance I did not bring
to fruition.

Woe to Babylon, which I planted like a luxuriant
orchard, but never tasted its fruit.

Woe to Babylon, which I have thrown on to the
neck of Anu like a cylinder seal of
elmešu-stone.

Woe to Babylon, which I have taken in my hands
like the Tablet of Destinies and will not deliver
to anyone else."'

Then prince Marduk spoke thus,

'[   ] which from time immemorial [   ]

Henceforth he who would cross from the
quayside shall cross on foot.

Henceforth the rope which would go down into
the pit shall not save the life of a single man.

Henceforth they shall drive out the deep-sea

fisherman's boat a hundred leagues into the
vast expanse of sea-water with a pole.
Even Sippar, the eternal city, which the Lord of
Lands did not allow the Flood to overwhelm,
because it was so dear to him;
You destroyed its wall without Shamash's
permission and dismantled its parapet.[43]
Even Uruk, the dwelling of Anu and Ishtar, city
of prostitutes, courtesans, and call-girls,
Whom Ishtar deprived of husbands and kept in
her (*lit.* their) power:
Sutean men and women hurl their abuse;
They rouse Eanna, the party-boys and festival
people
Who changed their masculinity into femininity to
make the people of Ishtar revere her.
The dagger-bearer, bearers of razors, pruning-
knives, and flint blades
Who frequently do abominable acts to please the
heart of Ishtar:
You set over them an insolent governor who will
not treat them kindly.
He persecuted them and violated their rites.
Ishtar was enraged and became angry with Uruk.
She summoned an enemy and despoiled the land
like (standing) corn before (flood-) water.
The inhabitants of Parsay would not cease ritual
wailing because of E-ugal, which had been
contaminated.
The enemy whom you had summoned would not
agree to stop.'
Angal replied,
'You have made the city of Der into a wilderness;
You have snapped the people within it like
reeds!
Like scum (?) on the surface of water you have
stopped their hubbub,
And you did not spare me; you delivered me up
to the Suteans.[44]
So I, because of my city Der,[45]

Shall not give fair justice, I shall not make
   decisions for the land.
I shall not give any orders, nor will I open my ear.
The people abandoned justice and took to
   atrocities.
They deserted righteousness and planned
   wickedness.
I made the seven winds rise up against the one
   country.
Anyone who has not died in battle will die in an
   epidemic.
Anyone who has not died in the epidemic, the
   enemy will carry off as spoil.
Anyone whom the enemy has not carried off as
   spoil, thieves will murder.
Anyone whom thieves have not murdered, the
   king's weapon will overcome.[46]
Anyone whom the king's weapon has not
   overcome, a prince will fell.
Anyone whom a prince did not fell, Adad will
   wash away.
Anyone whom Adad has not washed away,
   Shamash will parch.[47]
Anyone who goes out on to the land, the wind
   will infect.
Anyone who enters his own home, the Croucher
   will hit.
Anyone who goes up into the heights will die of
   thirst,
Anyone who goes down into the depths will die
   by water,
For you encompass the heights and the depths
   alike.
The city governor will say thus to his mother,
"Would that I had been obstructed in your womb
   on the day you bore me,
Would that my life had ended and that we had
   died together,
Because you delivered me to a city whose walls
   were to be demolished,

Its people treated like cattle, their god turned
    smiter,[48]
And because his net is of such fine mesh, even
    picked men could not draw (their swords), but
    died by the sword."[49]
He who sired a son will say, "This is my son
And I reared him and he does good in return,"—
Yet shall I put the son to death and his father
    shall bury him.
Afterwards I shall put the father to death, and he
    shall have nobody to bury him.
He who builds a house and says, "This is my
    home,
I have built it and I shall find peace within it,
And when Fate carries me off I shall rest there
    (forever)"—[50]
Yet shall I put him to death and vandalize his
    home.
Afterwards it will be wrecked, and I shall give it
    to someone else.'

(*Ishum answers*)

'O warrior Erra, you have put the just to death,
You have put the unjust to death.
You have put to death the man who sinned
    against you,
You have put to death the man who did not sin
    against you.
You have put to death the *en*-priest who made
    taklīmu-offerings promptly,
You have put to death the courtier who served
    the king,
You have put old men to death on the porch,
You have put young girls to death in their
    bedrooms.
Yet you will not rest at all,
Yet you say to yourself, "They despise me!"
Yet this is what you tell yourself, Warrior Erra,
"I shall smite the strong and terrify the weak,

I shall murder the leader of the army and rout
    the army,
I shall ruin the shrine on top of the temple
    (-tower) and the wall's crenellations, and
    destroy the city's vitality.
I shall tear out the mooring poles and let boats
    drift downstream,
I shall break the rudder, so that it cannot reach
    the bank,
I shall rip out the mast and tear out its rigging.
I shall dry out the breast so that the baby cannot
    live,
I shall block springs, so that small channels
    cannot bring the waters of fertility.
I shall make Erkalla quake, so that the skies
    billow,
I shall fell the rays of Shulpae and throw away
    the stars of heaven,
The roots of trees shall be cut through so that
    their new growth will not flourish,
I shall destroy the base of the wall so that the top
    of it sways.
To the dwelling of the king of gods I shall go, so
    that counsel shall not prevail." '
Warrior Erra listened to him,
And the words that Ishum spoke to him were as
    pleasing as the best oil.
And Warrior Erra spoke thus,
    'Sea (people) shall not spare sea (people), nor
    Subartian (spare) Subartian, nor Assyrian
    Assyrian,[51]
Nor shall Elamite spare Elamite, nor Kassite
    Kassite,
Nor Sutean spare Sutean, nor Gutian Gutian,
Nor shall Lullubean spare Lullubean, nor country
    country, nor city city,
Nor shall tribe spare tribe, nor man man, nor
    brother brother, and they shall slay one
    another.
But afterwards a man of Akkad shall rise up and

fell them all and shepherd all (the rest) of
          them.'[52]
Warrior Erra addressed his words to Ishum, who
          marches before him,
     'Go, Ishum! Take full discretion for the words
          you spoke!'
Ishum set his face towards the mountain Hehe.
The Sebitti, unrivalled warrior, stormed (?) behind
          him.
The warrior arrived at the mountain Hehe,
Raised his hand and destroyed the mountain,
Counted the mountain Hehe as (flat) ground.
He lopped the tree trunks in the forest of
          hašūru-trees[53]
Like [   ].
He finished off the cities and made of them a
          wilderness,
Destroyed mountains and struck down their cattle,
Stirred up the seas and destroyed their produce,
Devastated reed-beds and groves, and burnt them
          like Gerra
Cursed the cattle and turned them into clay.
(*Catchline*)
When Erra had rested and settled in his dwelling

TABLET V

When Erra had rested and settled in his dwelling,
All the gods began to look at his face.
The Igigi and the Anunnaki, all of them, were
          standing in awe.
Erra made his voice heard and spoke to all the gods,
     'Keep quiet, all of you, and learn what I have to
          say!
     What if I did intend the harm of the wrong I
          have just done?
     When I am enraged, I devastate people!
     Like a hired man among the flocks, I let the
          leading sheep out of the pen.

Like one who does not plant the orchard, I am
    not slow to cut it down.
Like one who plunders a country, I do not
    distinguish just from unjust, I fell (them both).
One does not snatch a corpse from the mouth of
    a marauding lion,
And where one man is beside himself, another
    man cannot give him advice!
What would happen if Ishum, who goes before
    me, were not there?
Where would your provider be, wherever would
    your *en*-priest be?
Where would your *nindabû*-offerings be? You
    would not (even) smell the *qutrinnu*-offering!'
Ishum made his voice heard and spoke,
Addressed his words to warrior Erra,
    'Warrior, be still and listen to my words!
    What if you were to rest now, and we would
        serve you?
    We all know that nobody can stand up to you in
        your day of wrath!'
Erra heard him and his face brightened;
His features lit up like the dawning of a (new) day.
He entered into Emeslam and settled in his dwelling.
Ishum called out and said the key word,
Began to confirm the decision concerning the
    scattered people of Akkad.
    'May the reduced people of the land become
        numerous again,
    May the short man and the tall man go along its
        paths,
    May the weak man of Akkad fell the strong
        Sutean,
    May one man drive away seven (of them) as if
        they were flocks!
    You shall make *their* towns into ruins and *their*
        hills into wildernesses,
    You shall bring their heavy spoils into Shuanna,[54]
    You shall put the country's gods who were angry
        safely back into their dwellings,

You shall let Shakkan and Nissaba go down into
   the country,
You shall let the mountains bear their wealth and
   the sea its produce,
You shall let the meadowlands, which you
   allowed to be devastated, bear their produce!
Then let the governors of all cities, every one of
   them, haul their heavy tribute into Shuanna,
Let the temples, which were allowed to become
   damaged, lift their heads (up) as high as the
   rising sun,
Let the Tigris and Euphrates bring the waters of
   abundance,
Let the governors of all cities, every one of them,
   deliver up to the provider of Esagila and
   Babylon!'
For countless years shall the praises of the great
   lord Nergal and the warrior Ishum (be
   sung):
How Erra became angry and set his face towards
   overwhelming countries and destroying their
   people,
But Ishum his counsellor placated him so that he
   left a remnant!

The one who put together the composition about
   him was Kabti-ilani-Marduk son of Dabibi.[55]
(Some god) revealed it to him in the middle of the
   night, and when he recited it upon waking, he
   did not miss anything out,
Nor add a single word to it.
Erra heard and approved it,
And it was pleasing also to Ishum who marches in
   front of him.
All the other gods gave praise with him.
And the warrior Erra spoke, saying,
   'Wealth shall be piled up in the shrine of the god
      who praises this song![56]
   But whoever discards it shall never smell the
      qutrinnu-offering!

The king who magnifies my name shall rule the
world,
The prince who recites the praise of my valiant
deeds shall have no rival,
The musician who sings it shall not die in an
epidemic.
The words of it will find favour with kings and
princes.
The scribe who learns it will survive even in
enemy country, and will be honoured in his
own.
In the shrine of craftsmen where they ever
proclaim my name, I shall make them wise,[57]
In the house where this tablet is placed, even if
Erra becomes angry and the Sebitti storm,
The sword of judgement shall not come near him,
but peace is ordained for him.
Let this song endure forever, let it last for
eternity!
Let all countries listen to it and praise my valour!
Let settled people see and magnify my name!'
(*Colophon*)
Fifth tablet, series 'Erra'.
I, Assurbanipal, great king, mighty king, king of the
world, king of Assyria,
Son of Esarhaddon king of Assyria, son of
Sennacherib king of Assyria,
Wrote, checked, and collated this tablet in the
company of scholars
In accordance with clay tablets and wooden writing
boards, exemplars from Assyria, Sumer, and
Akkad,
And put it in my palace for royal reading.
Whoever erases my written name and writes his
own name,
May Nabu, the scribe of all, erase his name.

NOTES TO *ERRA AND ISHUM*

Text: Cagni 1969 and 1977.

Although an epic formula to introduce direct speech is sometimes used, many of the speeches in this work occur abruptly. In some cases, especially where there are breaks in the text, the precise points at which a speech begins and ends are not certain.

1. The opening lines are modelled on the opening of *Anzu*. Some commentators would restore the name of Marduk or of Erra/Nergal at the end of the line, but it is very doubtful whether there is a lacuna at the ends of lines 1 or 2, and Hendursanga is definitely a name for Ishum. Therefore I have followed Edzard, RlA, s.v. Irra; the prologue, like the epilogue, is addressed to Ishum and Erra. The epilogue shows that Erra and Nergal are two names for the one god.
2. Unusual vocabulary for the phrase 'fierce axes' is also found in the letter describing Sargon's eighth campaign, line 122 (Thureau-Dangin 1912).
3. The second person address, only briefly maintained, perhaps implies that the dialogue within the poem was a hymn sung around a statue of Ishum.
4. These two lines read like the exclamation of a chorus, tinged with sarcasm.
5. Literally, 'him'. The Sebitti, 'The Seven Gods', can be regarded both as a singular and as a plural deity.
6. Reading *[te-n]e-di-ru*, from *edēru* N, 'band together'.
7. Cagni translated 'be razed to the ground' rather than 'flee'.
8. This speech echoes *Atrahasis*, I–II in which the gods recommend that overpopulation be curbed by plague, although the idea comes from Ellil, not Anu in the version known to us.
9. 'Black-headed people': see note 41 on *Epic of Creation*.
10. Another use of the overpopulation theme from *Atrahasis*.
11. Reading *lupqi[d]*, 'appoint', rather than *luppi[t]*, 'draw (them)' (Cagni).
12. Variant: 'He felt compassion and . . .'
13. The word for 'smiter', *māhisu*, can also be translated 'hunter'.
14. 'Sheepfolds' or 'pastureland'.
15. Here Marduk takes responsibility for the Flood; in *Atrahasis* it was Ellil's idea.
16. Literally: 'To the extent that I held their seed in my hand like a ploughman.'
17. In this speech Marduk refers to himself as a cult statue made of precious metals, gems, and timbers.
18. Variant has: 'Should you raise your weapons . . .' The line may equally be taken as an affirmative statement, not as interrogative.
19. These Craftsmen are the Seven Sages. See Glossary, s.v. Seven Sages.
20. Or, 'of the *mēsu*-tree (which bears) *elmešu*-stone'. Although a translation 'amber' has been suggested for *elmešu*, amber seems not to have

been used in ancient Mesopotamia. The word is sometimes used with *būṣu*, 'glass', and may perhaps be rock crystal. *mēsu* may have been a rosewood (Dalbergia) with wider mythical connotations.

21. i.e. the wood was used to make the gods' basic statues, which were then adorned with inlay etc.

22. This is a pun on *mes* as a logographic value for *eṭlu*, 'youth', and *mēsu*-timber (Cagni 1969, 194). The same pun occurs in a late third millennium poem known as *Shulgi King of Abundance* (Klein 1981, 11).

23. Literally, 'a hundred double hours'.

24. A blue stone, possibly top-quality lapis lazuli.

25. When a divine statue was made or repaired, rituals known as 'washing the mouth' and 'opening the mouth' were carried out with incantations, Ea's speciality, to bring the statue to 'life'. In an inscription of Esarhaddon (680–669 BC) '(the newly fashioned statues) entered the city with rituals by sages, with "washing the mouth" and "opening the mouth".' (Borger 1956, 89).

26. The idea that a god is made powerless when divested of his rays or mantle of radiance is also found in the episode of Humbaba in *Gilgamesh*.

27. This restoration and those which follow are based on a new, fragmentary tablet from Tell Haddad, kindly made available by Dr Farouk al Rawi and Dr Jeremy Black. That tablet shows that Tablet II had about 160 lines.

28. Cagni translates: 'Where the god does not go, they draw near.'

29. The Fox Star was equated with Erra.

30. The main restorations using the Tell Haddad tablet end here.

31. The new passage shows that Innina, not Erra, should be restored here.

32. Tentatively reading *išâlma ramānuš*.

33. Tentatively reading *tuš-bi mìn-su*.

34. Shamash and Adad were gods of extispicy (the reading of entrails) and omens.

35. If the total number of lines for this tablet should be about 160 as indicated by the tablet from Tell Haddad, this and the following gap represent about forty-three missing lines.

36. Certain cities were accorded the privileged status of protection called *kidinnūtu* in which its citizens were exempted from military service, and professional soldiers were forbidden to bear arms within the city walls. Such places proclaimed their status with standards set up at the gates of the city. They may in return have supported permanent encampments of professional soldiers. In Babylonia the cities Sippar, Nippur, Babylon, and Borsippa, in Assyria the cities Assur and Harran, enjoyed the status, at least in the early first millennium, although not without interruption. *kidinnu*-men in such cities appear to have had a special relationship with the two gods Anu and Dagan. It is not certain whether the *kidinnu*-men were citizens exempt from military service or the soldiery stationed in those cities.

37. Or, 'storm', rather than 'moment'. This line assimilates Nergal with Ninurta, who defeated Asakku in the Sumerian story *Lugal-e* (Van Dijk 1983).

38. This literary allusion is not understood. According to one text 'the ruined gods were in the sea', and the *Epic of Creation*, VI may allude to the same event. It is possible that a feat of Ninurta is involved.

39. The reference is to the myth of Anzu, but a different version from the one known to us in which no net is used. As in previous lines here, assimilation with Ningirsu and Ninurta is implied. However, the text may be corrupt; cf. *Etana*, note 18.

40. This speech is quoted on plague amulets (Reiner 1960).

41. Erra/Nergal may have been equated with Heracles, whose ambivalent nature as a god and as a mortal hero is stressed by Herodotus (Dalley 1987).

42. For 'wings' see Tsevat 1987. The second phrase probably implies a wrestler's strength, arm muscles.

43. The historical event to which this line alludes cannot be pinpointed.

44. The Suteans were traditional enemies of Assyria and had raided Der, Nippur, and Parsay in the eleventh century (Heltzer 1981, 90–4); they are attested again on the fringes of Babylonia in the eighth and early seventh centuries; Sargon II in the late eighth century claimed to have driven Sutean bandits from Babylonian countryside.

45. This allusion to Der is not clear. The Assyrians were defeated there by Elam in 720 BC, perhaps with Babylonian help (Brinkman 1984, 48) but retained control of the city.

46. Probably a reference to the winged disk, symbol of royalty on which oaths of loyalty to the king were sworn under threat of horrific penalties for perjury. Such symbols were regularly referred to as weapons because of their power to harm and kill.

47. Or, 'will take away' rather than 'will parch'.

48. Or, 'hunter' rather than 'smiter', both meanings of *māhiṣu*.

49. The word *ha'īru*, 'chosen one', normally means a lover, bridegroom, first husband. A widower was often obliged to marry the widow of a relative, and had little choice upon remarriage.

50. People were commonly buried under the floors of their houses.

51. The Sea probably refers to southern Mesopotamia, where the marsh-lands were inhabited by several different tribes or 'houses'.

52. 'Man of Akkad' probably refers to an urban Babylonian as opposed to a nomad or a foreigner. This line indicates that there is an important element of pseudo-prophecy in the epic.

53. *hašūru*: a kind of cypress.

54. Veenhof has pointed out an identical phrase used in an inscription of Merodach-Baladan II, who ruled Babylon in 721–710 and 703 BC. See Brinkman, 1984, 49, n. 230.

55. See Introduction, p. 284.

56. This and the following lines are paraphrased in the subscripts of plague amulets (Reiner 1960).

57. Literally, 'I shall make them open their ears'.

1. Anzu
2. The Bull-man
3. The Horned serpent
4. Two *lahmu*-heroes
5. Head of Humbaba
6. The *mušhuššu*-dragon
7. The Scorpion-man
8. The *ugallu*-demon

Fig. 2. Mythical monsters referred to in the translations

GLOSSARY OF DEITIES,
PLACES, AND KEY TERMS

abūbu—'flood-weapon', personified weapon of floods, flash-floods, and torrents. Used as an epithet and as a weapon by various gods including Ninurta, Nergal, and Adad. Also describes the voice of Humbaba.

Adad (Sumerian Ishkur, west semitic Hadad and Addu)—storm-god, canal-controller, son of Anu. Symbols: bull and forked lightning. Lord of omens and extispicy. Cult centre: Aleppo.

Adapa—son of Ea, priest in Eridu. Also known as Uan (Oannes), the first of the Seven Sages, who brought the arts and skills of civilization to mankind.

Addu—see Adad.

Akkad—name for northern Babylonia.

Akkadian—east semitic language related to Hebrew and Arabic; includes dialects of the Babylonians and Assyrians, written with cuneiform (wedge-shaped) signs that have a combination of logographic, syllabic, and determinative values. In use from about 2400 to 100 BC.

Alexander—great king of Macedonia who won Babylon in 330 BC and died there in 323 BC.

Alala—harvest song, god of harvest song.

Amurru—'the western god'. Nature, shrines, and precise attributes uncertain.

Anduruna—name of the gods' dwelling.

Angal—a name of Ishtaran, patron god of Der, a city east of the Tigris.

Anshan (modern Tell Malyan)—capital of the most ancient Iranian civilization, near Persepolis. Included in the Sumerian king list.

Anshar—'whole sky', a Sumerian god of the old generation, father of Anu, paired with Kishar, assimilated with Assur by phonetic similarity. His vizier is the god Kakka.

Antu—wife of Anu in Uruk, mother of Ishtar. Also called Anunitu, especially in Sippar.

Anu (Sumerian An)—'sky', god of Uruk, temple Eanna; son of Anshar and Kishar, consort of Antu, father of Ellil, Adad, Gerra, Shara, and (in some traditions), Ishtar. His vizier is the god Ilabrat. Head of the older generation of gods. Paired with Dagan in connection with the *kidinnūtu*-status of cities (see *Erra and Ishum*, note 36). Symbol: horned crown on a shrine.

Anunitu—see Antu.

Anunna, Anunnaki, Anukki, Enunaki—Sumerian group term for the old, chthonic deities of fertility and the Underworld, headed by Anu. They later became judges in the Underworld. Often paired with the Igigi. See Sommerfeld 1985, 11–15.

Anzu (Sumerian Imdugud, previously read Zu in Akkadian. Also pronounced Azzu.)—lion-headed eagle, doorkeeper of Ellil, born in the mountain Hehe. Portrayed as a wicked thief in *Anzu*, but benevolent in the Sumerian epic of Lugalbanda. Often shown in iconography in the pose of 'master of animals'. See fig. 2:1.

Apsu—domain of sweet, fresh water beneath the earth, home of Ea and of the Seven Sages. Name of Ea's temple in Eridu. Husband of Tiamat, father of the primeval gods.

Arali, Arallu—name of desert between Bad-tibira and Uruk, where Dumuzi was killed; perhaps also a semi-mythical land from which gold was obtained, also known as Harallum. Evolved into a name for the Underworld.

Aruru—a name for the great mother goddess; see Ninhursag.

Asakku—see Demons.

Asarluhi (also spelt Asalluhi)—god of Ku'ara, son of Ea, assimilated with Marduk. Has powers of magic and healing. Often invoked in incantations and magical literature.

Ashnan—god of cereal grain, often paired with Shakkan.

ašqulālu-weapon—unidentified object which is 'weighed' or balanced for throwing, comparable with a throw-stick. The word also means a plant (also known as 'sunspit'), and an atmospheric phenomenon.

Assur (Ashur)—national god of Assyria, epithet 'Assyrian Ellil'. Replaces Marduk as hero of the *Epic of Creation* in the Assyrian version, eponymous patron of the city Assur.

Atrahasis—'extra wise', epithet of Ut-napishtim, q.v. and of Adapa.

Aya—spouse of Shamash. Epithet: 'the daughter-in-law'.

Ayabba—the sea, ocean: mainly a west semitic term. See also Tiamat.

Babylon—'gate of god' (secondary etymology?), capital city of the Babylonians, situated on the river Euphrates. Patron: Marduk. Residence of major kings from the second millennium onwards. Also known as Shuanna.

Babyloniaca—see Berossus.

Bel—title, 'Lord', taken by various gods as head of their local pantheon; refers to Marduk in Babylon, Assur in Assyria, and Ninurta in *Anzu*.

Belet-ili—'mistress of the gods', a name for the great mother goddess. See Ninhursag.

Belet-ṣeri—'mistress of open country' (where restless ghosts resided), goddess who was recorder of the Underworld. Epithet: 'scribe of Earth'.

Belili—a name of the goddess Geshtin-anna, sister of Dumuzi, wife of Nin-gishzida. Epithet: 'she who always weeps'.

Berossus—priest of Marduk in Babylon. Wrote *Babyloniaca* in Greek around 281 BC for Antiochus I, to narrate ancient Mesopotamian cultural traditions to the Greeks. The work is known only in parts, from quotations in later Greek writers.

Birdu—name possibly means 'pimple'. An Underworld god, consort of the little-known deity Manungal. Assimilated with Meslamta'ea, a name of Nergal.

Bull-man—word *kusarikku* formerly translated 'bison'. Composite creature, slain in the sea by Ninurta in Sumerian mythology; one of Tiamat's brood slain by Marduk in the *Epic of Creation*. Attested in iconography from the Early Dynastic period onwards. See fig. 2:2.

Buluqiya—hero-king who searched for immortality in the *Arabian Nights'* tale 'Queen of the Serpents'. May be a diminutive of Gilgamesh's name.

Dagan—chthonic god of fertility and of the Underworld. Name means 'grain' in Ugaritic. Cult centres at Tuttul and Terqa on the middle Euphrates. Paired with Anu in connection with the *kidinnūtu*-status of cities.

Damascius—born *c*.AD 480. Worked in Alexandria, Athens, and in Iran at the court of Chosroes I (AD 531–79) in the time of Justinian. Writings show knowledge of the *Epic of Creation*.

Damkina—'faithful wife', Sumerian name used also in Akkadian. Wife of Ea.

Dannina—'stronghold(?)', term for the Underworld, q.v.

Demons—illnesses and misfortunes were personified as demons, both male and female, with Akkadian or Sumerian names. Groups of demons are: *asakku/ašakku* (Sumerian *asag*), seven created by Anu and defeated by Ninurta, a victory also attributed to Nergal; *gallū*, a term which originally referred to police officers; Sebitti, 'The Seven', q.v. Individuals with Akkadian names are: 'Lord of the Roof', *bēl ūri*; 'Fits', *bennu*; 'Wind', *idiptu*; 'Scab', *libu*; Lamashtu—a female demon, a disease; 'Something Evil', *mimma lemnu*; 'Stroke', *miqit*; 'Flashes of Lightning', *muttabriqu*; 'She who Erases', *pašittu* (an epithet of the demon Lamashtu); a lion-demon *ugallu*, see fig. 2:8; 'The Croucher', *rābiṣu*; 'Bailiff', *šarabda*; 'Staggers', *ṣidana*; a disease brought on by flood water, *šuruppu*; 'Expulsion', *ṭirid*; 'Feverhot', *umma*; a storm demon, *ūmu*. Individuals with Sumerian names are: 'Upholder of Evil', *saghulhaza*; and doorkeepers of the Underworld: Engidudu (also an epithet of Erra, q.v.), Endushuba, Endukuga, Endashurimma, Ennu-gigi, Enuralla/Nerulla, Nerubanda.

Der—city east of the Tigris in northern Babylonia. Patron god Ishtaran.

Dimkurkurra—'creator of lands', Sumerian epithet of Marduk in the *Epic of Creation*; 'bond of lands', epithet of Babylon.

Duku—'holy mound', Sumerian name for a cosmic place in Ubshu-ukkinakku, where the ancestors of Ellil lamented, where the Sun-god and the Anunnaki decided fates; represented in the temple of each major deity.

Dumuzi—'faithful son', Sumerian god, lover of Ishtar, brother of Geshtin-anna, shepherd of Uruk, doorkeeper of Anu, paired with Gishzida, fisherman of Ku'ara. Spent half of each year in the Underworld and so was the subject of the annual *taklimtu*-ritual of lying-in-state. Name pronounced Tammuz in Syria, Du'uzi in Assyria.

Dunnu—town in the vicinity of Isin and Larsa in central Mesopotamia, important in the Old Babylonian period.

Duranki—'bond of heaven and earth', name of Ellil's temple, also used for the god himself.

Ea (Sumerian Enki)—god of fresh water, wisdom, and incantations, helper of mankind who sent the Seven Sages to teach the arts and skills of civilization to men. Lived in the Apsu. Cult centre Eridu. Temple named E-engurra and E-abzu. Spouse Damkina. Symbols: a goat-fish, a horned crown on a shrine, and probably the overflowing vase. Also known as Nudimmud, a name associated with function as a creator god. Epithet: *niššiku*, q.v., translated here 'far-sighted'.

E-akkil—temple of the god Papsukkal in Kish.

Eanna—'house of the sky', name of Anu's and Ishtar's temple in Uruk, also called 'the pure treasury'.

Earth—primeval goddess in *Theogony of Dunnu*; a name for the Underworld.

Ea-sharru—'Ea the king', a form of Ea's name.

E-engurra—temple of the god Ea in Eridu.

E-galgina—'the everlasting palace', name of a place in the Underworld.

E-galmah—temple of the goddess Gula in Isin.

E-igi-kalama—temple of Lugal-Marada in Marad.

E-halanki—shrine of the goddess Zarpanitum in Babylon.

Ekur—'mountain house', temple of Ellil in Nippur, where Ninurta was born.

E-kurmah—'great mountain house', temple of Ninazu.

Elam—country east of Babylonia in modern Iran. Capital cities: Susa and Anshan. Language of no known group, written in cuneiform.

Ellil (also Illil; Sumerian Enlil)—god whose nature and attributes are still uncertain. Head of the younger generation of Sumerian and Akkadian gods. Cult centre Nippur. Temple called Ekur. Spouse Mulliltu; son Ninurta. Old interpretation of his name as 'Lord wind/air' is disputed. Epithet: 'king of (all) populated lands'. Symbol: a horned crown on a shrine.

E-meslam—'Meslam house' (see Underworld). Temple of Nergal in Kutha.

Enbilulu—a Sumerian god of irrigation, canals, and farming, meaning of name unknown. Assimilated with Adad in Babylon.

E-nimma-anku—name of an unknown temple.

E-ninnu—'house of fifty', temple of Ningirsu in Girsu.

Enki—see Ea.

Enkidu (previously read Ea-bani)—primitive, wild man who lived among wild animals until tamed by a harlot and introduced to Uruk to rival Gilgamesh. Epitomizes the wise, skilful hunter. Name may mean 'created by Ea', 'lord of the good place', or 'the wild one'. Assimilated partly with Shakkan as master of animals, and partly with the *lahmu*-hero as a primeval hero. Equivalent of the wise counsellor Affan in *Story of Buluqiya*.

Enkurkur—'lord of the lands', Sumerian title.

Enmesharra—a Sumerian Underworld god.

Engidudu—see Demons and Erra.

Ennugi—Sumerian god, throne-bearer of Ellil.

Eresh—cult centre of Ninhursag, the great mother goddess. Unidentified site in central Mesopotamia.

Ereshkigal (also pronounced Arshigingal)—'queen of the great Earth', 'Mistress of Earth'. Sumerian goddess, sister of Ishtar, spouse of Nergal, mother of Ninazu.

Eridu—very ancient city at the shore of the Arabian Gulf, cult centre of Ea. Also the name of a quarter of Babylon.

Erkalla—'great city'; see Underworld.

Erra—god of war, hunting, and plague. Etymology 'scorched (earth)' probably incorrect. Assimilated with Nergal and Gerra. Temple Emeslam in the city Kutha. Epithet Engidudu, 'lord who prowls by night' (see Demons). See also Nergal.

Erragal, Erakal—probably a pronounced form of Nergal, may mean 'Erra the great', probably pronounced Herakles in Greek.

E-sagila—'house with the lofty top', temple of Marduk in Babylon. Epithet: 'the palace of heaven and earth'.

E-sharra—name of several temples, including one of Anu in Uruk and one of Assur in Assur city.

Eshgalla—'great shrine'.

Eshnunna—kingdom east of Tigris. Included Ishchali where some of OBV *Gilgamesh* was excavated, and Tell Haddad, where some of *Erra and Ishum* was excavated.

E-sizkur—'house of prayer'.

E-sikil—'pure house', name of the temple of Tishpak (formerly of Ninazu) in Eshnunna.

Etana—twelfth king of Kish after the Flood, father of Balih.

E-temen-anki—name of the ziggurrat tower of Marduk in Babylon.

E-ugal—name of the temple of Ellil in Dur-Kurigalzu (see also Parsay).

Euphrates—river of Mesopotamia. Akkadian name Purattu, Hittite name Mala.

Flocks god—deity in the *Theogony of Dunnu*, may be read as Gaiu or Lahar.

gallū-demons—see Demons.

Gerra (Sumerian Gibil)—fire-god, partly assimilated with Erra and Nergal, son of Anu and Anunitu.

Geshtu-e (formerly read We-ila)—'ear', name of otherwise unknown god who was slain in order that his blood and intelligence might be used as ingredients in man's creation. Now read Ilawela.

Gilgamesh (Bilgamesh, Galgamishul, Buluqiya(?), previously read Izdubar)—king of Uruk, son of Lugalbanda and Ninsun in the Epic. Name may mean 'the old man is a young man' in Sumerian. Listed with gods in very early texts. Late epithet: 'king of Earth'.

Girsu—important Sumerian city in the third millennium BC, patron god Ningirsu, identified as modern Tello (which was once wrongly identified as Lagash).

Gishzida (sometimes pronounced Gizzida, also called Nin-gishzida)— 'trusty timber', Sumerian god paired with Dumuzi, son of Ninazu, consort of Belili, doorkeeper of Anu. Cult centre: Gishbanda, between Lagash and Ur. Symbol: horned snake.

Gudea—local ruler of Lagash c.2199–2180 BC. Author of long inscriptions in Sumerian.

Gushkin-banda—Sumerian name for the patron god of gold-working.

Gutian—barbarous enemies of Mesopotamian cities who invaded and caused much destruction in the late third millennium BC.

Haharnu—a god, functions and meaning of name unknown.

Hammurabi—king of Babylon 1848–1806 BC. Author of famous law code.

Hanigalbat—name given to the Hurrian kingdom of Mittani, northwest of Assyria, varying in extent as that kingdom's empire varied. Chiefly in the upper Habur region in Syria and in the vicinity of modern Diarbekir in Turkey.

Hanish—minor god, servant of the weather-god, paired with Shullat.

Hattusas (modern Bogazköy)—Hittite capital city in northern Anatolia where Akkadian, Hittite, and Hurrian fragments of *Gilgamesh* have been found.

Hayyashum—a god, function and meaning of name ('Hasty'?) uncertain.

Hehe—name of a mythical mountain, birthplace of Anzu.

Hendursanga—'lofty mace', epithet of Ishum as herald of Sumer.

Heracles—see Nergal.

Horned serpent (Akkadian *bašmu*)—mythical monster created in the sea, 60 leagues long with multiple mouths and tongues. See fig. 2:3.

Hermon—see Sirara.

Hubur (Sumerian Ilurugu)—river of the Underworld, and the river ordeal used to settle disputes. Same word means a tributary of the Euphrates in Syria, and 'hubbub'.

Humbaba (also pronounced Huwawa)—guardian of the Pine Forest, fire-breathing servant of the god Wer, depicted with a face lined like coiled intestines, ancestor of the Greek Gorgon. His voice is the *abūbu*-weapon. See fig. 2:5.

Hurabtil—an Elamite god also known as Lahurabtil.

Igigi—Sumerian group term for the great gods of the younger generation, sky-gods headed by Ellil. Often paired with the Anunnaki.

Ilabrat—vizier of Anu.

Illil—see Ellil.

Imgur-Ellil—name of the defensive wall of Babylon.

Inninna—see Ishtar.

Irnini (Irnina)—a goddess of war assimilated with Ishtar.

Ishhara—goddess of marriage and childbirth, enforcer of oaths. Cult centre: Kisurra in Babylonia. Symbol: a scorpion.

Ishtar (Sumerian Innin, Inninna, Inanna)—goddess of love and war, patron of Uruk, Nineveh, and Erbil. In Uruk traditions her father is Anu, in others, Sin the moon-god. Sister of Ereshkigal. Her name is also used as a generic term for 'goddess', and can have a plural form. Symbols: morning star and evening star; rosette.

Ishtaran (previously read Sataran and Kadi)—patron god of Der.

Ishullanu—gardener of the god Anu.

Ishum—a fire-god(?), war leader of the gods, herald and adviser of Erra. Assimilated with Hendursanga. Epithets: 'wise', and 'pious slaughterer'.

Kabti-ilani-Marduk—descendant of Dabibi, author of *Erra and Ishum*.

Kakka—vizier of Anshar and of Anu.

Kalah (modern Nimrud)—capital city of Assyrian kings in the early first millennium BC. Cult centre of Ninurta.

Kalkal—doorkeeper of Ellil in Nippur.

Kar-usakar—'quay of the crescent moon' in Eridu.

Kassites—horsemen from outside Mesopotamia who seized power as resident aliens in the mid-second millennium BC, and ruled from Babylon for almost 500 years. Although they had their own, non-semitic language, they were fully assimilated to Akkadian culture and appear to have introduced no particular innovations of their own.

kašûšu-weapon—a destructive weapon used by various gods.

Kish—an ancient city, the first to regain kingship after the Flood according to the Sumerian king list. East of Babylon, connected to it by canal. Cult centre of Ishtar (temple E-hursag-kalama), and Zababa (temple E-mete-ursag).

Kishar—'whole earth', Sumerian god of old generation, paired with Anshar.

Kulla—patron god of bricks.

Kullab—name of a quarter in the city Uruk; also the name of a quarter of Babylon.

kurgarrû—a cult person who appears to have been effeminate and to have been some kind of an actor.

Kurnugi—'land of no return', a Sumerian term for the Underworld.

Kush—a herdsman god.

Kutha—cult centre of Nergal, city near Babylon. Temple Emeslam.

lahmu, lahamu—'the hairy one', perhaps also 'muddy', term for a primeval hero with three pairs of curls, shown naked except for a triple sash. Creature of Ea in the Apsu. Ea's temple in Eridu contained fifty of them. They controlled the bolt of the sea and the availability of fish. Often shown holding the overflowing vase. See also Enkidu. See fig. 2:4.

Lamashtu—see Demons.

Lebanon—name of a mountain in *Gilgamesh*.

Lugalbanda—king of Uruk, son of Enmerkar, father of Gilgamesh. Deified hero of several Sumerian stories. Consort of the goddess Ninsun, native of Kullab.

Lugal-dimmer-ankia—Sumerian title 'king of the gods of heaven and earth'.

Lugal-Marada—'king of Marad', name of the patron god of Marad, temple E-igi-kalama.

Lullubu—a savage tribe which lived in the area of Suleimaniya in north-eastern Iraq.

Malah—'Boatman'. See also Sirsir, Puzur-Amurri, and Ur-shanabi.

Mami, Mammi, Mammitum—names for the great mother goddess Ninhursag, q.v.

Manungal—little-known Sumerian Underworld deity. Spouse of Birdu. Epithet:'The Snatcher'.

Marduk—patron god of Babylon, consort of Zarpanitum. Temple Esagila, ziggurrat E-temen-anki. Epithet: Bel, 'Lord'. Agricultural god. Symbols: a spade, a *mušhuššu*-dragon. Name may mean 'bull-calf of the Sun' and/or 'son of Duku'. For assimilation with other gods, see seven names and epithets in *Epic of Creation*, VI, and fifty in VII.

Mashu—a mountain at the edge of the world where the sun rises. Guarded by the scorpion-men. Name means 'twin'.

Melqart—Phoenician god, equivalent of Nergal. Name means 'King of the City'. Patron god of Tyre.

Muhra—'Face both ways(?)', name of the two-faced gatekeeper of the Underworld. See also Ushmu.

Mulliltu (Assyrian Mullissu, Sumerian Ninlil, Greek Mylitta)—goddess, spouse of Ellil, and of Assur as the Assyrian Ellil.

Mummu—vizier of Apsu.

mušhuššu—'red/furious snake'. A dragon or composite monster, symbol of Marduk. See fig. 2:6. (Previously read *şirruš*.)

Nabonassar (Nabu-naṣir)—king of Babylon 747–734 BC, under whom a new era was reckoned to have begun.

Nabu—god of writing and wisdom. Temples called Ezida. Main shrine in Borshippa. Spouse Tashmetum. Prominent from the eighth century onwards.

Nammu—Sumerian birth-goddess, mother of Ea, associated with fresh water.

Namtar, Namtara—Sumerian god, 'decider of fate', vizier of Ereshkigal, demonic god of the Underworld.

Nash (pronounced form of Nanshe)—daughter of Ea. Cult centre: Sirara near Lagash.

Neberu—'crossing place', name of the planet Jupiter.

Nedu, Neti—'doorkeeper', name of the doorkeeper of the Underworld.

Nergal (also pronounced Erakal)—'lord of Erkalla (the Great City)'. Chief god of the Underworld, consort of Ereshkigal (and of Mammitum; see s.v. Ninhursag). Assimilated with Erra and called Herakles in Greek. Patron god of Kutha and Tarbiṣu. Temple Emeslam. Partly assimilated with Gilgamesh as judge of the Underworld and with Ninurta.

Nimush (previously read Niṣir)—mountain on which the ark came to rest when the Flood receded, according to a Nineveh version of *Gilgamesh*, XI.

Nin-agal—'lord strong-arm'. Name of the patron god of smiths.

Nin-azu—god of Eshnunna. Temple called E-sikil and E-kurmah. Son of Ereshkigal, father of Nin-gishzida. Replaced by Tishpak as patron of Eshnunna.

Nineveh (modern Küyünjik and Nebi Yunus)—capital of the late Assyrian kings, in the late eighth and early seventh centuries BC. Cult centre of Ishtar.

Nin-girsu—'lord of Girsu', patron god of Girsu, son of Ninmah (Ninhursag). Temple Eninnu. God of fertility, vegetation, and war. Symbol: Anzu, the lion-headed eagle. Weapon: Sharur, a personified and deified mace.

Nin-gishzida—'Lord of the trusty timber'. See Gishzida.

Nin-hursag—'mountain lady', also known as Ninmah 'supreme lady', Nintu 'birth(?)lady', Mamma, Mammi, Mami, Mammitum, 'mummy', Belet-ili 'mistress of the gods', Aruru (meaning unknown). Epithets: *šassuru*, 'womb-goddess'; *tabsūt īlī*, 'midwife of the gods'; and *qurqurrat īlī*, 'smelter of the gods', 'mother of the gods', and 'mother of all children'. Spouse of Shulpae and then of Nergal. Shrine at Kesh in central Mesopotamia, still not identified.

Nin-ildu—patron god of carpenters.

Nin-sun—'lady wild cow', Sumerian goddess, mother of Gilgamesh. Epithets: 'wise' and 'wild cow' (in Akkadian). The epithet 'wild cow' can alternatively be read as part of the personal name, Rimat-Ninsun.

Nin-shubur—female deity in Sumerian, male in Akkadian. Vizier of Anu and of Ishtar. Assimilated with Ilabrat and with Papsukkal.

Nin-tu—a name of Ninhursag, q.v.

Nin-urta (probably pronounced Nimrod and Enurta at times)—Sumerian warrior-god, heroic winner of many famous victories, god of agricultural and pastoral fertility. Son of Ellil. Assimilated with Ningirsu. Temple E-padun-tila (previously read E-patu-tila), chief shrine perhaps in Nippur. Leader of the Anunnaki in *Anzu*. Epithet: 'avenger/champion of Ellil'.

Nippur—city in central Mesopotamia. Cult centre of Ellil. Main temple Ekur.

Nissaba—Sumerian goddess of writing, learned knowledge, and of cereal fertility. Patron of Eresh. Daughter of Anu, spouse of Haya.

niššiku (previously misread as a Sumerian phrase *nin-igi-kù*, translated 'lord of the bright eye')—epithet of Ea. Meaning not exactly certain, partly synonymous with 'wise'. Translated here as 'far-sighted'.

Nudimmud—name of Ea as a Sumerian creator-god.

Nusku—god of light. Important shrines with the moon-god at Harran and Neirab. Vizier of Anu and of Ellil. Symbol: lamp.

Oannes—Greek form of Uan, a name of Adapa, q.v.

Offerings—flour offering *mashatu* which was roasted and scattered; smoke offering, *qutrinnu*, which the gods could smell from heaven; incense offering, *muššakku*; scattered offering, *surqinnu*; presentation offering, *taqribtu*; displayed offering, *taklīmu*; food offering, *nindabû*, often of bread; regular offerings, *ginû*; sacrifices, *niqû*, often of sheep.

Pabilsag—god of Larak, a city of importance before the Flood.

Pagalguenna—'great canal of the Guenna (governor of Nippur)', title of Marduk in *Epic of Creation*.

Panigara (written Pap-nigin-gara)—a warrior-god assimilated with Ninurta. Epithet: 'lord of the boundary stone.'

Papsukkal—vizier of the great gods. Temple E-akkil in Kish. Assimilated with Ilabrat and Ninshubur.

Parsay—name of Dur-Kurigalzu, Kassite capital city near Baghdad.

Pasture and Poplar—goddess Ua-ildak.

Plough—Akkadian *harab*, previously read Hain. Personification of the kind of plough used for opening up virgin soil.

Priests and Priestesses—*enu* (Sumerian *en*), high priest, a role sometimes filled in early times by a city ruler; *entu*, high priestess, sometimes the king's daughter dedicated to the moon-god at Ur, may have acted for the goddess in sacred marriage ceremony; *ugbabtu*, *egisītu*, *kulmašītu*, and *qadištu*, cloistered females under cultic regulations that prohibited normal marriage and childbirth; *pašīšu*; anointed priest, *išippu* and *lumahhu*, kinds of purification priests; *gudapsû*, *lagaru*, names for priestly personnel whose roles are uncertain; *šakkanakku* city governor with priestly functions.

Puzur-Amurri—'secret of the West(ern god)', name of Ut-napishtim's boatman at the Flood in *Gilgamesh*.

Qingu (previously read Kingu)—name of Tiamat's chosen battle leader. Holder of the Tablet of Destinies. Meaning of name unknown.

River—Sumerian goddess Ida.

Sargon II—king of Assyria, 721–705 BC. Wrote a long description of his eighth campaign in the form of a letter to the gods.

Scorpion-man and -woman—composite creatures sometimes helpful to man, used as apotropaic figurines. Guardians of mountain Mashu. See fig. 2:7.

Sea—see Ayabba and Tiamat.

Sebitti—'The Seven', group of seven warrior-gods who march with Erra into battle. The Pleiades. Demonic and evil in some traditions, good and helpful in others. Offspring of Anu and Earth.

Sennacherib—king of Assyria 704–681 BC. Sacked Babylon, 689 BC. Established Nineveh as capital city with royal palace library.

Seven Sages—according to cuneiform traditions, known only from indirect references and from Berossus, Ea sent seven divine sages, *apkallu*, in the form of *purādu*-fish (carp?) from the Apsu to teach the arts (Sumerian *me*) of civilization to mankind before the Flood. They were: Adapa (U-an, called Oannes by Berossus), U-an-duga, En-me-duga, En-me-galama, En-me-buluga, An-Enlilda, and Utu-abzu. Each is also known by other names or epithets, and is paired with an antediluvian king, hence their collective name 'counsellors', *muntalkū*. In this capacity they were credited with building walled cities. Responsible for technical skills, they were also known as 'craftsmen', *ummiānu*, a word which puns with Adapa's name U-an. They were banished back to the Apsu forever after angering Ea. After the Flood, certain great men of letters and exorcists were accorded sage-status, although only as mortals. Deities other than Ea—Ishtar, Nabu, and Marduk—claimed to control the sages. In iconography sages are shown either as fish-men, or with bird attributes appropriate to Underworld creatures.

Shakkan (also called Sumuqan and Amakandu)—god of cattle and of herdsmen, often paired with Ashnan the grain-god. Also pronounced Shahhan.

Shamash (Sumerian Utu)—sun-god. Patron god of Sippar and Larsa, temples called E-babbar. Spouse Aya/Anunitum; god of justice, omens, and extispicy. Title 'my sun' means 'his majesty', conferred on mortal kings and on gods who were the head of a particular pantheon.

Shamhat (also pronounced Shamkat)—'harlot, voluptuous one', name of the prostitute sent to Enkidu. Probably belonged to the cult personnel of Ishtar's temple in Uruk.

Shara—Sumerian city god of Umma, modern Tell Djoha, north-east of Uruk. Son of Ishtar. Epithet: 'hero of Anu'.

Sharur—personified weapon of Ninurta/Ningirsu, a lesser god, probably represented as a mace.

Shuanna—name for Babylon, originally the quarter of Babylon in which the main temples were situated.

Shullat—a little-known god paired with Hanish. Servant of the sun-god.

Shulpae—major Sumerian god with very wide range of attributes, including fertility and demonic powers. Consort of Ninhursag. Identified with planet Jupiter.

Shuruppak—city of Ut-napishtim in central southern Mesopotamia. Identified with modern Tell Fara.

Shushinak—patron god of Susa in western Elam.

Siduri—name of alewife, meaning of name unknown. Goddess of brewing and of wisdom. Word 'alewife', *sabītum*, may also mean 'woman from the land of Sabum'.

Sililu—mother of the horse; not otherwise known.

Sin (also spelt Su'en; Sumerian Nanna, west semitic Erah)—moon-god of Ur, Harran, and Neirab. Consort of Nikkal (Sumerian Ningal). Symbol: crescent disk. Lord of oaths. Associated with skin diseases.

Sippar—city of Shamash and Aya/Anunitum, on the Euphrates, upstream from Babylon. Epithet: 'the eternal city'.

Sirara (also called Saria)—name of Mount Hermon in the Lebanon.

Sirsir—boatman-god, patron of sailors.

Subartu—probably a general term for the countries north of Assyria.

Sultantepe (ancient Huzirina)—site near Harran in which archaeologists found school texts including exercise tablets of literary compositions. They probably all stem from versions in the libraries of Assyria of the eighth and seventh centuries.

Sur-sunabu—see Ur-shanabi.

Susa—western capital of the Elamite kingdom, in the Zagros mountains. Patron god: Shushinak.

Suteans—west semitic nomads of the late second and early first millennia, mainly attested on the middle Euphrates, but threatened Der, east of the Tigris, in the eleventh century BC. Traditional enemies of settled Akkadians.

Tablet of Destinies (previously translated 'Tablets of Destiny')—the cuneiform clay tablet on which fates were written. It gave supreme power to its possessor. Antecedent of the Book of Fate in the Book of Jubilees, and of the pre-Islamic and Islamic *Lawh al-mahfuz*, 'Preserved Tablet', on which the decrees of Allah were written (See *Encyclopaedia of Islam*), s.v. LAWH). Accompanied by the Seal of Destinies (George 1986).

Tarbisu—ancient town just north of Nineveh. Cult centre of Nergal.

Tell Haddad—site on the Diyala river, east of Tigris, ancient Me-Turan.

Tell Harmal—site near Baghdad, ancient Shaduppum.

Tiamat (also pronounced Tiwawat and Tamtu, probably pronounced Tethys in Ionian Greek; also known as Ayabba chiefly in west Semitic)—'Sea', salt water personified as a primeval goddess. Mother of the first generation of gods in the *Epic of Creation*. Spouse of Apsu. Epitomizes chaos.

Tigris—river of eastern Mesopotamia, ancient Idiglat.

Tirannu—name of Uruk, means 'rainbow', used in Seleucid times.

Tiruru—largely unknown deity, about whom a myth must have existed in extreme antiquity.

Tishpak—patron god of Eshnunna. Nature uncertain. Probably assimilated with Ninazu.

Tutu—name of a Sumerian creator-god.

Ua-ildak—previously read Ga'um; goddess of pasture and poplar.

Ubara-Tutu—father of Ut-napishtim, king of Shuruppak, who ruled for 18,600 years according to the Sumerian king list.

Ubshu-ukkina, Ubshu-ukkinakku—Sumerian name for the divine assembly hall which had its earthly counterpart in various chief temples. Contained the holy mountain Duku, q.v.

Ugarit (modern Ras Shamra)—Bronze Age city in Syria where many Akkadian cuneiform tablets were unearthed, as well as tablets written in alphabetic cuneiform for the Canaanite language now known as Ugaritic.

Ukur—a demonic Underworld god, vizier of Nergal, perhaps also assimilated with Nergal.

Ulaya—river Karkheh in western Iran.

Underworld—known as 'The Earth', *erṣetum*; 'The Stronghold(?)', Dannina; Arali, q.v.; Kutha (city where Nergal was patron god); Meslam (Nergal's temple in Kutha); 'The Lower Regions', *šaplātu*; 'The Great Place', *kigallu, gingal*; 'The Land of No Return', Kurnugi; and 'The Great City', Erkalla. Great gate called Ganzir, palace Egalgina. Ruled by Ereshkigal and by Nergal. Recorder: Belet-ṣeri. Judges: the Anunnaki gods, and Gilgamesh. The Greek Hades may be derived from Akkadian *adêšu*, 'oaths, consequences of perjury'.

Ur—city port on the Euphrates near the Arabian Gulf. Patron god: Sin. Temple E-kishnugal, holy seat of the royal *entu*-priestess.

Ur-shanabi (Sumerian Sur-sunabu)—boatman of Ut-napishtim after he became immortal and lived at the 'Mouth of the Rivers'.

Uruk (modern Warka)—city in lower Mesopotamia. Kings included Enmerkar, Lugalbanda, and Gilgamesh. Patron deities Anu and Ishtar. Main temple Eanna. Epithet: sheepfold (also means cattle-pen) of Eanna. Also known as Tiranna, 'Rainbow City' in the Seleucid period.

Ushmu, Usmu, Isimud—Sumerian god, two-faced vizier of Apsu. Perhaps known in Akkadian as Muhra, q.v.

Ut-napishtim—also known as Uta-na'ishtim and Ut-napushte, meaning perhaps 'he found life' and/or 'day of life', Hebrew Noah, Sumerian Ziusudra, and Xisuthros in Berossus' Greek rendering. Epithet/name: *atrahasis*, 'extra wise', and 'far-distant' (see Introduction, pp. 2–3). Precursor of the Islamic sage Al-Khiḍr/Al-Khaḍir.

Weapons of gods—see *abūbu*, 'flood-weapon', *kašūšu*, Sharur, Winds, and *ašqulālu*; also net of Shamash in *Etana*.

Wer (also known as Mer, Ber, and Ilwer)—a storm-god, Humbaba's patron god, identified with Amurru and with Adad. One of his cult centres was at Afis, 45 km. south-west of Aleppo.

Winds—four winds of the compass points: South Wind, *šūtu*, capricious and female, also known as 'Ea's breath'; North Wind, *ištānu*, pleasant and moderate; East Wind, *šadû*, literally 'mountain wind'; West Wind, *amurru*. Seven evil winds, variously referred to as 'Evil Wind', *imhullu*; 'Tempest', *mehû*; 'Whirlwind', *ašamšatu*; 'Tornado', *imsuhhu*; and *šaparziqqu*-wind.

Zababa (also known as Zamama)—warrior-god, patron of Kish, temple E-meteursag.

Zarpanitum (previously read Ṣarpanitum)—goddess of pregnancy. Spouse of Marduk in Babylon. Also called Erua.

Ziggurrat—temple tower, either stepped in tiers or spiral, symbolizing mountain peak on which gods dwelt. Topped by a small shrine.

Note. Certain terms, notably Igigi, Anunnaki, and Sebitti, are very seldom declined in Akkadian texts, so the forms given have been taken as probably *status absolutus*, although they are sometimes declined in esoteric, scholarly texts.

SELECT BIBLIOGRAPHY

Items which incorporate long and detailed bibliographies are marked with an asterisk. References to the publication of copies of the cuneiform tablets can be found in the editions, and are not given separately here. Recent additions to the bibliography are given in the preface to the revised edition, pp. ix–x above.

Borger, R. 1956, 'Die Inschriften Asarhaddons, Königs von Assyrien', *Archiv für Orientforschung Beiheft*, 9 (Graz).
—— 1979, *Babylonisch-assyrische Lesestücke* (2nd edn; Rome).
—— 1980, 'Note brève, Enuma eliš IV 72', *Revue d'Assyriologie*, 74 (1980), 95–6 (Paris).
Bottéro, J. 1977, 'Les noms de Marduk', in *Essays in honor of J. J. Finkelstein*, ed. M. de J. Ellis (Connecticut).
Brinkman, J. A. 1984, *Prelude to Empire: Babylonian society and politics 747–626 BC* (Philadelphia).
Buccellati, G. 1982, 'The Descent of Inanna as a ritual journey to Kutha?', *Syro-Mesopotamian Studies*, 4/3 (Malibu).
Burkert, W. 1982, 'Literarische Texte und funktionaler Mythos: zu Ištar und Atrahasis', in *Funktionen und Leistungen des Mythos, drei altorientalische Beispiele, Orbis Biblicus et Orientalis*, 48, ed. J. Assmann *et al.* (Freiburg and Göttingen).
—— 1983, 'Oriental Myth and Literature in the Iliad', in *The Greek Renaissance of the 8th century BC*, ed. R. Hägg (Sweden).
—— 1984, *Die orientalisierende Epoche in der griechischen Religion und Literatur* (Heidelberg).
*Cagni, L. 1969, 'L'Epopea di Erra', *Studi Semitici*, 34 (Rome).
—— 1977. *The poem of Erra*. Sources and Monographs, Sources from the Ancient Near East, 1/3 (Malibu).
Campbell Thompson, R. 1930, *The Epic of Gilgamesh: Text, Transliteration, and Notes* (Oxford).
Chicago Assyrian Dictionary, 1956–88 (still in progress).
Clayden, T. 1989, 'The Archaeology and History of the Kassite period (circa 1600–1150 BC) in Iraq'. Unpublished D.Phil. thesis, Oxford University.
Collon, D. 1982, *Catalogue of the Western Asiatic Seals in the British Museum. Cylinder Seals II* (London).
Cooper, J. S. 1978, *The Return of Ninurta to Nippur* (Rome).

Craig, J. A. 1895–7, *Assyrian and Babylonian Religious Texts I and II* (Leipzig).

Dalley, S. 1987, *Near Eastern patron deities of mining and smelting*, Reports of the Department of Antiquities in Cyprus.

—— 1991, 'Gilgamesh in the Arabian Nights', *JRAS* 1, pp. 1–17.

van Dijk, J. 1976, *Texts in the Iraq Museum IX, Cuneiform Texts of Varying Content* (Leiden).

—— 1983, *Lugal ud me-lám-bi nir-gál, le récit épique et didactique des Travaux de Ninurta, du Déluge et de la Nouvelle Création* (Leiden). With review of S. N. Kramer, *Journal of the American Oriental Society*, 105/1, 1985.

Driver, S. 1926, *The Book of Genesis* (12th edn; London).

During Caspars, E. 1983, *Northeastern Arabian Archaeology in Retrospect*, Bibliotheca Orientalis XL, pp. 39–46.

Ebeling, E. 1931. *Tod und Leben nach den Vorstellungen der Babylonier* (Berlin).

—— 1949, 'Ein Heldenlied auf Tiglatpileser I und der Anfang einer neuer Version von "Ištars Höllenfahrt" nach einer Schülertafel aus Assur', *Orientalia*, 18, pp. 30 ff.

Edzard, D. O. 1986, Review of Kinnier Wilson 1985, *Zeitschrift für Assyriologie*, 76/1, pp. 134–7.

Ellis, M. de J. 1981–2, 'Gilgamesh' Approach to Huwawa: A new text', *Archiv für Orientforschung*, 28, pp. 123–31.

Encyclopaedia of Islam 1936, s.v. Al-Khaḍir (Al-Khiḍr) and s.v. LAWḤ (London and Leiden).

Frazer, J. G. 1919, *Folk-Lore in the Old Testament*, i. 104–360 (London).

—— 1921, *Apollodorus* (Loeb edn; Harvard and London).

Friedrich, J. 1930, 'Die hethitischen Bruchstücke des Gilgameš-Epos', *Zeitschrift für Assyriologie*, 39, Neufolge 5, pp. 1–82.

George, A. 1985a, 'Observations on a passage of "Inanna's Descent"', *Journal of Cuneiform Studies*, 37 (1985), pp. 109–13.

—— 1985b, 'Notes on two extremes of weather', *Revue d'assyriologie*, 79, pp. 69–71.

—— 1986, 'Sennacherib and the Tablet of Destinies', *Iraq*, 48, pp. 133–46 (London).

—— 1987, 'The Day the Earth Divided: a geological aetiology in the Babylonian Gilgameš epic', paper read at the *Rencontre Assyriologique Internationale* in Istanbul.

Greengus, S. 1979, *Old Babylonian tablets from Ishchali and vicinity* (Istanbul).

Gressmann, H. 1926, 'Der Eingang ins Paradies', *Archiv für Orientforschung*, 3, p. 12.

Gurney, O. R. 1957, 'The Sultantepe Tablets (continued) VI, A letter of Gilgamesh', *Anatolian Studies*, 7, pp. 127–36.

—— 1960, 'The Sultantepe Tablets', *Anatolian Studies*, 10, pp. 105–31.

—— 1979, 'Note brève, Gilgamesh XI, 78', *Revue d'assyriologie*, 73, pp. 89–90.

Haas, V. 1979. 'Remarks on Hurrian Ištar-Sawuska of Nineveh in the second millennium BC', *Sumer*, 35, pp. 397–401.

Hallo, W. and Moran, W. 1979, 'The first tablet of the SB recension of the Anzu myth', *Journal of Cuneiform Studies*, 31, pp. 65–115.

Hassan, F. A. and Robinson, S. W. 1987, 'High precision radiocarbon chronometry', *Antiquity*, 61/231, pp. 119–35.

Heltzer, M. 1981, *The Suteans*. Istituto Universitario Orientale, seminario di studi asiatici, series minor XIII (Naples).

Hesiod, *Theogony*, translated by R. Lattimore (Ann Arbor, 1959).

Hruška, B. 1975, *Der Mythenadler Anzu in Literatur und Vorstellung* (Budapest).

Huber, P. J. 1982, 'Astronomical dating of Babylon I and Ur III', *Occasional Papers on the Near East*, 1/4 (Malibu).

Hunger, H. 1976, *Spätbabylonische Texte aus Uruk I* (Berlin).

Jacobsen, T. 1939, 'The Sumerian King List', *Assyriological Studies*, 11 (Chicago).

*—— 1984, 'The Harab Myth', *Studies in the Ancient Near East*, 2/3 (Malibu).

Jensen, P. 1906, *Das Gilgamesch-Epos in der Weltliteratur* (I, Strasburg; II, 1928, Marburg).

Kilmer, A. D. 1971, 'How was Queen Ereshkigal tricked?', *Ugarit-Forschungen*, 3 (1971), 229–311.

—— 1982, 'Word play in Gilgamesh', in *Zikir Šumim, Festschrift for F. R. Kraus*, ed. K. R. Veenhof (Leiden).

—— 1987, 'The symbolism of the flies in the Mesopotamian flood myth and some further implications', in *Language, Literature and History: philological and historical studies presented to E. Reiner*, ed. F. Rochberg-Halton (New Haven), pp. 175–80.

*Kinnier Wilson, J. V. 1985, *The Legend of Etana* (Warminster).

Klein, H. 1983, 'Tudittum', *Zeitschrift für Assyriologie*, 73, pp. 255–84.

Klein, J. 1976, 'Šulgi and Gilgameš—two peer-brothers', in *Kramer Anniversary volume, Alter Orient und altes Testament*, 25 (Neukirchen-Vluyn).

—— 1981, 'The Royal Hymns of Shulgi, king of Ur', *Transactions of the American Philosophical Society*, 71/7.

Knudtzon, J. 1915, *Die El-Amarna Tafeln* (Leipzig, reprinted Aalen 1964), i. 964–8, Adapa; 968–74, Nergal and Ereshkigal.

Kramer, S. N. 1944, 'The Epic of Gilgamesh and its Sumerian sources', *Journal of the American Oriental Society*, 64, pp. 7–23.

—— 1983, 'The Sumerian Deluge Myth', *Anatolian Studies*, 33, pp. 115–21.

Labat, R. 1935, *Le poème babylonien de la création* (Paris).

Lambert, W. G. and Walcot, P. 1965, 'A new Babylonian theogony and Hesiod', *Kadmos*, 4, pp. 64 ff.

—— and Millard A. R. 1969, *Atra-hasis. The Babylonian story of the Flood* (Oxford).

—— 1969a, 'New evidence for the first line of Atra-hasis', *Orientalia*, 38, pp. 533–8.

—— 1969b, 'An eyestone of Esarhaddon's queen and other, similar gems', *Revue d'assyriologie*, 63, pp. 65–71.

—— 1979, 'Note brève, Gilgamesh I, i, 41', *Revue d'assyriologie*, 73, p. 89.

—— 1980a, 'The theology of Death. Death in Mesopotamia', in Papers from the Twenty-sixth *Rencontre Assyriologique Internationale, Mesopotamia*, 8, ed. B. Alster (Copenhagen), 53–66.

—— 1980b, 'New fragments of Babylonian epics', *Archiv für Orientforschung*, 27, pp. 71–82.

—— 1986, 'Note brève, Niṣir or Nimuš', *Revue d'assyriologie*, 80, pp. 185–6.

Lehmann-Haupt, C. F. 1910, *Armenien Einst und Jetzt I*, Chapter 14 *'Der Tigris Tunnel'* (Berlin).

McGinnis, J. 1987, 'A neo-Assyrian text describing a royal funeral', *State Archives of Assyria*, Bulletin 1/1, pp. 1–11.

Millard, A. R. 1964, 'Gilgamesh X: a new fragment', *Iraq*, 26, p. 99 ff.

Moran, W. L. 1970, 'The Creation of Man in Atrahasis I 192–248', *Bulletin of the American Schools of Oriental Research*, 200, pp. 48–56.

—— 1977, 'Note brève, Gilgamesh I, i, 41', *Revue d'assyriologie*, 71, pp. 190–1.

—— 1981, '*duppuru (dubburu)—ṭuppuru*, too?', *Journal of Cuneiform Studies*, 33, pp. 44–7.

—— 1985, 'Note brève, Atrahasis 78, iv, 9 ff.', *Revue d'assyriologie*, 79, p. 90.

*—— 1987, 'Some considerations of form and interpretation in Atrahasis', in *Language, Literature and History: philological and historical studies presented to Erica Reiner*, ed. F. Rochberg-Halton (New Haven), 245–56.

Oppert, J. 1903. *Jewish Encyclopaedia*, IV, s.v. Chronology, pp. 66 f. (New York and London).

Otten, H. 1958, 'Die erste Tafel des hethitischen Gilgamesh-Epos', *Istanbuler Mitteilungen*, 8, pp. 93–125.

Parpola, S. 1983, 'Letters of Assyrian Scholars, Commentary vol. II', *Alter Orient und Altes Testament*, 5 (Neukirchen-Vluyn).

*Picchioni, S. A. 1981, *Il poemetto di Adapa* (Budapest).

Pilcher, E. J. 1903, 'The Jews of the Diaspora in Roman Galatia', *Proceedings of the Society for Biblical Archaeology*, pp. 225–33 and 250–8.

Powell, M. A. 1982, 'The adverbial suffix -a and the morphology of the multiples of ten', *Zeitschrifte für Assyriologie*, 72, pp. 89–105.

Reallexikon der Assyriologie, ed. B. Meissner *et al.*, s.v. Elohim; Gilgamesh; Heilige Hochzeit; Irra; and *Literatur.

Reiner, E. 1960, 'Plague amulets and house blessings', *Journal of Near Eastern Studies*, 19, pp. 148–55.

Renger, J. 1972, 'Note brève, Gilgamesh P, ii, 32', *Revue d'assyriologie*, 66, p. 190.

*——— 1987, 'Zur fünften Tafel des Gilgamesch-Epos', in *Language, Literature and History: philological and historical studies presented to Erica Reiner*, ed. F. Rochberg-Halton (New Haven), 317–27.

*Saggs, H. W. F. 1986, 'Additions to Anzu', *Archiv für Orientforschung*, 33, pp. 1–29.

Schretter, H. 1974, *Alter Orient und Hellas* (Innsbruck).

Shaffer, A. 1963, *The Sumerian sources of Tablet XII of the Epic of Gilgamesh* (University Microfilms, Ann Arbor).

Sjöberg, A. 1984, 'Eve and the chameleon', in *In the Shelter of Elyon, essays in honour of G. W. Ahlström*, ed. W. Boyd Barrick and J. R. Spencer, *Journal of Society of Old Testament*, Supp. Series 31 (Sheffield), 217–25.

Sladek, W. 1974, *Inanna's Descent to the Netherworld* (University Microfilms, Ann Arbor).

von Soden, W. 1959–81, *Akkadisches Handwörterbuch* (Wiesbaden).

——— 1979, 'Konflikte und ihre Bewältigung in babylonischen Schöpfungs- und Fluterzählungen. Mit einer Teil-Übersetzung des Atram-hasis Mythos', *Mitteilungen der Deutsch-Orient Gesellschaft*, 111, pp. 1–34.

——— 1981, 'Untersuchungen zur babylonischen Metrik I', *Zeitschrift für Assyriologie*, 71, pp. 161–204.

Sommerfeld, W. 1982, 'Der Aufstieg Marduks', *Alter Orient und altes Testament*, 213 (Neukirchen-Vluyn).

——— 1985, 'Der Kurigalzu-Text MAH 15922', *Archiv für Orientforschung*, 32.

Speiser, E. A. 1926–7, 'Southern Kurdistan in the Annals of

Ashurnasirpal and Today', *Annual of the American Schools of Oriental Research*, 8, pp. 17–19.

Steinkeller, P. 1982, 'The Mesopotamian god Kakka', *Journal of Near Eastern Studies*, 41, pp. 289–94.

Stefanini, R. 1969, 'Enkidu's dream in the Hittite "Gilgamesh"', *Journal of Near Eastern Studies*, 28, pp. 40–7.

Streck, M. 1916, *Assurbanipal und die letzten assyrischen Könige bis zum Untergang Ninivehs* (Leipzig).

Strong, H. A. and Garstang, J. 1913, *The Syrian Goddess* (London).

Thureau-Dangin, F. 1912, *Une relation de la huitième campagne de Sargon*, Textes Cuneiformes du Louvre 3 (Paris).

Tigay, J. H. 1977, 'Was there an integrated Gilgamesh Epic in the Old Babylonian period?', in *Essays in Memory of J. J. Finkelstein*, ed. M. de J. Ellis (Connecticut), 215–18.

*—— 1982, *The Evolution of the Gilgamesh Epic* (Philadelphia).

Tsevat, M. 1987, 'Note brève, Erra IV, 7–10', *Revue d'assyriologie*, 81, p. 184.

Veenhof, K. R. 1975–6, An Old Akkadian private letter, with a note on *ṣiāhum/sīhtum*, *Jaarbericht Ex Oriente Lux*, 24.

Walker, C. B. F. 1983, 'The Myth of Girra and Elamatum', *Anatolian Studies*, 33, pp. 145–52.

von Weiher, E. 1988, *Spätbabylonische Texte aus Uruk* III (Berlin).

West, M. 1986, 'Review of Burkert 1984', *Journal of Hellenic Studies*, 106, pp. 233–4.

Wiggermann, F. A. M. 1981–2, 'Exit *Talim*! Studies in babylonian demonology I', *Jaarbericht Ex Oriente Lux*, 27, pp. 90–105.

—— 1986, *Babylonian prophylactic figures: the ritual texts* (Amsterdam).

Wilcke, C. 1969, *Das Lugalbanda Epos* (Wiesbaden).

—— 1977, 'Die Anfänge der akkadischen Epen', *Zeitschrift für Assyriologie*, 67, pp. 153–216.

—— 1985a, 'Familiengründung im Alten Babylonien', in *Geschlechtsreife und Legitimation zur Zeugung*, ed. J. Martin and Th. Nipperdey, Historische Anthropologie 3, *Kindheit, Jugend, Familie* I (Freiburg/München).

—— 1985b, 'Liebesbeschwörungen aus Isin', *Zeitschrift für Assyriologie*, 75, pp. 188–209.

Wiseman, D. J. 1975, 'A Gilgamesh Epic fragment from Nimrud', *Iraq*, 37, pp. 157–63.

Woolley, C. L. 1982, *Ur of the Chaldees*, rev. by P. R. S. Moorey.

Zimmern, H. 1901, *Beiträge zur Kenntnis der babylonischen Religion* (Leipzig).

'This man whose [prayers reach me (?)]—
Do go quickly and bring me news of him,
And ask him to give me a report about his country.'
They crossed the wide seas
[Until they arrived] at the harbour of Apsu.
They repeated Ea's message to Atra-hasis.
'Are you the man who is weeping?
Is it your plea that went down to the Apsu?
Ea has heard your voice
And he has sent us to you.'
'If Ea has really heard me,
What [has reached him]?'
They answered straight away,
They addressed Atra-hasis:
'As sleep began to overtake (you)
The irrigation-water took (the offering), the river
carried (it),
The gift was placed in front of Ea your lord.
Ea saw it and thought of you,
And so he sent us to you.'
He bowed down, kissed the ground in front of them.
The *lahmu*-creatures [returned] into the seas.
Ea made his voice heard and spoke,
He addressed Usmu his vizier:
'Go out to Atra-hasis and tell him my order,
Saying: "The state of the country is according to the
behaviour of its people."'
Usmu, Ea's vizier, addressed Atra-hasis
Saying: 'The state of the country is according to the
behaviour of its people.
If water has left it, if grain has left [the fields (?)],
[It is because   ] to me,
[   ] they have left them.
The country is like a young man who falls flat on
his face,
He has fallen down [and is not nourished] from the
teats [of the sky].

The land has been shaken off like a dried fig on
    to [the ground].
Above, the teats of the sky are sealed,
And below, the water from the depths is bolted, it
    does not flow.
(That is why) the dark ploughland has whitened,
(That is why) in the pastureland grass does not sprout.'

SUPPLEMENT 2 *(see p. 65)*

(An unpublished fragment with 27 lines of text continues the speech of Ninsun. She invokes the help of Aya to persuade Shamash, to send 13 winds against Humbaba so that the weapons of Gilgamesh will prevail, and to remind Shamash to look after Gilgamesh at every moment of danger. She prays that Gilgamesh may win a place among the great gods of sky, earth and underworld. Aya was the daughter-in-law of Shamash, so she was well-placed to intercede for Ninsun.)

SUPPLEMENT 3 (see p. 66)

(Within column vi of Tablet III which contained up to 35 lines, an unpublished fragment with 4 lines of text contains the last two lines of a speech, perhaps Gilgamesh addressing the city elders, telling them to maintain law and order in his absence, then a farewell in which the elders gather and address Gilgamesh:)

'Do not trust entirely, Gilgamesh, in your own strength.
When you have looked long enough, trust to your first
    blow.
He who leads the way will save his comrade.
He who knows the paths, he will (?) guard his friend.
Let Enkidu go in front of you,
He knows the way of the Pine Forest.
He can look at the fight and instruct in the battle.'

SUPPLEMENT 4 (*see p. 242*)

Anshar shouted furiously,
He addressed Anu his son:
> 'Steadfast son, heroic *kašūšu*-weapon,
> Whose strength is mighty, whose attack is unfaceable,
> Go against Tiamat and stand your ground!
> Let her anger abate, let her fury be quelled.[10]
> If she will not listen to your word,
> Speak words of supplication to her, that she may be
>   calmed.'

He listened to the words of his father Anshar.
He took the road, went straight on his way.
He went, he searched for Tiamat's strategy,
But then stayed silent and turned back.
He entered into the presence of the ruler Anshar,
In supplication he addressed him.
> 'My father, Tiamat's actions were too much for me.
> I searched for her course, but my spell was not equal
>   to her.
> Her strength is mighty, she is completely terrifying.
> Her crowd is too powerful, nobody could defy her.
> Her noise never lessens, it was too loud for me.
> I feared her shout, and I turned back.
> But father, you must not relax, you must send someone
>   else to her.
> However strong a woman's strength, it is not equal to
>   a man's.
> You must disband her regiments, confuse her advice,
> Before she can impose her power over us.'

[10] Alliteration, *libbuš lippuš*.

The Oxford World's Classics Website

www.worldsclassics.co.uk

- Information about new titles
- Explore the full range of Oxford World's Classics
- Links to other literary sites and the main OUP webpage
- Imaginative competitions, with bookish prizes
- Peruse the Oxford World's Classics Magazine
- Articles by editors
- Extracts from Introductions
- A forum for discussion and feedback on the series
- Special information for teachers and lecturers

www.worldsclassics.co.uk

American Literature

British and Irish Literature

Children's Literature

Classics and Ancient Literature

Colonial Literature

Eastern Literature

European Literature

History

Medieval Literature

Oxford English Drama

Poetry

Philosophy

Politics

Religion

The Oxford Shakespeare

A complete list of Oxford Paperbacks, including Oxford World's Classics, Oxford Shakespeare, Oxford Drama, and Oxford Paperback Reference, is available in the UK from the Academic Division Publicity Department, Oxford University Press, Great Clarendon Street, Oxford OX2 6DP.

In the USA, complete lists are available from the Paperbacks Marketing Manager, Oxford University Press, 198 Madison Avenue, New York, NY 10016.

Oxford Paperbacks are available from all good bookshops. In case of difficulty, customers in the UK can order direct from Oxford University Press Bookshop, Freepost, 116 High Street, Oxford OX1 4BR, enclosing full payment. Please add 10 per cent of published price for postage and packing.